Scoring High

Iowa Tests of Basic Skills®

A Test Prep Program for ITBS®

Book 1
Now with Science

Columbus, OH

The McGraw·Hill Companies

SRAonline.com

 SRA

Copyright © 2007 by SRA/McGraw-Hill.

All rights reserved. Except as permitted under the United States
Copyright Act, no part of this publication may be reproduced or
distributed in any form or by any means, or stored in a database
or retrieval system, without the prior written permission of the
publisher, unless otherwise indicated.

Send all inquiries to:
SRA/McGraw-Hill
4400 Easton Commons
Columbus, OH 43219

Printed in the United States of America.

ISBN 0-07-604380-0

3 4 5 6 7 8 9 QPD 09

The McGraw-Hill Companies

On Your Way to Scoring High

On the Iowa Tests of Basic Skills®

Book 1

Family Letter

Greetings!

Your child, like many students across the country, will take standardized tests throughout his or her educational experience. Standardized tests are administered for several reasons.

- It gives us a snapshot of what your child has learned (achieved). It is one of many ways we assess the skills and knowledge of students because no one test or assessment tool can give an accurate, ongoing picture of your child's development.

- We use these tests to help us determine where to strengthen our curriculum to better meet the needs of the students. It also helps us see if we are meeting the learning goals set previously.

In order to give students the best opportunity to prepare for standardized achievement tests, we will be using SRA/McGraw-Hill's test preparation program, *Scoring High on the Iowa Tests of Basic Skills*. Why will we be spending time using this program?

- Test-taking skills can be learned. When preparing, we focus on such skills as reading and listening carefully to directions; budgeting time; answering the easy questions first so more time can be spent on the harder ones; eliminating answer choices that are obviously wrong; and more. These are life skills that students will take with them and use again and again.

- Preparing for standardized tests assures that students won't be surprised by the format of the test. They won't be worried about the type of questions they will see, or how hard the questions will be. They'll know how to fill in answers appropriately. These, and other skills learned ahead of time, will free students to focus on the content of the test and thus give a much more accurate picture of what they know.

How can you help?

- Talk to us here at school if you have any questions. Remember, we are a team with the **same** goals in mind—the improvement of your child's educational experience.

- Encourage reading at home, and spend time together talking about what you read.

Please feel free to contact me if you have any questions.

Sincerely,

_____

Your child's teacher

Scoring High on the Iowa Tests of Basic Skills®
A program that teaches achievement test behaviors

Scoring High on the Iowa Tests of Basic Skills is designed to prepare students for these tests. The program provides instruction and practice in reading, spelling, language, mathematics, study, and science skills. *Scoring High* also familiarizes students with the kinds of test formats and directions that appear on the tests and teaches test-taking strategies that promote success.

Students who are used to a comfortable learning environment are often unaccustomed to the structured setting in which achievement tests are given. Even students who are used to working independently may have difficulty maintaining a silent, sustained effort or following directions that are read to a large group. *Scoring High*, with its emphasis on group instruction, teaches these test-taking skills systematically.

Using *Scoring High* to help prepare students for the Iowa Tests of Basic Skills will increase the probability of your students doing their best on the tests. Students' self-confidence will be at a maximum, and their proficiency in the skills tested will be higher as a result of the newly learned test-taking strategies and increased familiarity with test formats.

Scoring High can be used effectively along with your regular reading, language arts, mathematics, and science curriculums. By applying subject-area skills in the context of the test-taking situation, students will not only strengthen their skills, but will accumulate a reserve of test-taking strategies.

Eight Student Books for Grades 1–8

To choose the most appropriate book for each student, match the level of the *Iowa Tests of Basic Skills* that the student will take to the corresponding *Scoring High* book.

Grade Levels	Test Levels
Book 1	Level 7
Book 2	Level 8
Book 3	Level 9
Book 4	Level 10
Book 5	Level 11
Book 6	Level 12
Book 7	Level 13
Book 8	Level 14

Sequential Skill Development

Each student book is organized into units reflecting the subject areas covered in the corresponding levels of the Iowa Tests of Basic Skills. This book covers reading, spelling, language, mathematics, study, and science skills. Each lesson within a unit focuses on one or two of the subject-area skills and the test-taking strategies that complement the skills. The last lesson in each unit is designed to give students experience in taking an achievement test in that subject area.

The Test Practice section at the end of each book also provides practice in taking achievement tests and will increase students' confidence in their test-taking skills.

Note: The lessons in this book are arranged in the order that comparable items appear on the ITBS. You may find it helpful to review the lessons and administer them in the order that is most appropriate for the reading level of your students.

Features of the Student Lessons

Each student lesson in subject-area skills contains:

- A Sample(s) section including directions and one or more teacher-directed sample questions
- A Tips section providing test-taking strategies
- A Practice section

Each Test Yourself lesson at the end of a unit is designed like an achievement test in the unit's subject area(s).

How the Teacher's Edition Works

Since a program that teaches test-taking skills as well as subject-area skills may be new to your students, the Teacher's Edition makes a special effort to provide detailed lesson plans. Each lesson lists subject-area and test-taking skills. In addition, teaching suggestions are provided for handling each part of the lesson—Sample(s), Tips, and Practice. The text for the subject-area and Test Yourself lessons is designed to help students become familiar with following oral directions and with the terminology used on the tests.

Before you begin Lesson 1, you should use the Orientation Lesson on pages xii–xiii to acquaint students with the program organization and the procedure for using the student book.

Scope and Sequence: Test-taking Skills

	UNIT										
	1	2	3	4	5	6	7	8	9	10	11
Analyzing problems or answer choices			✓		✓		✓				✓
Choosing a picture to answer a question										✓	✓
Comparing or evaluating answer choices									✓	✓	✓
Computing carefully								✓			✓
Considering every answer choice	✓	✓	✓	✓	✓	✓	✓	✓			✓
Converting items to a workable format								✓			✓
Following oral directions	✓	✓	✓	✓	✓	✓	✓	✓	✓	✓	✓
Identifying and using key words, numbers, and pictures			✓	✓	✓	✓					✓
Indicating that the correct answer is not given							✓	✓			✓
Listening carefully	✓	✓	✓	✓	✓	✓	✓	✓	✓	✓	✓
Performing the correct operation								✓			✓
Recalling error types					✓						✓
Referring to a passage to answer questions			✓								✓
Referring to a reference source									✓		✓
Substituting answer choices		✓									✓
Subvocalizing answer choices		✓			✓						✓
Taking the best guess when unsure of the answer	✓	✓	✓	✓	✓						✓
Transferring numbers accurately								✓			✓
Using graphs						✓					✓
Using context to find an answer			✓								✓
Working methodically		✓	✓		✓	✓	✓		✓	✓	✓

Scope and Sequence: Reading Skills

	UNIT 1	2	3	4	5	6	7	8	9	10	11
Associating words and pictures	✓										✓
Identifying the best word to complete a statement	✓										✓
Identifying beginning letters		✓									✓
Identifying middle letters		✓									✓
Matching beginning sounds		✓									✓
Matching rhyming sounds		✓									✓
Matching vowel sounds		✓									✓
Substituting beginning sounds		✓									✓
Completing sentences that match a picture			✓								✓
Drawing conclusions			✓								✓
Identifying feelings			✓								✓
Making inferences			✓								
Making predictions			✓								
Matching pictures and text clues			✓								✓
Recognizing details			✓								✓
Recognizing setting			✓								
Understanding reasons			✓								✓
Understanding sequence			✓								
Understanding the main idea			✓								✓

Scope and Sequence: Language Skills

	UNIT 1	2	3	4	5	6	7	8	9	10	11
Matching graphic answers and oral prompts				✓							✓
Identifying capitalization errors					✓						✓
Identifying errors in usage or expression					✓						✓
Identifying punctuation errors					✓						✓
Identifying spelling errors					✓						✓
Identifying a word that does not fit an implied class					✓						✓
Understanding oral language					✓						

Scope and Sequence: Mathematics Skills

	UNIT										
	1	2	3	4	5	6	7	8	9	10	11
Comparing and ordering whole numbers						✓					✓
Counting						✓					✓
Counting by tens						✓					✓
Estimating measurement						✓					✓
Identifying measurement tools						✓					✓
Identifying parts of a figure						✓					✓
Naming numerals						✓					✓
Recognizing fractional parts						✓					
Recognizing plane figures						✓					✓
Recognizing value of coins and bills						✓					✓
Representing problems with number sentences						✓					✓
Sequencing numbers or shapes						✓					✓
Telling time						✓					✓
Understanding number sentences						✓					✓
Understanding place value						✓					✓
Using mathematical language						✓					✓
Identifying problem solving strategies							✓				✓
Interpreting tables and graphs							✓				✓
Solving oral word problems							✓				✓
Adding and subtracting whole numbers								✓			✓
Solving oral addition and subtraction problems								✓			✓

Scope and Sequence: Study Skills

	UNIT										
	1	2	3	4	5	6	7	8	9	10	11
Alphabetizing words									✓		✓
Understanding a map									✓		✓
Using a dictionary									✓		✓
Using a table of contents									✓		✓

Scope and Sequence: Science Skills

	UNIT											
	1	2	3	4	5	6	7	8	9	10	11
Classifying things based on characteristics										✓	
Differentiating living and nonliving things										✓	
Differentiating real and imaginary living things										✓	
Differentiating the source of natural and manufactured products										✓	✓
Recalling characteristics and functions of the human body										✓	✓
Recalling characteristics of Earth and bodies in space										✓	✓
Recognizing characteristics of a habitat										✓	✓
Recognizing forms, sources, and principles of energy										✓	
Recognizing health and safety practices										✓	✓
Recognizing moon phases										✓	
Recognizing states and properties of matter										✓	✓
Understanding characteristics of bodies of water										✓	
Understanding diseases and their sources										✓	✓
Understanding foods and food groups										✓	✓
Understanding the history and language of science										✓	
Understanding life cycles and reproduction										✓	✓
Understanding magnetism										✓	
Understanding plant and animal behaviors and characteristics										✓	✓
Understanding properties of light										✓	
Understanding scientific instruments, measurement, and processes											✓
Understanding weather, climate, and seasons										✓	✓
Understanding work and the principles of machines										✓	✓

Orientation Lesson

Focus
Understanding the purpose and structure of *Scoring High on the Iowa Tests of Basic Skills*

Note: Before you begin Lesson 1, use this introductory lesson to acquaint the students with the program orientation and procedures for using this book.

Say Taking a test is something that you do many times during each school year. What kind of tests have you taken? *(math tests, reading tests, spelling tests, daily quizzes, etc.)* Have you ever taken an achievement test that covers many subjects? An achievement test shows how well you are doing in these subjects compared to other students in your grade. Do you know how achievement tests are different from the regular tests you take in class? *(many students take them on the same day; special pencils, books, and answer sheets are used; etc.)* Some students get nervous when they take achievement tests. Has this ever happened to you?

Encourage the students to discuss their feelings about test taking. Point out that almost everyone feels anxious or worried when facing a test-taking situation.

Display the cover of *Scoring High on the Iowa Tests of Basic Skills.*

Say Here is a new book that you'll be using for the next several weeks. The book is called *Scoring High on the Iowa Tests of Basic Skills.*

Distribute the books to the students.

Say This book will help you improve your reading, language, mathematics, study, and science skills. It will also help you gain the confidence and skills you need to do well on achievement tests. What does the title say you will be doing when you finish this book? *(scoring high)* Scoring high on achievement tests is what this program is all about. If you learn the skills taught in this book, you will be ready to do your best on the *Iowa Tests of Basic Skills.*

Inform the students about the testing date if you know when they will be taking the *Iowa Tests of Basic Skills.* Then make sure the students understand that the goal of their *Scoring High* books is to improve their reading, mathematics, and other skills.

Tell the students to turn to the table of contents at the front of their books.

Say The first two pages show the contents of this book. They are also a progess chart. How many units are there? *(11)* Let's read the names of the units together. *(Read the names of the units aloud.)* **In these units you will learn reading, spelling, language arts, mathematics, study science, and test-taking skills. The last lesson in each unit is called Test Yourself. It reviews what you have learned in the unit. In Unit 11, the Test Practice section, you will have a chance to use all of the skills you have learned on tests that are somewhat like real achievement tests. These pages will also help you keep track of the lessons you have completed. Do you see the box beside each lesson number? When you finish a lesson, you will write your score in the box to show your progress.**

Make sure the students understand the information presented on this page.

Say Now let's look at two of the lessons. Turn to Lesson 1a on page 1.

Check to be sure that the students have found page 1.

Say The lesson number and title are at the top of the page. The page number is at the bottom of the page. This page is about vocabulary words. When we start a lesson, you will find the lesson by its page number. The page number is always at the bottom of the page.

Familiarize the students with the lesson layout and sequence of instruction. Have them locate the directions and sample items. Explain that you will work through the Samples section together. Then have the students find the GO sign in the lower right-hand corner of the page.

On Your Way to Scoring High
On the **Iowa Tests of Basic Skills**®

Book 1

Name _____

Say Near the bottom of some pages is a GO sign. When you see the GO sign at the bottom of a page, it means you should turn the page and continue working.

Have the students turn to page 2.

Say At the bottom of other pages is a STOP sign. When you see the STOP sign at the bottom of a page, it means you should stop working. Then we will either do different items, or we will go over the answers to the items you have already completed. I will also explain anything that you did not understand.

Have the students turn to page 1 and locate the Tips sign above the Samples section.

Say What does the sign point out to you? *(the tips)* Each lesson has tips that suggest new ways to work through the items. Tests can be tricky. The tips will tell you what to watch out for. They will help you find the best answer quickly.

Explain to the students that the questions in this book and on an achievement test are also called items. Tell the students that each lesson has several practice items that they will answer by themselves.

Say Now I'll show you how to fill in the spaces for your answers.

Draw several circles on the chalkboard and demonstrate how to fill them in. Explain to the students that they should make dark, heavy marks and fill in the circles completely. Allow volunteers to demonstrate filling in answer circles that you have drawn on the chalkboard.

Ask the students to turn to the Test Yourself lesson on page 5 of their books. Tell the students the Test Yourself lessons may seem like real tests, but they are not. The Test Yourself lessons are designed to give them opportunities to apply the skills and tips they have learned in timed, trial-run situations. Explain that you will go over the answers together after the students complete each lesson. Then they will figure out their scores and record the number of correct answers in the boxes on the progress chart. Be sure to point out that the students' scores are only for them to see how well they are doing.

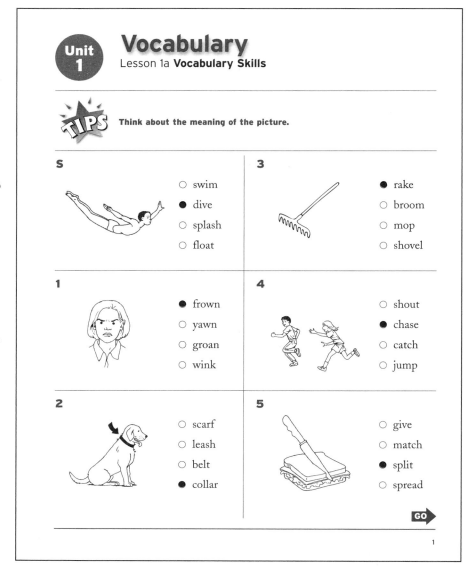

Say Each lesson will teach you new skills and tips. What will you have learned when you finish this book? *(vocabulary, reading, spelling, language arts, mathematics, study science, and test-taking skills; how to do my best on an achievement test)* **When you know you can do your best, how do you think you will feel on test day? You may be a little nervous, but you should also feel confident that you are ready to do your best.**

Background

This unit contains three lessons that deal with vocabulary skills. Students are asked to match words and pictures and to choose the best word to complete a sentence.

• **In Lesson 1a,** students match words and pictures. Students are encouraged to follow oral directions and listen carefully. They consider every answer choice and take the best guess when unsure of the answer.

• **In Lesson 1b,** students identify words to complete sentences. They review the test-taking skills introduced in Lesson 1a.

• **In the Test Yourself lesson,** the vocabulary skills and test-taking skills introduced and used in Lessons 1a and 1b are reinforced and presented in a format that gives students the experience of taking an achievement test.

Instructional Objectives

Lesson 1a	**Vocabulary Skills**	Given a picture and four words, the student identifies which of the words goes best with the picture.
Lesson 1b	**Vocabulary Skills**	Given an incomplete sentence and four words, the student identifies which of the words best completes the sentence.
	Test Yourself	Given questions similar to those in Lessons 1a and 1b, the student utilizes vocabulary skills and test-taking strategies on achievement test formats.

Focus

Reading Skill
• associating words and pictures

Test-taking Skills
• following oral directions
• listening carefully
• considering every answer choice
• taking the best guess when unsure of the answer

Sample S

Say Turn to Lesson 1a on page 1. The page number is at the bottom of the page on the right. This page has pictures and words on it.

Check to see that the students have found the right page.

Say In this lesson you will choose words that tell about a picture. Look at the picture for S. It is at the top of the first column. Now look at the words beside the picture. Which word best tells about the picture? *(pause)* The second answer, *dive,* is correct because it best tells about the picture. Fill in the circle beside the word *dive,* the second answer. Be sure your answer circle is completely filled in with a dark mark and that you have marked the correct answer circle.

Check to see that the students have marked the correct circle.

★TIPS

Say Now let's look at the tip.

Read the tip aloud to the students.

Say Look at the picture and think about what the picture is showing. Then look at the answer choices. Decide which word goes best with the picture.

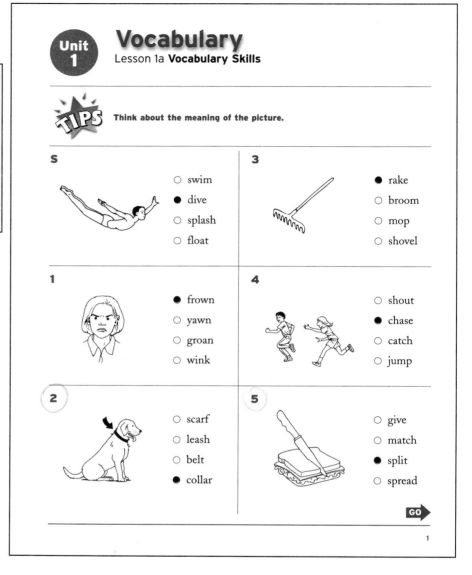

Unit 1

Vocabulary
Lesson 1a **Vocabulary Skills**

TIPS   Think about the meaning of the picture.

S
○ swim
● dive
○ splash
○ float

3
● rake
○ broom
○ mop
○ shovel

1
● frown
○ yawn
○ groan
○ wink

4
○ shout
● chase
○ catch
○ jump

2
○ scarf
○ leash
○ belt
● collar

5
○ give
○ match
● split
○ spread

GO

1

Practice

Say Now we will do the Practice items in the same way we did S. You will work by yourself. Look at each picture. Read each answer choice. Fill in the circle beside the word that goes best with the picture. If you are not sure which answer is correct, take your best guess.

When you come to the GO sign at the bottom of the page, turn the page and continue working. Work until you come to the STOP sign at the bottom of the next page. Fill in your answer circles with dark marks. If you change your answer, be sure to completely erase any other marks. Do you have any questions? Start working now.

Allow time for the students to do Numbers 1 through 11.

Say It's time to stop. You have finished Lesson 1a.

Review the answers with the students. Ask them if they remembered to look at all of the answer choices and to take the best guess if they were unsure of the correct answer. Did they have any difficulty marking the circles in the answer rows? If any questions caused particular difficulty, work through each of the answer choices.

Have the students indicate completion of the lesson by entering their score for this activity on the progress chart at the beginning of the book. Provide the students whatever help is necessary to record their scores.

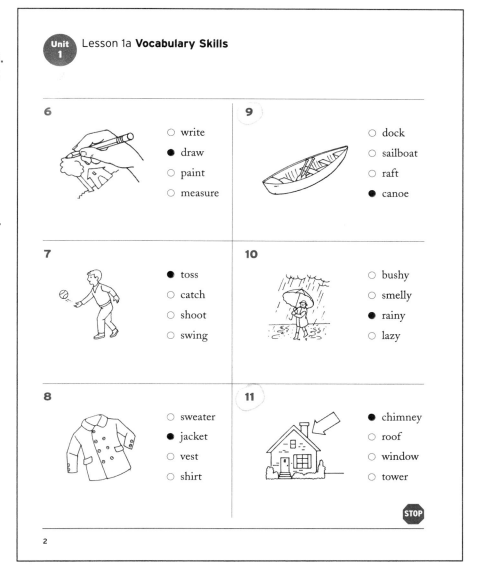

Unit 1   Lesson 1a **Vocabulary Skills**

6
○ write
● draw
○ paint
○ measure

7
● toss
○ catch
○ shoot
○ swing

8
○ sweater
● jacket
○ vest
○ shirt

9
○ dock
○ sailboat
○ raft
● canoe

10
○ bushy
○ smelly
● rainy
○ lazy

11
● chimney
○ roof
○ window
○ tower

STOP

2

Unit 1 Lesson 1b Vocabulary

Focus

Reading Skill
- identifying the best word to complete a statement

Test-taking Skills
- following oral directions
- listening carefully
- considering every answer choice
- taking the best guess when unsure of the answer

Sample S

Say Turn to Lesson 1b on page 3. The page number is at the bottom of the page on the right.

Check to see that the students have found the right page.

Say In this lesson you will choose words to complete a sentence. Look at the sentence for S at the top of the page. Read the sentence and the answer choices to yourself while I read them out loud.

Read the sentence and answer choices out loud.

Say Which word fits best at the end of the sentence? *(pause)* The second answer, *desert,* is correct because a desert is a place with little water. Fill in the circle beside the word *desert.* Be sure your answer circle is completely filled in with a dark mark.

Check to see that the students have marked the correct circle.

★ TIPS

Say Let's review the tip.

Read the tip aloud to the students.

Say Whenever you are not sure which answer is correct, take your best guess. If you guess, you will be right some of the time. If you leave an item blank, it will always be wrong.

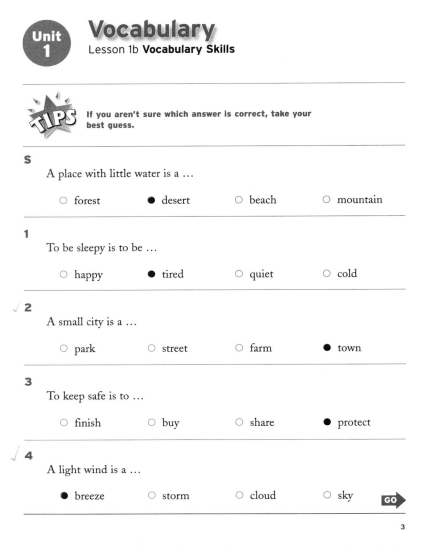

Practice

Say Now we will do the Practice items in the same way we did S. You will work by yourself. Read each sentence. Fill in the circle beside the word that fits best at the end of the sentence. If you are not sure which answer is correct, take your best guess.

When you come to the GO sign at the bottom of the page, turn the page and continue working. Work until you come to the STOP sign at the bottom of the next page. Fill in your answer circles with dark marks and completely erase any marks for answers that you change. Do you have any questions? Start working now.

Allow time for the students to do Numbers 1 through 10.

Say It's time to stop. You have finished Lesson 1b.

Review the answers with the students. Ask them if they remembered to guess when they were not sure of the answer. If any questions caused particular difficulty, work through each of the answer choices.

Have the students indicate completion of the lesson by entering their score for this activity on the progress chart at the beginning of the book. Provide the students whatever help is necessary to record their scores.

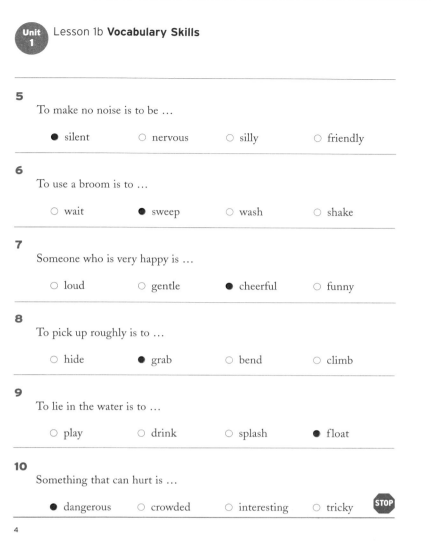

Unit 1   Lesson 1b **Vocabulary Skills**

5 To make no noise is to be …

● silent   ○ nervous   ○ silly   ○ friendly

6 To use a broom is to …

○ wait   ● sweep   ○ wash   ○ shake

7 Someone who is very happy is …

○ loud   ○ gentle   ● cheerful   ○ funny

8 To pick up roughly is to …

○ hide   ● grab   ○ bend   ○ climb

9 To lie in the water is to …

○ play   ○ drink   ○ splash   ● float

10 Something that can hurt is …

● dangerous   ○ crowded   ○ interesting   ○ tricky   **STOP**

4

Test Yourself: Vocabulary

Focus

Reading Skills
- associating words and pictures
- identifying the best word to complete a statement

Test-taking Skills
- following oral directions
- listening carefully
- considering every answer choice
- taking the best guess when unsure of the answer

This lesson simulates an actual test-taking experience. Therefore, it is recommended that the directions be read verbatim and the suggested procedures be followed.

Directions

Administration Time: approximately 20 minutes

Say Turn to the Test Yourself lesson on page 5. There is a picture of a person in a boat at the top of the page.

Check to be sure the students have found the right page. Point out to the students that this is not a real test and that they will score it themselves to see how well they are doing.

Say This lesson will check how well you understand word meanings. Remember to make sure that the circles for your answer choices are completely filled in. Press your pencil firmly so that your marks come out dark. Completely erase any marks for answers that you change. Do not write anything except your answer choices in your books.

In this part of the lesson you will choose words that tell about a picture. Look at the picture for S. It is at the top of the first column. Now look at the words beside the

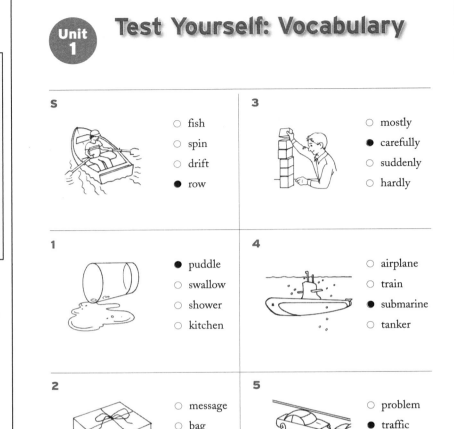

picture. Which word best tells about the picture? *(pause)* The last answer, *row,* is correct because it best tells about the picture. Fill in the circle beside the word *row,* the last answer. Be sure your answer circle is completely filled in with a dark mark and that you have marked the correct answer circle.

Check to see that the students have marked the correct circle.

Say Now we will do more items like S. Look at each picture. Read each answer choice. Fill in the circle beside the word that goes best with the picture. If you are not sure which answer is correct, take your best guess.

When you come to the GO sign at the bottom of the page, turn the page and continue working. Work until you come to the STOP sign at the bottom of the next page. Fill in your answer circles with dark marks and completely erase any marks for answers that you change. Do you have any questions? Start working now.

Allow time for the students to do Numbers 1 through 11.

Say Look at the next page, page 7.

Check to be sure the students have found the right page. Allow the students a moment to rest.

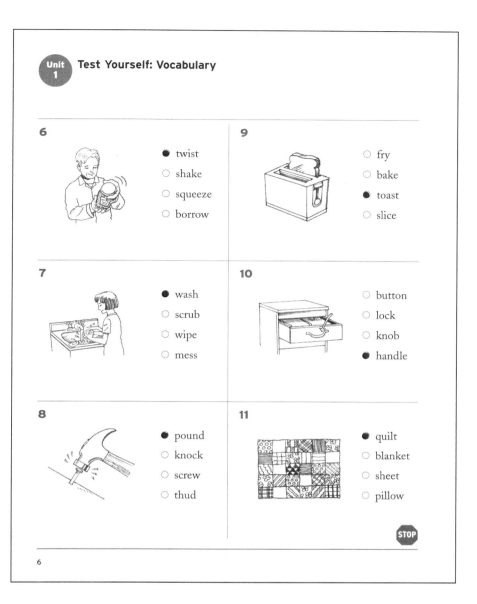

Unit 1 | **Test Yourself: Vocabulary**

6
- ● twist
- ○ shake
- ○ squeeze
- ○ borrow

9
- ○ fry
- ○ bake
- ● toast
- ○ slice

7
- ● wash
- ○ scrub
- ○ wipe
- ○ mess

10
- ○ button
- ○ lock
- ○ knob
- ● handle

8
- ● pound
- ○ knock
- ○ screw
- ○ thud

11
- ● quilt
- ○ blanket
- ○ sheet
- ○ pillow

6

Say Now you will answer different questions. In this part of the lesson, you will read a sentence in which a word is missing. You will choose the word that fits best at the end of the sentence. Fill in the circle beside the answer you think is best. Work until you come to the STOP sign at the bottom of the page. When you have finished, you can check over your answers to this test. Then wait for the rest of the group to finish. Any questions?

Answer any questions that the students have.

Say Start working now.

Allow time for the students to do Numbers 12 through 17.

Say It's time to stop. You have completed the Test Yourself lesson. Check to see that you have completely filled in your answer circles with dark marks. Make sure that any marks for answers that you changed have been completely erased. Now you may close your books.

Review the answers with the students. Have the students indicate completion of the lesson by entering their score for this activity on the progress chart at the beginning of the book. Provide the students whatever help is necessary to record their scores.

Unit 1 · **Test Yourself: Vocabulary**

12
Something loud is …

● noisy　　○ pleasant　　○ hushed　　○ busy

13
To feel rough is to be …

○ smooth　　○ fluffy　　● scratchy　　○ thick

14
People marching in the street is a …

○ concert　　○ party　　○ race　　● parade

15
To be scared is to be …

● afraid　　○ cold　　○ hungry　　○ sick

16
A deep valley is a …

○ meadow　　○ river　　● canyon　　○ tunnel

17
To look for something is to …

○ wait　　● search　　○ dream　　○ taste　　**STOP**

7

Unit 2

Background

This unit contains nine lessons that deal with word analysis skills. Students are asked a variety of questions that demonstrate familiarity with letters and their sounds.

• **In Lessons 2a and 2b,** students match beginning and rhyming sounds. Students are encouraged to follow oral directions and listen carefully. They practice considering every answer choice and taking their best guess.

• **In Lessons 3a and 3b,** students substitute letters that make initial sounds. They review the test-taking skills introduced in previous lessons and learn the importance of subvocalizing answer choices.

• **In Lessons 4a and 4b,** students complete words with missing letters. They review the test-taking skills introduced in previous lessons and learn how to substitute answer choices.

• **In Lessons 5a and 5b,** students identify words with specific vowel sounds. They review the test-taking skills introduced in previous lessons and learn how to substitute answer choices.

• **In the Test Yourself lesson,** the word analysis skills and test-taking skills introduced and used in Lessons 2a through 5b are reinforced and presented in a format that gives students the experience of taking an achievement test.

Instructional Objectives

Lesson 2a **Letter Recognition** Lesson 2b **Letter Recognition**	Given three words, the student identifies which word begins with the same sound as a spoken word. Given three words, the student identifies which word rhymes with a spoken word.
Lesson 3a **Initial Sounds** Lesson 3b **Initial Sounds**	Given a word and three pictures, the student identifies which of the picture names can be created from the word by substituting one or more initial letters.
Lesson 4a **Word Formation** Lesson 4b **Word Formation**	Given an incomplete word, the student identifies which of three letters or groups of letters completes the word.
Lesson 5a **Vowel Sounds** Lesson 5b **Vowel Sounds**	Given three pictures or words, the student identifies which contains the vowel sound in a specified word.
Test Yourself	Given questions similar to those in Lessons 2a through 5b, the student utilizes word analysis skills and test-taking strategies on achievement test formats.

Lesson 2a
Letter Recognition

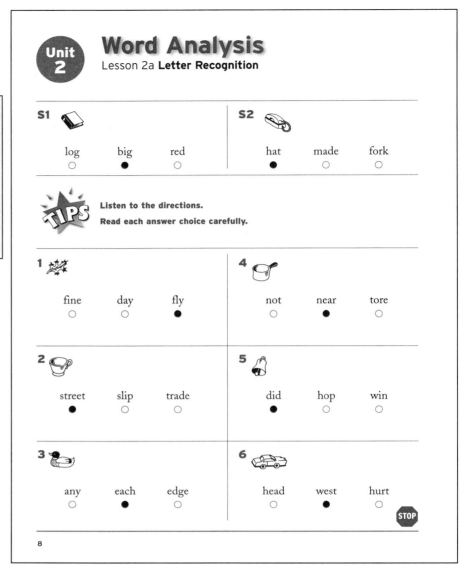

Unit 2

Focus

Reading Skills
- matching beginning sounds
- matching rhyming sounds

Test-taking Skills
- following oral directions
- listening carefully
- considering every answer choice

Samples S1 and S2

Say Turn to Lesson 2a on page 8. In this lesson you will answer questions about words and sounds.

Check to be sure the students have found the right page.

Say Let's begin by doing S1, the row of words below the picture of the book. Which word begins with the same sound as *book...book*? *(pause)* Fill in the circle under the second word, *big*. It begins with the same sound as *book*.

Check to see that the students have marked the correct answer circle.

Say Now let's do S2. Look at the words below the picture of the phone. Which word rhymes with *sat...sat*? *(pause)* Fill in the circle under the first word, *hat*. It rhymes with *sat*.

Check to see that the students have marked the correct answer circle.

 TIPS

Say Now let's look at the tips.

Read the tips aloud to the students.

Say Listen carefully to what I say. The directions I give you will tell you what to do. Read each word carefully. This will help you decide which answer is correct.

Practice

Say Now we are ready for Practice. Listen to what I say. Fill in the circle under the answer you think is correct. Are you ready? Let's begin.

Allow time between items for the students to mark their answers.

1. Look at the row with the leaf. Which word in this row begins with the same sounds as *flow*? Fill in the circle under the word that begins with the same sounds as *flow* ... *flow*.

2. Look at the row with the cup. Which word in this row begins with the same sounds as *string*? Fill in the circle under the word that begins with the same sounds as *string* ... *string*.

3. Look at the row with the duck. Which word in this row begins with the same sound as *even*? Fill in the circle under the word that begins with the same sounds as *even* ... *even*.

4. Listen carefully. This item is a little different. Look at the row with the pot. Fill in the circle under the word that rhymes with *fear* ... *fear*.

5. Look at the row with the bell. Fill in the circle under the word that rhymes with *hid* ... *hid*.

6. Move down to the last row, the one with the car. Fill in the circle under the word that rhymes with *best* ... *best*.

It's time to stop. You have finished Lesson 2a.

Review the answers with the students. Have the students indicate completion of the lesson by entering their score for this activity on the progress chart at the beginning of the book.

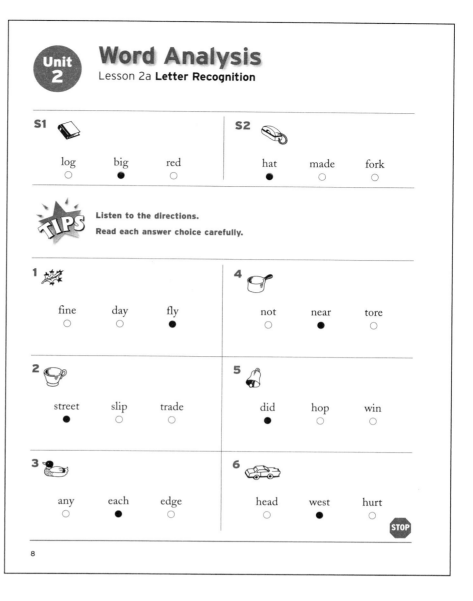

Unit 2 Lesson 2b Letter Recognition

Focus

Reading Skills
• matching beginning sounds
• matching rhyming sounds

Test-taking Skills
• following oral directions
• listening carefully
• considering every answer choice
• taking the best guess when unsure of the answer

Say Turn to Lesson 2b on page 9. In this lesson you will answer more questions about words and sounds.

Check to be sure the students have found the right page.

Practice

Say The items in this lesson are just like those we did in Lesson 2a. You will choose words that have the same beginning or rhyming sound. Listen to what I say. Fill in the circle under the answer you think is correct. Are you ready? Let's begin.

Allow time between items for the students to mark their answers.

1. Look at the row with the book. Which word in this row begins with the same sound as *oink*? Fill in the circle under the word that begins with the same sound as *oink ... oink.*

2. Look at the row with the phone. Which word in this row begins with the same sounds as *broke*? Fill in the circle under the word that begins with the same sounds as *broke ... broke.*

3. Look at the row with the leaf. Which word in this row begins with the same sound as *gave*? Fill in the circle under the word that begins with the same sound as *gave ... gave.*

4. Look at the row with the cup. Which word in this row begins with the same sounds as *step*? Fill in the circle under the word that begins with the same sounds as *step ... step.*

5. Look at the row with the bell. Which word in this row begins with the same sound as *ocean*? Fill in the circle under the word that begins with the same sound as *ocean ... ocean.*

Look at the row with the car at the top of the next column.

Unit 2 Word Analysis
Lesson 2b Letter Recognition

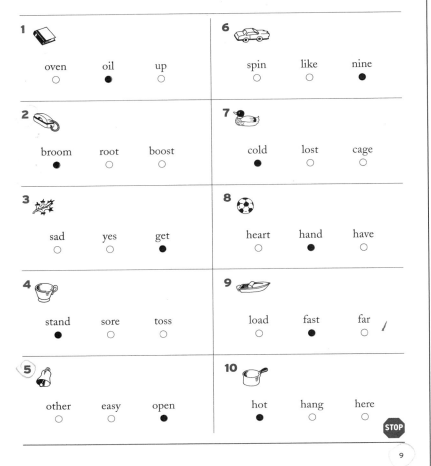

1. oven ○   oil ●   up ○
2. broom ●   root ○   boost ○
3. sad ○   yes ○   get ●
4. stand ●   sore ○   toss ○
5. other ○   easy ○   open ●
6. spin ○   like ○   nine ●
7. cold ●   lost ○   cage ○
8. heart ○   hand ●   have ○
9. load ○   fast ●   far ○
10. hot ●   hang ○   here ○

STOP

9

6. Listen carefully. This item is a little different. Fill in the circle under the word that rhymes with *mine ... mine.*

7. Look at the row with the duck. Fill in the circle under the word that rhymes with *hold ... hold.*

8. Look at the row with the ball. Fill in the circle under the word that rhymes with *sand ... sand.*

9. Look at the row with the boat. Fill in the circle under the word that rhymes with *last ... last.*

10. Move down to the last row, the one with the pot. Fill in the circle under the word that rhymes with *cot ... cot.*

    It's time to stop. You have finished Lesson 2b.

Review the answers with the students. Have the students indicate completion of the lesson by entering their score for this activity on the progress chart at the beginning of the book.

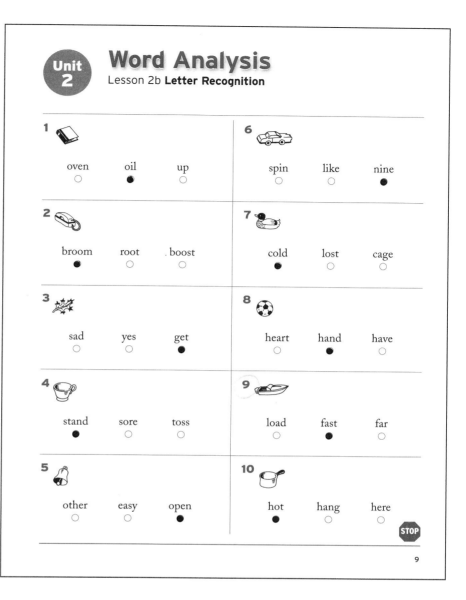

Unit 2 Lesson 3a
Initial Sounds

Focus

Reading Skill
- substituting beginning sounds

Test-taking Skills
- following oral directions
- listening carefully
- subvocalizing answer choices

Sample S

Say Turn to Lesson 3a on page 10. In this lesson you will answer questions about beginning sounds in words.

Check to be sure the students have found the right page.

Say Let's begin by doing S, the row at the top of the page. Look at the first word, *teen*. Take away the *t* (*say the letter t and all subsequent letters where needed*) and put *s-c-r* in its place. This makes a new word. Which new word do you make? (*pause*) Fill in the circle under the second answer, a *screen*. The word *screen* begins with the letters *s-c-r*.

Check to see that the students have marked the correct answer circle. If necessary, elaborate on the instructions if you are not sure the students understand what they are supposed to do.

★**TIPS**

Say Now let's look at the tips.

Read the tips aloud to the students.

Say Listen carefully to the directions for each item. Look at each picture, think about it, and then say the name of each picture to yourself. This will help you find the right answer.

Unit 2 Word Analysis
Lesson 3a **Initial Sounds**

S				
	teen			
	scr	○	●	○

Listen carefully to the directions.
Say the name of each picture to yourself.

1				
	dome			
	h	○	●	○
2				
	jump			
	p	○	○	●
3				
	down			
	cl	●	○	○
4				
	fair			
	ch	○	●	○

STOP

10

---

14   Unit 2 Lesson 3a **Initial Sounds**

Practice

Say Now we are ready for Practice. Listen to what I say. Fill in the circle under the answer you think is correct. Are you ready? Let's begin.

Allow time between items for the students to mark their answers.

1. Look at row 1. The word is *dome*. Take away the *d* and put *h* in its place. Fill in the circle under the picture of the new word.

2. Look at row 2. The word is *jump*. Take away the *j* and put *p* in its place. Fill in the circle under the picture of the new word.

3. Look at row 3. The word is *down*. Take away the *d* and put *c-l* in its place. Fill in the circle under the picture of the new word.

4. Look at row 4. The word is *fair*. Take away the *f* and put *c-h* in its place. Fill in the circle under the picture of the new word.

   It's time to stop. You have finished Lesson 3a.

Review the answers with the students. Have the students indicate completion of the lesson by entering their score for this activity on the progress chart at the beginning of the book.

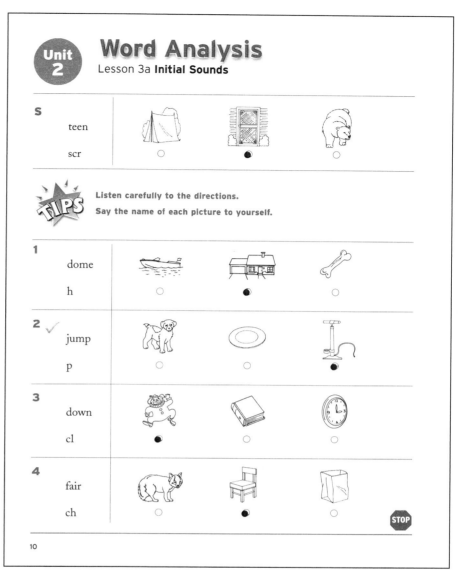

Unit 2 — Lesson 3b
Initial Sounds

Focus
Reading Skill
• substituting beginning sounds

Test-taking Skills
• following oral directions
• listening carefully
• subvocalizing answer choices

Say Turn to Lesson 3b on page 11. In this lesson you will answer more questions about beginning sounds in words.

Check to be sure the students have found the right page.

Practice

Say Now we will do more items just like we did in Lesson 3a. Listen to what I say. Fill in the circle under the answer you think is correct. Are you ready? Let's begin.

Allow time between items for the students to mark their answers.

1. Look at row 1. The word is *mess*. Take away the *m* and put *d-r* in its place. Fill in the circle under the picture of the new word.

2. Look at row 2. The word is *show*. Take away the *s-h* and put *s-n* in its place. Fill in the circle under the picture of the new word.

3. Look at row 3. The word is *camp*. Take away the *c* and put *l* in its place. Fill in the circle under the picture of the new word.

4. Look at row 4. The word is *rest*. Take away the *r* and put *n* in its place. Fill in the circle under the picture of the new word.

5. Look at row 5. The word is *make*. Take away the *m* and put *c* in its place. Fill in the circle under the picture of the new word.

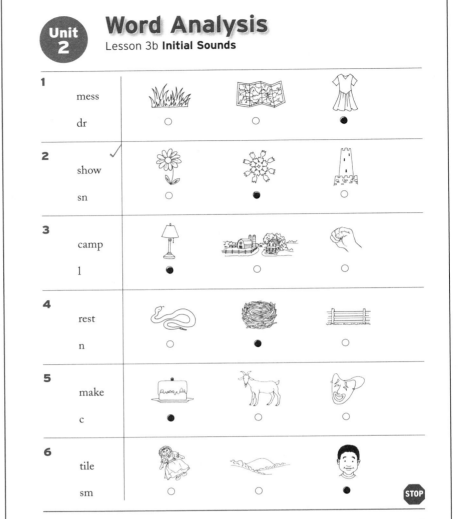

Unit 2 — Word Analysis
Lesson 3b **Initial Sounds**

1 mess / dr
2 show / sn
3 camp / l
4 rest / n
5 make / c
6 tile / sm

STOP

11

6. Look at row 6. The word is *tile*. Take away the *t* and put *s-m* in its place. Fill in the circle under the picture of the new word.

It's time to stop. You have finished Lesson 3b.

Review the answers with the students. Have the students indicate completion of the lesson by entering their score for this activity on the progress chart at the beginning of the book.

Lesson 4a
Word Formation

Focus

Reading Skill
• identifying beginning letters

Test-taking Skills
• following oral directions
• listening carefully
• considering every answer choice
• substituting answer choices

Sample S

Say Turn to Lesson 4a on page 12. In this lesson you will find the beginning letters in words.

Check to be sure the students have found the right page.

Say Look at S, the row at the top of the page. The picture shows a *ghost*. Find the letters that go before *o-s-t* (*Say the letters and all subsequent letters where needed.*) to make the word *ghost*. *(pause)* Fill in the circle under the second answer, *g-h*. The word *ghost* is spelled *g-h-o-s-t*.

Check to see that the students have marked the correct answer circle. If necessary, elaborate upon the instructions.

★TIPS

Say Now let's look at the tips.

Read the tips aloud to the students.

Say Listen carefully to what I say while you look at the pictures. If you are not sure which answer is correct, try each of the answer choices in the blank. This will help you find the right answer.

Explain the tips further, if necessary.

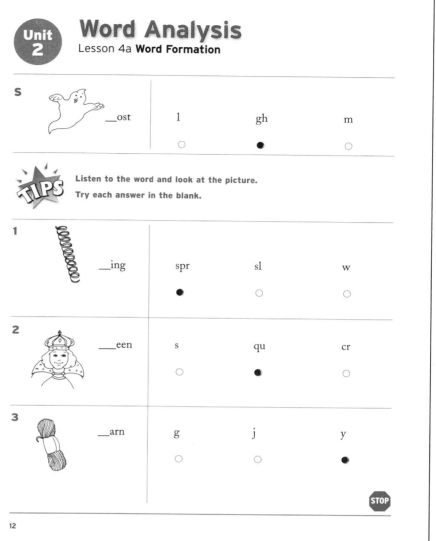

Practice

Say Now we are ready for Practice. Listen to what I say. Fill in the circle under the answer you think is correct. Are you ready? Let's begin.

Allow time between items for the students to mark their answers.

1. Look at row 1, the picture of the *spring*. Fill in the circle under the letters that go before *i-n-g* to make the word *spring*.

2. Look at row 2, the picture of the *queen*. Fill in the circle under the letters that go before *e-e-n* to make the word *queen*.

3. Look at row 3, the picture of the *yarn*. Fill in the circle under the letter that goes before *a-r-n* to make the word *yarn*.

    It's time to stop. You have finished Lesson 4a.

Review the answers with the students. Have the students indicate completion of the lesson by entering their score for this activity on the progress chart at the beginning of the book.

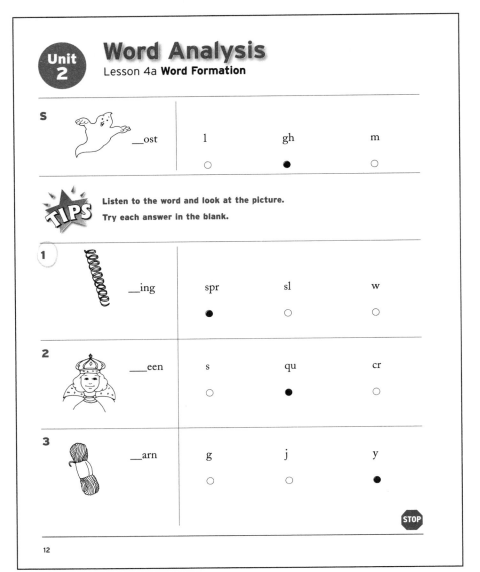

Unit 2 Lesson 4b Word Formation

Focus

Reading Skill
• identifying middle letters

Test-taking Skills
• following oral directions
• listening carefully
• considering every answer choice
• working methodically

Sample S

Say Turn to Lesson 4b on page 13. In this lesson you will find the letters that make the middle sounds in words.

Check to be sure the students have found the right page.

Say Look at S at the top of the page. The picture shows a *mitten*. Find the answer that goes with the letters beside the picture to make the word *mitten. (pause)* Fill in the circle under the third answer, *i.* The word *mitten* is spelled *m-i-t-t-e-n.*

Check to see that the students have marked the correct answer circle. If necessary, elaborate upon the instructions.

⭐**TIPS**

Say Now let's look at the tips.

Read the tips aloud to the students.

Say Listen carefully to what I say while you look at the pictures. If you are not sure which answer is correct, try each of the answer choices in the blank. This will help you find the right answer.

Explain the tips further, if necessary.

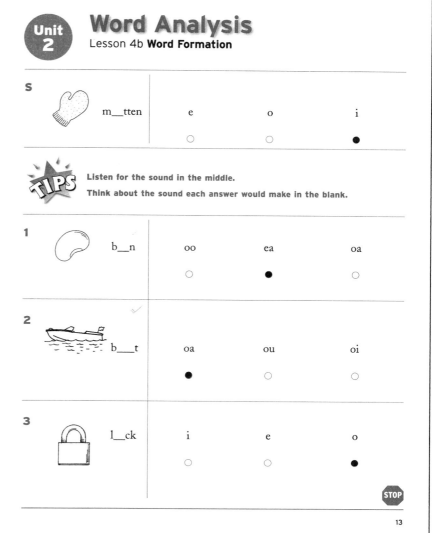

Practice

Say Now we are ready for Practice. Listen to what I say. Fill in the circle under the answer you think is correct. Are you ready? Let's begin.

Allow time between items for the students to mark their answers.

1. Look at row 1, the picture of the *bean*. Fill in the circle under the letters that go in the middle to make the word *bean*.

2. Look at row 2, the picture of the boat. Fill in the circle under the letters that go in the middle to make the word *boat*.

3. Look at row 3, the picture of the lock. Fill in the circle under the letter that goes in the middle to make the word *lock*.

    It's time to stop. You have finished Lesson 4b.

Review the answers with the students. Have the students indicate completion of the lesson by entering their score for this activity on the progress chart at the beginning of the book.

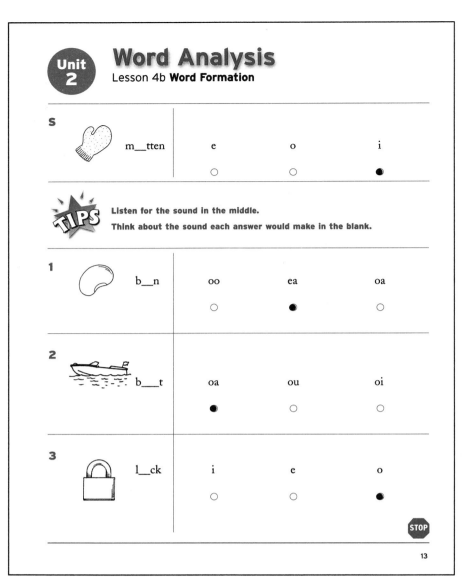

Unit 2

Word Analysis
Lesson 4b **Word Formation**

S   m__tten

e	o	i
○	○	●

TIPS

Listen for the sound in the middle.

Think about the sound each answer would make in the blank.

1   b__n

oo	ea	oa
○	●	○

2   b__t

oa	ou	oi
●	○	○

3   l__ck

i	e	o
○	○	●

STOP

13

Unit 2 Lesson 5a
Vowel Sounds

Focus

Reading Skill
• matching vowel sounds

Test-taking Skills
• following oral directions
• listening carefully
• considering every answer choice
• working methodically

Sample S

Say Turn to Lesson 5a on page 14. In this lesson you will answer questions about vowel sounds.

Check to be sure the students have found the right page.

Say Look at the pictures for S at the top of the page. Listen carefully. Which picture has a name with the same vowel sound as *wire ... wire*? *(pause)* Fill in the circle under the second answer, *fire*. It has the same vowel sound as *wire*.

Check to see that the students have marked the correct answer circle. If necessary, elaborate upon the directions until you are sure the students understand what they are supposed to do.

★TIPS

Say Now let's look at the tip.

Read the tip aloud to the students.

Say For the items in this lesson, you are supposed to find the word with the same vowel sound as the word I say. The vowel sound you should listen for is in the middle of the word. The correct answer will be the picture whose name has the same vowel or middle sound as the word I say.

Explain the tip further, if necessary.

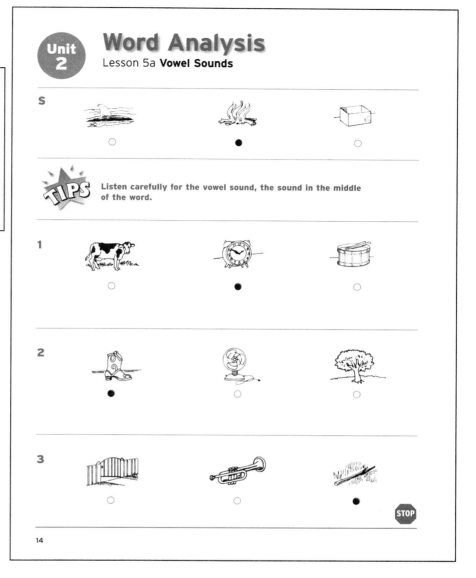

Unit 2 **Word Analysis**
Lesson 5a **Vowel Sounds**

Listen carefully for the vowel sound, the sound in the middle of the word.

14

Practice

Say Now we are ready for Practice. Listen to what I say. Fill in the circle under the answer you think is correct. Are you ready? Let's begin.

Allow time between items for the students to mark their answers.

1. Look at row 1. Fill in the circle under the picture whose name has the same vowel sound as *shop ... shop*.

2. Look at row 2. Fill in the circle under the picture whose name has the same vowel sound as *food ... food*.

3. Look at row 3. Fill in the circle under the picture whose name has the same vowel sound as *hit ... hit*.

    It's time to stop. You have finished Lesson 5a.

Review the answers with the students. Have the students indicate completion of the lesson by entering their score for this activity on the progress chart at the beginning of the book.

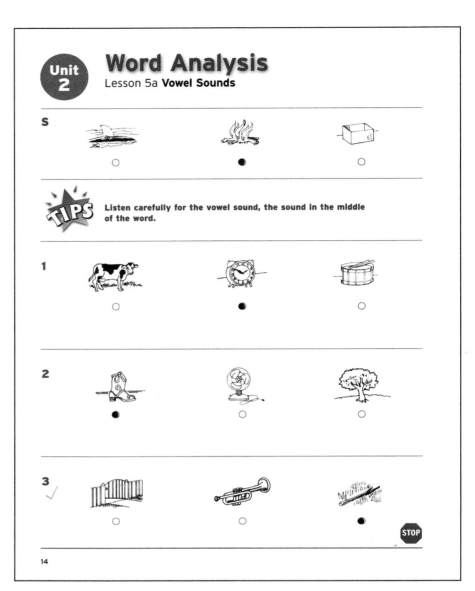

Unit 2

Word Analysis
Lesson 5a **Vowel Sounds**

S

TIPS Listen carefully for the vowel sound, the sound in the middle of the word.

1

2

3

14

Lesson 5b
Vowel Sounds

Unit 2

Focus

Reading Skill
• matching vowel sounds

Test-taking Skills
• following oral directions
• listening carefully
• considering every answer choice
• working methodically

Say Turn to Lesson 5b on page 15. In this lesson you will answer more questions about vowel sounds.

Check to be sure the students have found the right page.

Practice

Say Now we are ready for Practice. Listen to what I say. Fill in the circle under the answer you think is correct. Are you ready? Let's begin.

Allow time between items for the students to mark their answers.

1. Look at the row with the book. Fill in the circle under the word that has the same vowel sound as *fat...fat*.

2. Look at the row with the phone. Fill in the circle under the word that has the same vowel sound as *bounce...bounce*.

3. Look at the row with the leaf. Fill in the circle under the word that has the same vowel sound as *turn...turn*.

4. Look at the row with the cup. Fill in the circle under the word that has the same vowel sound as *bark...bark*.

5. Look at the row with the bell. Fill in the circle under the word that has the same vowel sound as *wheel...wheel*.

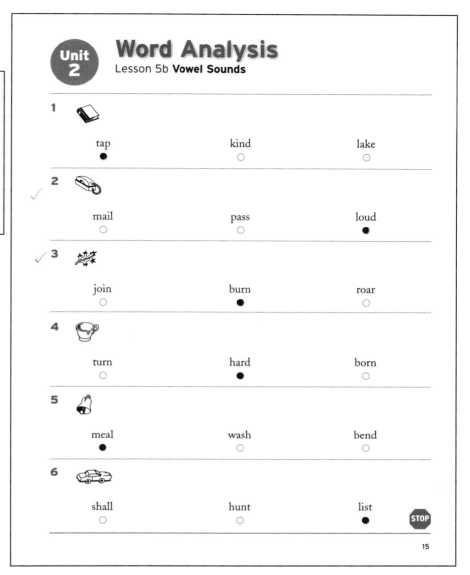

Word Analysis

Lesson 5b **Vowel Sounds**

Unit 2

1. tap ●   kind ○   lake ○

2. mail ○   pass ○   loud ●

3. join ○   burn ●   roar ○

4. turn ○   hard ●   born ○

5. meal ●   wash ○   bend ○

6. shall ○   hunt ○   list ●   STOP

15

6. Look at the row with the car. Fill in the circle under the word that has the same vowel sound as *mint...mint*.

   It's time to stop. You have finished Lesson 5b.

Review the answers with the students. Have the students indicate completion of the lesson by entering their score for this activity on the progress chart at the beginning of the book.

Test Yourself: Word Analysis

Focus

Reading Skills
- matching beginning sounds
- matching rhyming sounds
- substituting beginning sounds
- identifying beginning letters
- identifying middle letters
- matching vowel sounds

Test-taking Skills
- following oral directions
- listening carefully
- considering every answer choice
- taking the best guess when unsure of the answer
- subvocalizing answer choices
- substituting answer choices
- working methodically

This lesson simulates an actual test-taking experience. Therefore, it is recommended that the directions be read verbatim and the suggested procedures be followed.

Directions

Administration Time: approximately 30 minutes

Say Turn to the Test Yourself lesson on page 16.

Check to be sure the students have found the right page. Point out to the students that this is not a real test and that they will score it themselves to see how well they are doing.

Say This lesson will check how well you know letters and sounds. Remember to make sure that the circles for your answer choices are completely filled in. Press your pencil firmly so that your marks come out dark. Completely erase any marks for answers that you change. Do not write anything except your answer choices in your books.

Find S1, the row of words below the picture of the book. Listen carefully. Which word begins with the same sound as *under... under*? Fill in the circle for your answer.

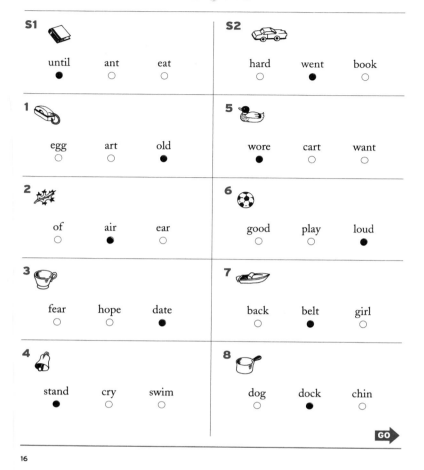

Allow time for the students to fill in their answers.

Say The first answer, *until*, is correct. If you chose another answer, erase yours and fill in the circle for the word *until* now.

Check to see that the students have correctly filled in their answer circles with a dark mark.

Say Now you will do more items like S1. Listen carefully to what I say. Fill in the circle under the answer you think is correct. If you are not sure which answer is correct, fill in the circle under the answer you think might be right. Are you ready? Let's begin.

Allow time between items for the students to mark their answers.

1. Look at the row with the phone. Which word in this row begins with the same sound as *oak*? Fill in the circle under the word that begins with the same sound as *oak ... oak*.

2. Look at the row with the leaf. Which word in this row begins with the same sounds as *area*? Fill in the circle under the word that begins with the same sound as *area ... area*.

3. Look at the row with the cup. Which word in this row begins with the same sound as *desk*? Fill in the circle under the word that begins with the same sound as *desk ... desk*.

4. Look at the row with the bell. Which word in this row begins with the same sound as *still*? Fill in the circle under the word that begins with the same sound as *still ... still*.

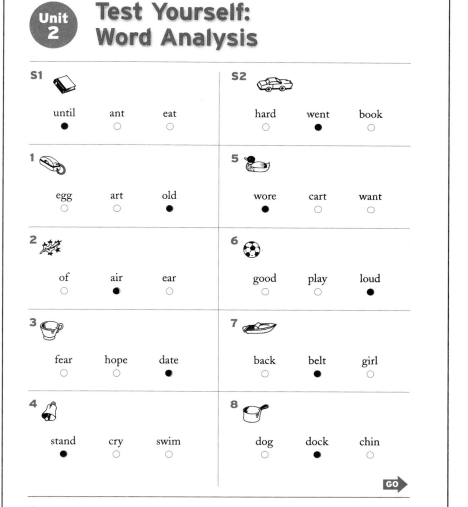

Unit 2 Test Yourself: Word Analysis

S1
until   ant   eat
●　○　○

S2
hard   went   book
○　●　○

1
egg   art   old
○　○　●

5
wore   cart   want
●　○　○

2
of   air   ear
○　●　○

6
good   play   loud
○　○　●

3
fear   hope   date
○　○　●

7
back   belt   girl
○　●　○

4
stand   cry   swim
●　○　○

8
dog   dock   chin
○　●　○

GO

16

Look at S2, the row of words below the picture of the car. It is at the top of the next column. Listen carefully. Which word rhymes with *rent*? Fill in the circle under the word that rhymes with *rent*... *rent*.

Allow time for the students to fill in their answers.

Say The second answer, *went*, is correct. If you chose another answer, erase yours and fill in the circle for the word *went* now.

Check to see that the students have correctly filled in their answer circles with a dark mark.

Say Now you will do more items like S2. Listen carefully to what I say. Fill in the circle under the answer you think is correct.

5. Look at the row with the duck. Fill in the circle under the word that rhymes with *tore*... *tore*.

6. Look at the row with the ball. Fill in the circle under the word that rhymes with *proud*... *proud*.

7. Look at the row with the boat. Fill in the circle under the word that rhymes with *felt*... *felt*.

8. Move down to the last row, the one with the pot. Fill in the circle under the word that rhymes with *knock*... *knock*.

Look at the next page, page 17.

Check to be sure the students have found the right page. Allow the students a moment to rest.

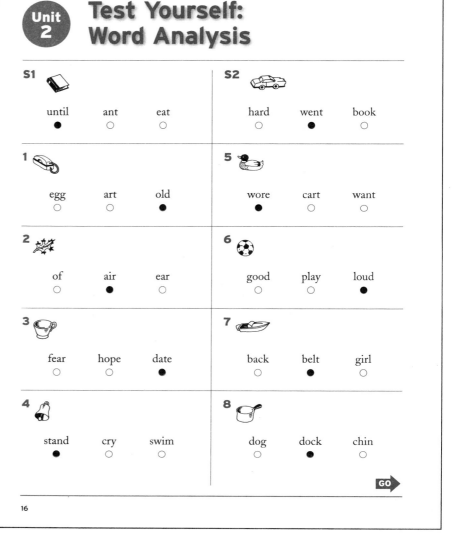

9. Look at row 9. The word is *wore*. Take away the *w* and put *s-t* in its place. Fill in the circle under the picture of the new word.

10. Look at row 10. The word is *say*. Take away the *s* and put *t-r* in its place. Fill in the circle under the picture of the new word.

11. Look at row 11. The word is *rock*. Take away the *r* and put *b-l* in its place. Fill in the circle under the picture of the new word.

12. Look at row 12. The word is *low*. Take away the *l* and put *c-r* in its place. Fill in the circle under the picture of the new word.

13. Look at row 13. The word is *hum*. Take away the *h* and put *d-r* in its place. Fill in the circle under the picture of the new word.

14. Look at row 14. The word is *dish*. Take away the *d* and put *f* in its place. Fill in the circle under the picture of the new word.

    Turn to the next page, page 18.

Check to be sure the students have found the right page. Allow the students a moment to rest.

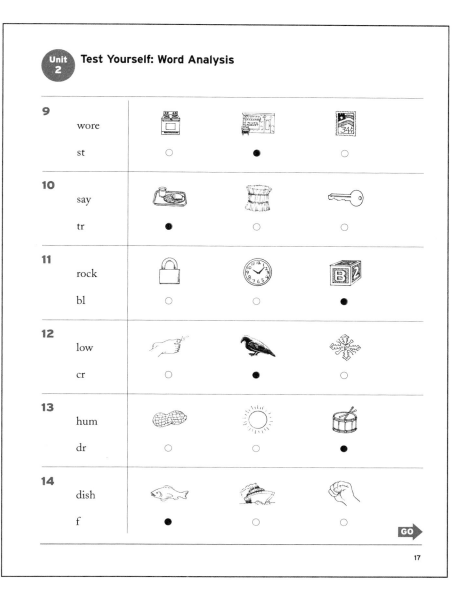

Unit 2   Test Yourself: Word Analysis

9   wore
    st

10 say
    tr

11 rock
    bl

12 low
    cr

13 hum
    dr

14 dish
    f

GO

17

15. Look at row 15, the picture of the *father*. Fill in the circle under the letter that goes before *a-t-h-e-r* to make the word *father*.

16. Look at row 16, the picture of someone going for a *swim*. Fill in the circle under the letters that go before *i-m* to make the word *swim*.

17. Look at row 17, the picture of the *jar*. Fill in the circle under the letter that goes before *a-r* to make the word *jar*.

18. Look at row 18, the picture of the *horse*. Fill in the circle under the letter that goes before *o-r-s-e* to make the word *horse*.

19. Look at row 19, the picture of the *loaf* of bread. Fill in the circle under the letters that go in the middle to make the word *loaf*.

20. Look at row 20, the picture of the *range*. Fill in the circle under the letter that goes in the middle to make the word *range*.

   Look at the next page, page 19.

Check to be sure the students have found the right page. Allow the students a moment to rest.

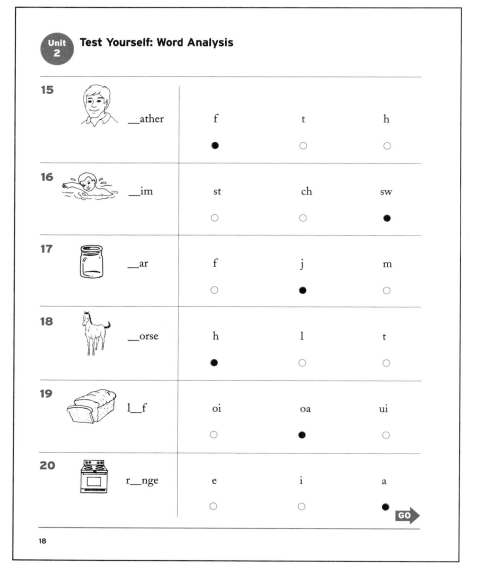

Unit 2	Test Yourself: Word Analysis			
15	__ather	f ●	t ○	h ○
16	__im	st ○	ch ○	sw ●
17	__ar	f ○	j ●	m ○
18	__orse	h ●	l ○	t ○
19	l__f	oi ○	oa ●	ui ○
20	r__nge	e ○	i ○	a ● GO

18

21. Look at row 21. Fill in the circle under the picture whose name has the same vowel sound as *bend ... bend*.

22. Look at row 22. Fill in the circle under the picture whose name has the same vowel sound as *main ... main*.

23. Look at row 23. Fill in the circle under the picture whose name has the same vowel sound as *noon ... noon*.

24. Look at row 24. Fill in the circle under the picture whose name has the same vowel sound as *lot ... lot*.

25. Look at row 25. Fill in the circle under the picture whose name has the same vowel sound as *reach ... reach*.

Turn to the next page, page 20.

Check to be sure the students have found the right page. Allow the students a moment to rest.

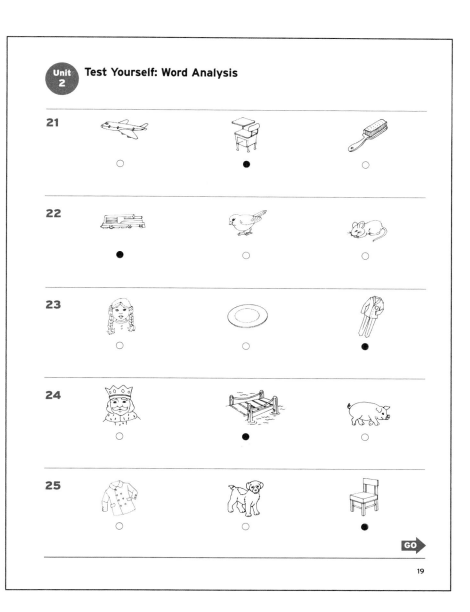

Unit 2 Test Yourself: Word Analysis

19

26. Look at the row with the cup. Fill in the circle under the word that has the same vowel sound as *wait ... wait*.

27. Look at the row with the bell. Fill in the circle under the word that has the same vowel sound as *sent ... sent*.

28. Look at the row with the car. Fill in the circle under the word that has the same vowel sound as *junk ... junk*.

29. Look at the row with the duck. Fill in the circle under the word that has the same vowel sound as *wig ... wig*.

30. Look at the row with the ball. Fill in the circle under the word that has the same vowel sound as *moist ... moist*.

31. Look at the row with the boat. Fill in the circle under the word that has the same vowel sound as *word ... word*.

Say It's time to stop. You have completed the Test Yourself lesson.

Review the answers with the students. Have the students indicate completion of the lesson by entering their score for this activity on the progress chart at the beginning of the book. Provide the students whatever help is necessary to record their scores.

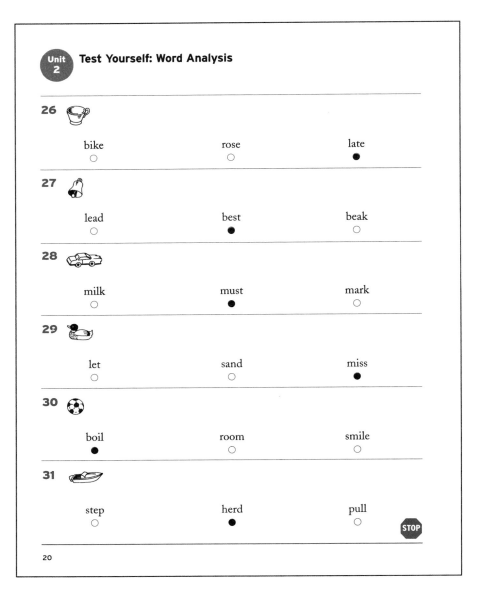

Unit 2 Test Yourself: Word Analysis

26.
bike ○   rose ○   late ●

27.
lead ○   best ●   beak ○

28.
milk ○   must ●   mark ○

29.
let ○   sand ○   miss ●

30.
boil ●   room ○   smile ○

31.
step ○   herd ●   pull ○

STOP

20

Unit 3

Background

This unit contains seven lessons that deal with reading skills. Students are asked to identify words, complete sentences, and answer questions about paragraphs they read.

• **In Lessons 6a and 6b,** students match a picture to a word in a sentence. Students are encouraged to follow oral directions and listen carefully. They consider every answer choice, use key words, and analyze answer choices.

• **In Lessons 7a and 7b,** students complete sentences about a picture. They review the test-taking skills introduced in Lessons 6a and 6b, use context to find the answer, and work methodically.

• **In Lessons 8a and 8b,** students answer questions about paragraphs they read. They review the test-taking skills introduced in previous lessons, refer to a passage, and take the best guess when unsure of the answer.

• **In the Test Yourself lesson,** the reading skills and test-taking skills introduced and used in Lessons 6a through 8b are reinforced and presented in a format that gives students the experience of taking an achievement test.

Instructional Objectives

Lesson 6a **Word Attack** Lesson 6b **Word Attack**	Given a sentence and three pictures, the student identifies which of the pictures matches a word in the sentence.
Lesson 7a **Pictures** Lesson 7b **Pictures**	Given a picture and incomplete sentences about it, the student identifies which of four words best completes the sentences.
Lesson 8a **Stories** Lesson 8b **Stories**	Given a written passage and a literal or inferential question based on the passage, the student identifies which of three answer choices is correct.
Test Yourself	Given questions similar to those in Lessons 6a through 8b, the student utilizes reading skills and test-taking strategies on achievement test formats.

Lesson 6a
Word Attack

Unit 3

Focus

Reading Skill
• matching pictures and text clues

Test-taking Skills
• following oral directions
• listening carefully
• considering every answer choice
• using key words to find an answer
• analyzing answer choices

Sample S

Say Turn to Lesson 6a on page 21. The page number is at the bottom of the page on the right. This page has sentences and pictures.

Check to see that the students have found the right page.

Say In this lesson you will choose a picture that matches the last word in the story. Read the story for S. It is at the top of the page. Now look at the pictures under the story. Which picture best matches the last word in the story? *(pause)* The second answer, *banana*, is correct. Fill in the circle under the banana, the second answer. Be sure your answer circle is completely filled in with a dark mark and that you have marked the correct answer circle.

Check to see that the students have marked the correct circle. Tell the students that even if they can't read the last word, they can use clues such as beginning, middle, and ending sounds to match the names of the pictures.

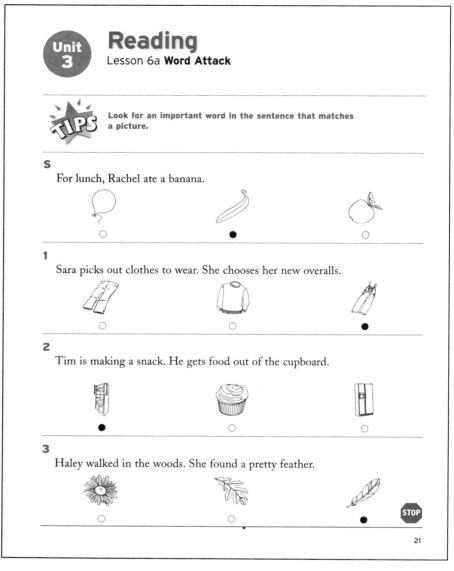

Unit 3

Reading
Lesson 6a **Word Attack**

TIPS Look for an important word in the sentence that matches a picture.

S For lunch, Rachel ate a banana.

1 Sara picks out clothes to wear. She chooses her new overalls.

2 Tim is making a snack. He gets food out of the cupboard.

3 Haley walked in the woods. She found a pretty feather.

STOP

21

★**TIPS**

Say Now let's look at the tip.

Read the tip aloud to the students.

Say Read the sentence and think about what it means. Pay close attention to the last word in the story. This is the word that should match the picture. If you aren't sure how to read the last word, look for clues such as beginning, middle, and ending sounds. Match these sounds with the names of the pictures.

Practice

Say Now we will do the Practice items in the same way we did S. You will work by yourself. Read each story and look at the pictures. Fill in the circle under the picture that goes best with the last word in the story. If you don't know what the last word is, use letter clues to help you find the right answer. Work until you come to the STOP sign at the bottom of the page. Do you have any questions? Start working now.

Allow time for the students to do Numbers 1 through 3.

Say It's time to stop. You have finished Lesson 6a.

Review the answers with the students. Have the students indicate completion of the lesson by entering their score for this activity on the progress chart at the beginning of the book. Provide the students whatever help is necessary to record their scores.

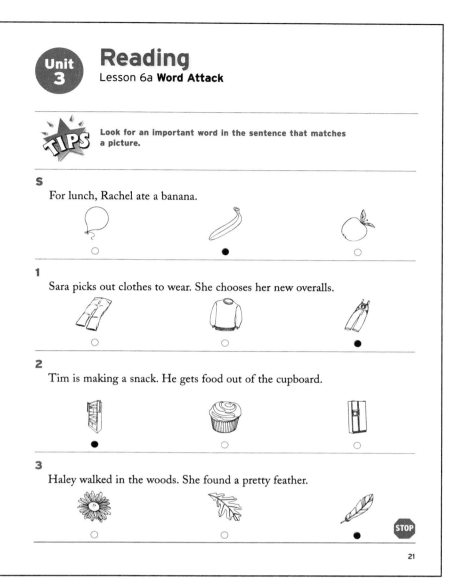

Focus

Reading Skill
• matching pictures and text clues

Test-taking Skills
• following oral directions
• listening carefully
• considering every answer choice
• using key words to find an answer
• analyzing answer choices

Say Turn to Lesson 6b on page 22. The page number is at the bottom of the page on the left. In this lesson you will choose a picture that matches the last word in a story.

Check to see that the students have found the right page.

Practice

Say Read each story and look at the pictures. Fill in the circle under the picture that goes best with the last word in the story. If you don't know what the last word is, use letter clues to help you find the right answer. Work until you come to the STOP sign at the bottom of the page. Do you have any questions? Start working now.

Allow time for the students to do Numbers 1 through 4.

Say It's time to stop. You have finished Lesson 6b.

Review the answers with the students. Have the students indicate completion of the lesson by entering their score for this activity on the progress chart at the beginning of the book. Provide the students whatever help is necessary to record their scores.

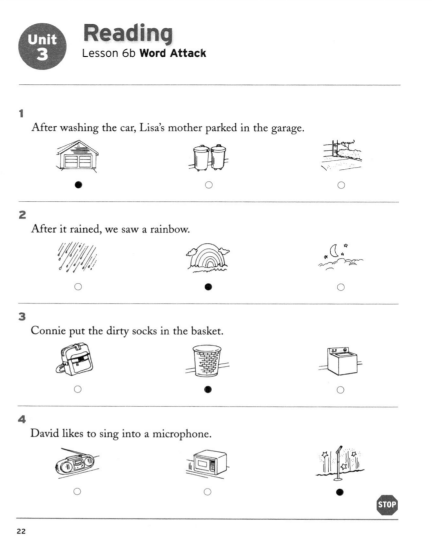

Unit 3
Reading
Lesson 6b **Word Attack**

1 After washing the car, Lisa's mother parked in the garage.

2 After it rained, we saw a rainbow.

3 Connie put the dirty socks in the basket.

4 David likes to sing into a microphone.

22

Unit 3 Lesson 7a Pictures

Focus

Reading Skill
- completing sentences that match a picture

Test-taking Skills
- following oral directions
- listening carefully
- considering every answer choice
- using context to find an answer
- working methodically

Sample S

Say Turn to Lesson 7a on page 23. There is a large picture near the top of the page.

Check to see that the students have found the right page.

Say In this lesson you will read sentences about a picture. The sentences have a missing word. You will choose a word that fits best in each sentence. Look at the picture. Now read the sentence for S. Which word fits best in the sentence? *(pause)* The third answer, *hang,* is correct. Dad will *hang* the picture. Fill in the circle beside the word *hang.* Be sure your answer circle is completely filled in with a dark mark and that you have marked the correct answer circle.

Check to see that the students have marked the correct circle.

⭐**TIPS**

Say Now let's look at the tip.

Read the tip aloud to the students.

Say Look at the picture, read the sentence with the blank, and then look back at the picture. The picture will give you clues about which word should go in the blank. You should also pay attention to the other words in the sentence. The meaning of the sentence will also help you find the answer.

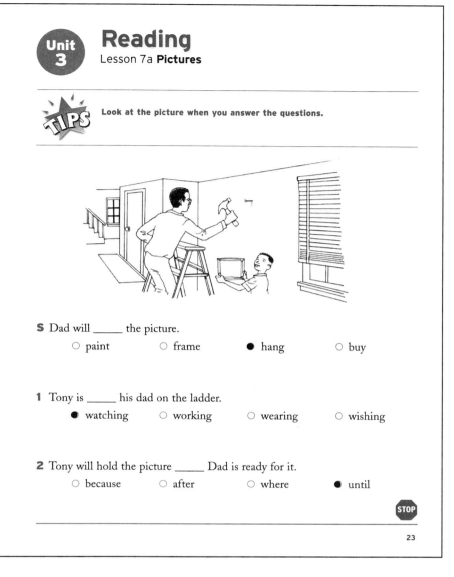

Unit 3 Reading

Lesson 7a **Pictures**

TIPS Look at the picture when you answer the questions.

S Dad will _____ the picture.
- ○ paint
- ○ frame
- ● hang
- ○ buy

1 Tony is _____ his dad on the ladder.
- ● watching
- ○ working
- ○ wearing
- ○ wishing

2 Tony will hold the picture _____ Dad is ready for it.
- ○ because
- ○ after
- ○ where
- ● until

STOP

23

Practice

Say Now we will do the Practice items in the same way we did the sample. You will work by yourself. Look at the picture and read the sentences. Fill in the circle beside the word that fits best in each sentence. Work until you come to the STOP sign at the bottom of the page. Do you have any questions? Start working now.

Allow time for the students to do Numbers 1 and 2.

Say It's time to stop. You have finished Lesson 7a.

Review the answers with the students. Have the students indicate completion of the lesson by entering their score for this activity on the progress chart at the beginning of the book. Provide the students whatever help is necessary to record their scores.

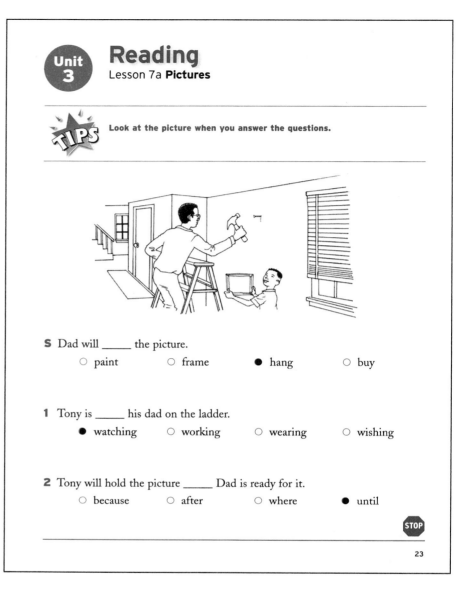

Unit 3

Reading
Lesson 7a **Pictures**

TIPS Look at the picture when you answer the questions.

S Dad will _____ the picture.
○ paint   ○ frame   ● hang   ○ buy

1 Tony is _____ his dad on the ladder.
● watching   ○ working   ○ wearing   ○ wishing

2 Tony will hold the picture _____ Dad is ready for it.
○ because   ○ after   ○ where   ● until

STOP

23

Unit 3 Lesson 7b
Pictures

Focus
Reading Skill
- completing sentences that match a picture

Test-taking Skills
- following oral directions
- listening carefully
- considering every answer choice
- using context to find the answer
- working methodically

Say Turn to Lesson 7b on page 24. There is a large picture near the top of the page. In this lesson you will complete sentences about a picture. You did items like this in Lesson 7a.

Check to see that the students have found the right page.

Practice

Say For the items in this lesson, you will look at the picture and read the sentences. Fill in the circle beside the word that fits best in each sentence. Use the information in the picture and the meaning of the sentence to find the answer. Work until you come to the STOP sign at the bottom of the page. Do you have any questions? Start working now.

Allow time for the students to do Numbers 1 through 3.

Say It's time to stop. You have finished Lesson 7b.

Review the answers with the students. Have the students indicate completion of the lesson by entering their score for this activity on the progress chart at the beginning of the book. Provide the students whatever help is necessary to record their scores.

Unit 3 Reading
Lesson 7b **Pictures**

1 Suzy is next to Mr. Miller's _____.

　　○ bulldozer　　● tractor　　○ truck　　○ car

2 Mr. Miller has been driving in the _____ fields.

　　● muddy　　○ rainy　　○ empty　　○ frozen

3 Suzy will help Mr. Miller _____ the wheels.

　　○ stop　　○ turn　　○ water　　● clean

STOP

24

Focus

Reading Skills
- understanding sequence
- recognizing details
- identifying feelings
- recognizing setting
- making inferences
- making predictions

Test-taking Skills
- considering every answer choice
- referring to a passage to answer questions
- taking the best guess when unsure of the answer

Sample S

Say Turn to Lesson 8a on page 25. This page has a story and some questions about it.

Check to see that the students have found the right page.

Say In this lesson you will answer questions about a story you read. Read the story for S and the question about it. Which answer is correct? *(pause)* The second answer is correct because the first thing the cat did was jump up on the chair. Fill in the circle beside the second answer. Be sure your answer circle is completely filled in with a dark mark.

Check to see that the students have marked the correct circle.

Say Let's review the tip.

Read the tip aloud to the students.

Say Don't try to know the story by heart. Just read it and try to understand it. Then read the questions. Look back at the story to find the answers.

Reading
Lesson 8a **Stories**

S

> The cat jumped up on the chair. She walked in a circle. Then she sat down. After a minute, she jumped down on the floor.

What did the cat do first?
- ○ Walked in a circle
- ● Jumped up on the chair
- ○ Sat down

TIPS Look back at the story to find the answer.

> It was time for Jack to go to school. He could not find his shoe. Jack looked all over the house. The shoe was nowhere.
> Jack's dog, Piper, came to Jack. Piper barked and went to the backyard. Jack followed him. Piper went into his doghouse. Jack looked inside. He was surprised. There was his shoe!
> "Now I know who took the shoe," Jack said.

1 What was Jack looking for?
- ○ His jacket
- ● His shoe
- ○ His books

2 Where was Jack going?
- ● School
- ○ The park
- ○ A baseball game

3 Where did Jack find his shoe?
- ○ Under the bed
- ○ In the closet
- ● In a doghouse

GO

25

Practice

Say Now we will do the Practice items in the same way we did S. You will work by yourself. Read each story and the questions that follow it. Fill in the circle beside the answer you think is correct. If you are not sure which answer is correct, take your best guess. When you come to the GO sign at the bottom of a page, turn the page and continue working. Work until you come to the STOP sign at the bottom of page 27. Fill in your answer circles with dark marks and completely erase any marks for answers that you change. Do you have any questions? Start working now.

Allow time for the students to read the passages and answer the questions.

 Unit 3 · Lesson 8a **Stories**

> Anna lived on a farm. Every day she collected eggs from the chickens.
> One spring day she went to the chicken house. There were no eggs. Then she heard a sound. She turned around. A chicken walked by. Ten yellow chicks ran behind her.
> Anna smiled. "That's where the eggs went!" she said.

4 Where did Anna live?
- ● On a farm
- ○ In a city
- ○ On a boat

5 What was Anna's job?
- ○ Mow the lawn
- ○ Set the table
- ● Collect eggs

6 How did Anna feel when she saw the chicks?
- ○ Sad
- ● Happy
- ○ Silly

GO

26

Say It's time to stop. You have finished Lesson 8a.

Review the answers with the students. Have the students indicate completion of the lesson by entering their score for this activity on the progress chart at the beginning of the book. Provide the students whatever help is necessary to record their scores.

 Lesson 8a **Stories**

> Mike's cat, Inky, is a strange cat. She loves to play outside in the yard. Inky's favorite outdoor game is "chase the stick." Mike throws a stick across the yard. Inky fetches it and brings it back.
>
> Inky has two favorite indoor games. One is "catch the feather." Inky's toy is a string with a feather on the end. Mike pulls the feather across the floor. Inky chases it and grabs it with her mouth. She has pink feathers all over her face!
>
> Inky's other favorite indoor game is "hide and seek." Inky takes small things like paper clips and pencils. She hides them under the couch. Whenever Mike needs a pencil, he looks under the couch.

7 How many games does Inky like to play?

○ One

○ Two

● Three

8 Why is it strange that Inky likes to fetch a stick?

● Dogs like that game.

○ Mike throws it.

○ Birds like that game.

9 Which of these might Mike find under the couch?

○ Furniture

○ Bicycle

● Ballpoint pen

27

Lesson 8b
Stories

Focus

Reading Skills
- recognizing details
- understanding reasons
- drawing conclusions
- understanding the main idea

Test-taking Skills
- considering every answer choice
- referring to a passage to answer questions
- taking the best guess when unsure of the answer

Say Turn to Lesson 8b on page 28. This page has a story and some questions about it.

Check to see that the students have found the right page.

Practice

Say In this lesson you will answer more questions about stories you read. You will work by yourself. Read each story and the questions that follow it. Fill in the circle beside the answer you think is correct. If you are not sure which answer is correct, take your best guess. When you come to the GO sign at the bottom of a page, turn the page and continue working. Work until you come to the STOP sign at the bottom of page 30. Fill in your answer circles with dark marks and completely erase any marks for answers that you change. Do you have any questions? Start working now.

Allow time for the students to read the passages and answer the questions.

Reading
Lesson 8b Stories

Emily's dad is a photographer. He loves to take pictures of animals. His dream is to take pictures of whales.

Last spring his wish came true. He and Emily were invited to ride on a big boat. The boat was filled with people studying whales. Emily's dad was hired to take pictures of the trip. They spent three weeks on the boat.

Every day Emily helped Dad with his cameras. Then they watched the sea. Soon the whales came. They were so big! Their huge tails slapped the water and made big splashes. Sometimes they swam next to the boat. One time Emily saw a baby whale.

1 **What was Emily's dad's dream?**
- ○ To ride on a boat
- ● To take pictures of whales
- ○ To go on a trip with Emily

2 **How long were Emily and her dad on the boat?**
- ○ Three days
- ● Three weeks
- ○ Three years

3 **Why were the people on the boat?**
- ○ They liked the ocean.
- ● They studied whales.
- ○ They wanted to take pictures.

GO

> Birthdays were important in David's family. His sister Jenny had a birthday coming up. Jenny loved to read. But David did not have enough money to buy her a new book.
>
> David and his mother had an idea. He found what he needed in the basement. He borrowed Dad's tools. Then he got to work.
>
> Jenny's birthday came. She opened up her gift. It was a bookshelf. David had painted it red and yellow. They were Jenny's favorite colors.
>
> "I will hang this on my wall," Jenny said. "It is the best present I ever got."

4 **What celebration is this story about?**

● Birthday
○ Wedding
○ Thanksgiving

5 **What is Jenny's favorite thing to do?**

○ Watch television
● Read books
○ Play games

6 **Where did David find the paint he used on the bookshelf?**

○ At the store
○ Outside
● In the basement

7 **Who helped David get the idea for the present?**

● His mother
○ His father
○ His teacher

29

Say It's time to stop. You have finished Lesson 8b.

Review the answers with the students. Have the students indicate completion of the lesson by entering their score for this activity on the progress chart at the beginning of the book. Provide the students whatever help is necessary to record their scores.

My best friend, Amy, was in the hospital. She had hurt her foot. She couldn't come to school. We all missed her a lot. I knew that she missed us too.

One day our teacher got an idea. "We can't visit Amy all the time," she said. "But maybe there is a way to show her that we are thinking about her." The teacher gave each of us a big piece of paper. We filled the paper with nice sayings and pretty pictures.

The next week we visited Amy. She was so surprised to get our presents! Her mom put our big drawings on the wall. It made the room look beautiful.

"Get well soon, Amy," we said. "We all miss you."

8 **What is the story mostly about?**
○ Drawing pictures
● Cheering up a friend
○ Visiting the hospital

10 **Why did Amy's mom put the drawings on the wall?**
● To make the room nicer
○ To cover the windows
○ To remind her of Amy

9 **Why was Amy not in school?**
● She was in the hospital.
○ She had moved.
○ She was home.

11 **What was wrong with Amy?**
○ She cut her hand.
○ She had a bad cold.
● She hurt her foot.

30

Unit 3 Test Yourself: Reading

Focus

Reading Skills
- matching pictures and text clues
- completing sentences that match a picture
- recognizing setting
- identifying feelings
- recognizing details
- understanding reasons
- making inferences
- drawing conclusions
- understanding the main idea

Test-taking Skills
- following oral directions
- listening carefully
- considering every answer choice
- using key words to find an answer
- analyzing answer choices
- using context to find the answer
- working methodically
- referring to a passage to answer questions
- taking the best guess when unsure of the answer

This lesson simulates an actual test-taking experience. Therefore, it is recommended that the directions be read verbatim and the suggested procedures be followed.

Directions

Administration Time: approximately 40 minutes

Say Look at the Test Yourself lesson on page 31. There is a sentence and pictures at the top of the page.

Check to be sure the students have found the right page. Point out to the students that this is not a real test and that they will score it themselves to see how well they are doing.

Say This lesson will check how well you understand the reading skills you practiced before. Remember to make sure that the circles for your answer choices are completely filled in. Press your pencil firmly so that your marks come out dark. Completely erase any

marks for answers that you change. Do not write anything except your answer choices in your books.

On this page you will choose a picture that matches the last word in a short story. Read the story for S. It is at the top of the page. Now look at the pictures under the story. Which picture best matches the last word of the story? *(pause)* The second answer, *mat*, is correct. Fill in the circle under the mat, the second answer. Be sure your answer circle is completely filled in with a dark mark and that you have marked the correct answer circle.

Check to see that the students have marked the correct circle.

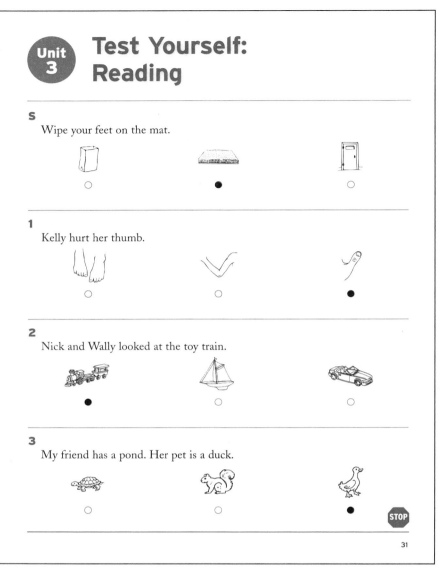

Say Now we will do more items like S. Look at each story and the pictures. Fill in the circle under the picture that goes best with the last word of the story. If you are not sure which answer is correct, take your best guess. Work until you come to the STOP sign at the bottom of the page. Fill in your answer circles with dark marks and completely erase any marks for answers that you change. Do you have any questions? Start working now.

Allow time for the students to do Numbers 1 through 3.

Say You may stop working now. Turn to the next page, page 32. For the items in this part of the lesson, you will look at a picture and read sentences with a blank in them. Fill in the circle beside the word that fits best in each sentence. Use the information in the picture and the meaning of the sentence to find the answer. Work until you come to the STOP sign at the bottom of the page. Do you have any questions? Start working now.

Allow time for the students to do Numbers 4 through 7. Walk around the room and make sure the students understand what they are supposed to do.

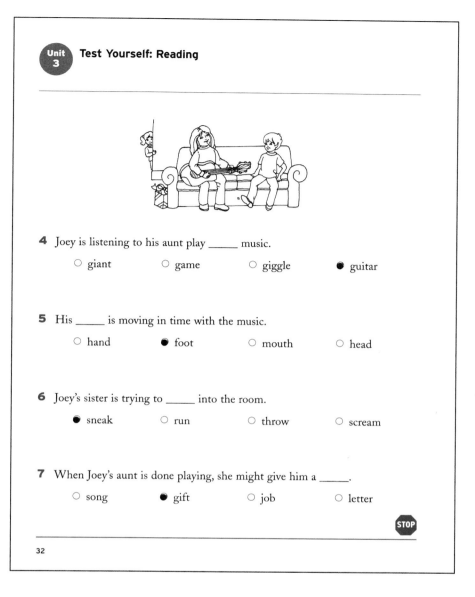

Unit 3 Test Yourself: Reading

4 Joey is listening to his aunt play _____ music.

○ giant   ○ game   ○ giggle   ● guitar

5 His _____ is moving in time with the music.

○ hand   ● foot   ○ mouth   ○ head

6 Joey's sister is trying to _____ into the room.

● sneak   ○ run   ○ throw   ○ scream

7 When Joey's aunt is done playing, she might give him a _____.

○ song   ● gift   ○ job   ○ letter

STOP

32

Say You may stop working now. Turn to the next page, page 33. For the items in this part of the lesson, you will read stories and answer questions about them. When you come to the GO sign at the bottom of a page, turn the page and continue working. Work until you come to the STOP sign at the bottom of page 35. Do you have any questions? Start working now.

Allow time for the students to do Numbers 8 through 18.

 Test Yourself: Reading

> Jonah's mom was at work. Jonah wanted to surprise her. He cleaned his room. He washed the dishes. He took out the trash.
>
> Mom came home. She was surprised. "The house looks great!" she said. Jonah smiled.
>
> Mom gave Jonah a present. It was a new game. Jonah was surprised. "Thank you for all your work," Mom said.

8 Where was Jonah's mom?
- ○ At home
- ● At work
- ○ At school

10 What did Jonah's mom give him?
- ○ A shirt
- ○ A dog
- ● A game

9 How did Jonah's mom feel when she came home?
- ● Surprised
- ○ Foolish
- ○ Tired

33

Mom wanted to have a yard sale. "We have too many things," she said. "It's time to get rid of some things."

Dad, Liz, and Penny got to work. They cleaned out the garage. Liz put all of her old toys in a box. Penny picked out the clothes that were too small. Mom set up tables in the yard. They put all of the things out to sell.

"No one will buy this stuff!" Penny said.

People came to the yard sale all day. Finally, it was over. "We worked hard and I am hungry," Mom said. She shook the money box. It was full. "We can buy a nice dinner," she said.

11 Why did Mom want to have a yard sale?

○ To buy a new table

● To get rid of some things

○ To buy dinner

12 Who put clothes in the yard sale?

○ Liz

○ Mom

● Penny

13 Why didn't Penny think anyone would buy their stuff?

○ She thought it was new.

○ She thought it was broken.

● She thought it was junk.

14 How do you know the family sold many things?

● The box was filled with money.

○ They cleaned out the garage.

○ Liz sold her old toys.

GO

Say It's time to stop. You have completed the Test Yourself lesson. Check to see that you have completely filled in your answer circles with dark marks. Make sure that any marks for answers that you changed have been completely erased. Now you may close your books.

Review the answers with the students. Have the students indicate completion of the lesson by entering their score for this activity on the progress chart at the beginning of the book. Provide the students whatever help is necessary to record their scores.

 Unit 3 **Test Yourself: Reading**

> Grandma was staying in a hotel for a while. Her house was being fixed. I liked to visit her. But the hotel was not the same as home. Grandma did not like it. Neither did I.
>
> "What can we do?" I said. "You will be here for a few more weeks."
>
> "I know," Grandma said. She whispered her plan to me. I grinned.
>
> The next day Dad took me to Grandma's house. It seemed empty and sad without her. I found her collection of colored glass bottles. I took some perfume from her dresser. Then we went back to the hotel.
>
> Grandma and I had so much fun hanging the bottles in front of her window. We put a drop of perfume in each one. The sun shone through the bottles and made colorful pictures on the floor.
>
> "Now it smells like home," she said.

15 Why didn't Grandma and the child like the hotel?

○ It was too far away.

○ It cost too much money.

● It wasn't the same as home.

16 What is this story mostly about?

○ Fixing a house that was old

● Making a grandmother feel better

○ Staying in a hotel

17 How did the child get to Grandma's house?

○ Her mother took her.

● Her father took her.

○ She walked by herself.

18 Why was the perfume so important?

● It smelled like Grandma's house.

○ It was something that Dad liked.

○ It was a pretty color.

35

Background

This unit contains three lessons that deal with listening skills. Students are asked to choose an answer that matches an oral prompt.

• **In Lesson 9a,** students identify the picture that best matches an oral prompt. Students are encouraged to follow oral directions and listen carefully. They consider every answer choice and use key words to find an answer.

• **In Lesson 9b,** students identify the picture that best matches an oral prompt. They review the test-taking skills introduced in Lesson 9a and take the best guess when unsure of the answer.

• **In the Test Yourself lesson,** the listening skills and test-taking skills introduced and used in Lessons 9a and 9b are reinforced and presented in a format that gives students the experience of taking an achievement test.

Instructional **Objectives**

Lesson 9a **Listening Skills** Lesson 9b **Listening Skills**	Given an oral prompt and three pictures, the student identifies which of the pictures matches the oral prompt.
Test Yourself	Given questions similar to those in Lessons 9a and 9b, the student utilizes listening skills and test-taking strategies on achievement test formats.

Lesson 9a
Listening Skills

Unit 4

Focus

Listening Skill
- matching graphic answers and oral prompts

Test-taking Skills
- following oral directions
- listening carefully
- considering every answer choice
- using key words to find an answer

Sample S

Say Turn to Lesson 9a on page 36. The page number is at the bottom of the page on the right. The answers on this page are pictures.

Check to see that the students have found the right page.

Say In this lesson you will choose a picture that matches what you hear. Let's do S together. Listen carefully and look at the pictures at the top of the page. Anna's family was planning a visit to her aunt's new house. Anna asked her mother, "What does Aunt Cara's new house look like?" Her mother answered: "It has a porch in the front, it is two stories tall, and there is a big tree in the front yard." Fill in the circle under the picture that shows Aunt Cara's house. *(pause)* The second answer is correct. Fill in the circle under the second picture. Be sure your answer circle is completely filled in with a dark mark and that you have marked the correct answer circle.

Check to see that the students have marked the correct circle. Explain why the second answer is correct and the other answers are wrong.

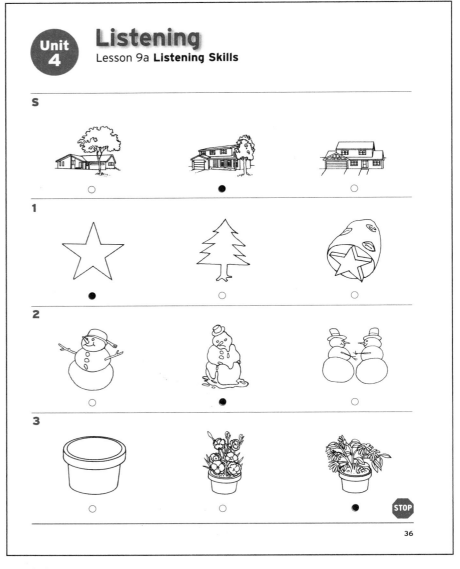

Practice

Say Now we will do the Practice items in the same way we did S. Listen to what I say and choose the answer you think is correct. Fill in the circle under the picture that goes best with what I say. Be sure your answer circle is completely filled in with a dark mark. Do you have any questions? Let's begin.

Allow time between items for students to fill in their answers.

1. Look at the pictures in row 1. Caleb's father showed him how to paint with potatoes. First, they cut a potato in half. Then, they carved shapes out of the potato's flat end. They dipped the potato in paint and pressed it on paper. It made a print of the carving. Caleb made a star. Look at the pictures in row 1. Fill in the circle under the picture of the print this potato would make.

2. Look at the pictures in row 2. Peter was excited when he saw that it was snowing outside. "I'm going to make a snowman," yelled Peter. He worked all afternoon. "I'll make a friend for my snowman tomorrow," said Peter. The next day, Peter looked outside. "I can't make another snowman now," he said. Fill in the circle under the picture that shows how the snowman looked the next day.

3. Look at the pictures in row 3. You should be at the bottom of the page. Nell took care of Mr. Shiko's yard while he was away. Before he left, Mr. Shiko said, "Be sure to water the flowers or they'll dry up." Nell accidentally missed one of the flowerpots. When Mr. Shiko came back, he said, "I'll just plant something else in that pot." Fill in the circle under the picture of the flowerpot Nell missed.

Say It's time to stop. You have finished Lesson 9a.

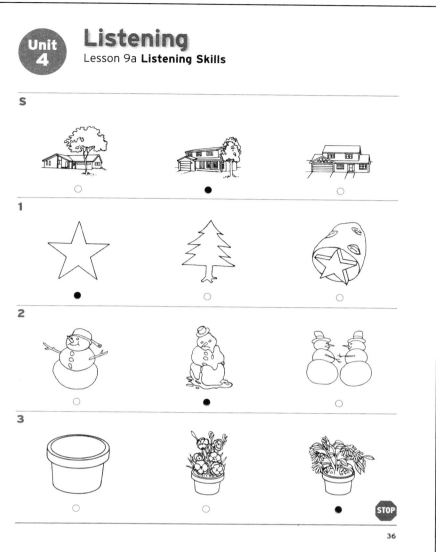

Review the answers with the students. Have the students indicate completion of the lesson by entering their score for this activity on the progress chart at the beginning of the book. Provide the students whatever help is necessary to record their scores.

Unit 4 — Lesson 9b
Listening Skills

Focus

Listening Skill
• matching graphic answers and oral prompts

Test-taking Skills
• following oral directions
• listening carefully
• considering every answer choice
• taking the best guess when unsure of the answer

Say Look at Lesson 9b on page 37. In this lesson you will choose a picture that matches what I say. This is the same thing you did in Lesson 9a.

Check to see that the students have found the right page.

Practice

Say For the Practice items in this lesson, listen to what I say and choose the answer you think is correct. Fill in the circle under the picture that goes best with what I say. If you are not sure which answer is correct, take your best guess. Be sure your answer circle is completely filled in with a dark mark. Do you have any questions? Let's begin.

Allow time between items for students to fill in their answers.

1. Look at the pictures in row 1. Joe wrote a letter to his new pen pal. When he was done, he put it in an envelope. He printed the address on the front. "I finished my letter," he called to his mother. She said, "Put a stamp on it. I'll take it to the post office later." Fill in the circle under the picture that shows what Joe should do with his letter.

2. Look at the pictures in row 2. People learn lots of new skills as they grow up. Sometimes a new skill is easy to learn. Other times we have to practice. This means doing it over and over again to get it right. Fill in the circle under the picture that shows someone practicing until she gets better.

Unit 4

Listening
Lesson 9b **Listening Skills**

1

2

3

4

STOP

37

3. Look at the pictures in row 3. Toby went for a walk with his mother. "I'm too hot," he complained. His mother said, "Take your hood off. Your body lets a lot of heat escape from your head, so doing that should cool you down." The next day it was very cold outside. "Better dress warmly for our walk," said his mother. Fill in the circle under the picture that shows how Toby should dress to stay as warm as he can.

4. Look at the pictures in row 4. You should be at the bottom of the page. Frances likes to play with her dog, Dizzy. One day she taught Dizzy to do a new trick. When Frances says "dance," Dizzy stands on his back legs. Then she gives him his favorite toy. Fill in the circle under the picture that shows Dizzy's new trick.

Say It's time to stop. You have finished Lesson 9b.

Review the answers with the students. Have the students indicate completion of the lesson by entering their score for this activity on the progress chart at the beginning of the book. Provide the students whatever help is necessary to record their scores.

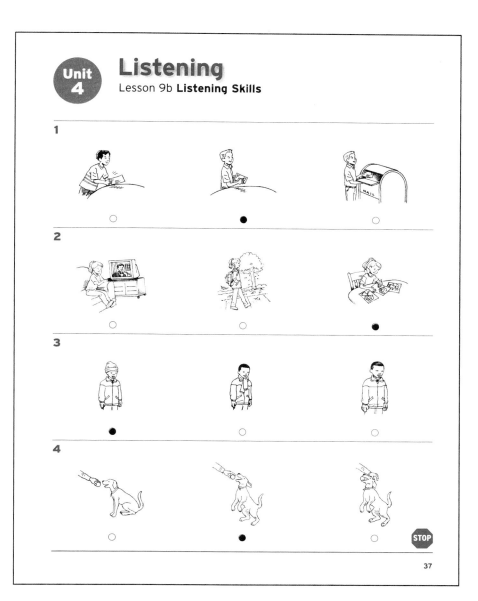

Unit 4 **Listening**
Lesson 9b **Listening Skills**

1

2

3

4

STOP

37

Test Yourself:
Listening

Unit 4

Focus
Listening Skill
• matching graphic answers and oral prompts

Test-taking Skills
• following oral directions
• listening carefully
• considering every answer choice
• using key words to find an answer
• taking the best guess when unsure of the answer

This lesson simulates an actual test-taking experience. Therefore, it is recommended that the directions be read verbatim and the suggested procedures be followed.

Directions
Administration Time:
approximately 20 minutes

Say Turn to the Test Yourself lesson on page 38. The page number is at the bottom of the page on the left.

Check to be sure the students have found the right page. Point out to the students that this is not a real test and that they will score it themselves to see how well they are doing.

Say This lesson will check how well you understand the listening skills you practiced before. Remember to make sure that the circles for your answer choices are completely filled in. Press your pencil firmly so that your marks come out dark. Completely erase any marks for answers that you change. Do not write anything except your answer choices in your books.

Listen carefully and look at the pictures at the top of the page. This is S. Jonathan's older sister, Ayesha, was getting ready for her first big concert. "I'm so excited," she said. "I love playing the piano." "Aren't you scared?" asked Jonathan. "No, I've practiced this music for a long time. I'm ready to play it for people."

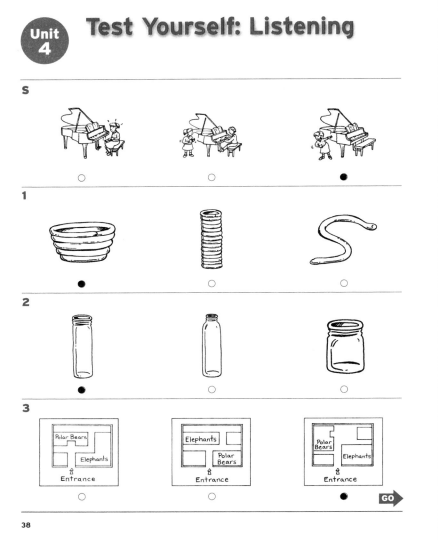

Later, Jonathan took a picture of his sister at her concert. Fill in the circle under the picture that Jonathan took. *(pause)* The last answer is correct because it best tells about the concert. If you chose another answer, erase yours and fill in the last answer circle now. Be sure your answer circle is completely filled in with a dark mark and that you have marked the correct answer circle.

Check to see that the students have marked the correct circle.

Say Now we will do more items like S. Look at the pictures and listen to what I say. Fill in the circle under the picture that goes best with what I say. If you are not sure which answer is correct, take your best guess. Do you have any questions? Let's begin.

Allow time between items for the students to fill in their answers.

1. Look at the pictures in row 1. In art class, Mrs. Devoe gave Tavion and the other students lumps of clay. She told them to roll it out into long, thin ropes, like skinny snakes. Then, she showed them how to coil it. By circling the clay rope on top of itself, Tavion made a shallow bowl. Fill in the circle under the picture that shows what Tavion made.

2. Look at the pictures in row 2. Kevin needed something to hold his paintbrushes. "Why don't you pick a jar out of the kitchen cupboard?" suggested his mother. Kevin sorted through all the tall jars. Finally, he found one he wanted. Its opening at the top was as wide as the rest of the jar. "This one is perfect," he said. Fill in the circle under the picture that shows Kevin's paintbrush jar.

3. Look at the pictures in row 3. You should be at the bottom of the page. Sarah asked one of the zoo helpers how to get to the polar bear exhibit. The helper said, "It's not far from here. Start at the zoo entrance. Go past the elephants, and then turn left. The polar bears are at the end of that path." Fill in the circle under the picture that shows how Sarah should get to the polar bear exhibit.

Say Look at the next page, page 39.

Check to be sure the students have found the right page.

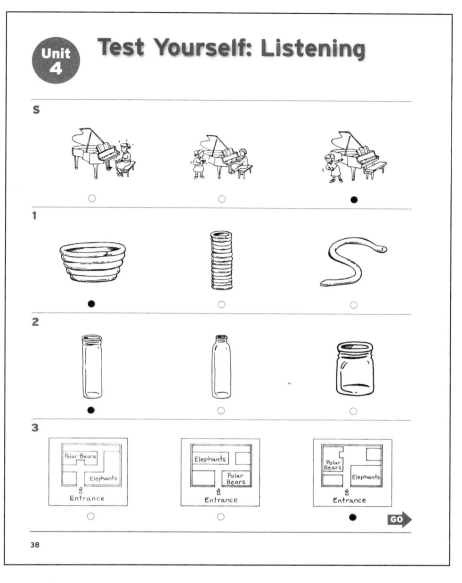

4. Look at the pictures in row 4 at the top of the page. Jane is buying a new collar for her cat, Squeaky. Squeaky lost the last collar because it was too big. Jane wants to be sure this collar fits better. Fill in the circle under the picture that shows what Jane should do.

5. Look at the pictures in row 5. At the beach, Kyle and Laura made a sand castle. All afternoon, they shaped the sand into tall towers. "You know," said Laura, "when the tide comes in the waves will wash over our castle." Fill in the circle under the picture that shows what will happen to the castle when the tide comes in.

6. There are three words in row 6, *SKIRT OR PANTS*. We will use the letters of these words to spell a new word. Listen carefully. Take the last letter in *SKIRT*, the first letter in *OR*, and the first letter in *PANTS*. Fill in the circle under the new word we spelled.

7. Look at the pictures in row 7. You should be at the bottom of the page. Every fall, Tyler's yard was covered with leaves. One day when all the trees had lost their leaves, Tyler raked his yard. He made a big pile of leaves. That night it was very windy. "Oh well," said Tyler when he looked outside, "It's good that I like raking leaves." Fill in the circle under the picture that showed what happened in Tyler's yard.

Say It's time to stop. You have completed the Test Yourself lesson. Check to see that you have completely filled in your answer circles with dark marks. Make sure that any marks for answers that you changed have been completely erased. Now you may close your books.

Review the answers with the students. Have the students indicate completion of the lesson by entering their score for this activity on the progress chart at the beginning of the book. Provide the students whatever help is necessary to record their scores.

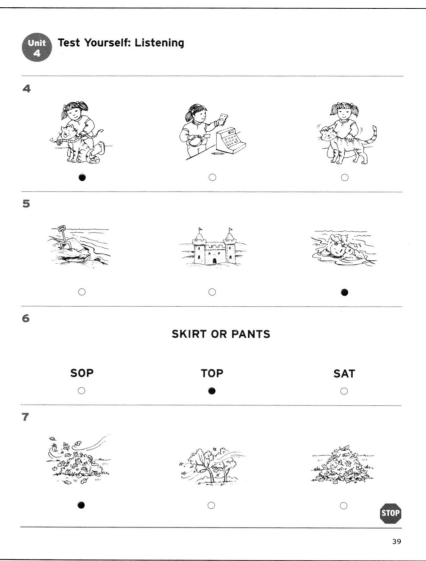

Unit 4 — Test Yourself: Listening

4

5

6
SKIRT OR PANTS

SOP   TOP   SAT

7

39

Unit 5

Background

This unit contains eleven lessons that deal with language skills.

• **In Lesson 10a,** students match a picture to an oral prompt. Students are encouraged to follow oral directions and listen carefully. They practice considering every answer choice and taking the best guess when unsure of the answer.

• **In Lesson 10b,** students choose a word that does not fit an implied class. Students are encouraged to follow oral directions and listen carefully. They review the test-taking skills introduced in previous lessons and learn the importance of using key words to find the answer.

• **In Lessons 11a and 11b,** students identify a misspelled word. They work methodically, analyze answer choices, and subvocalize answer choices.

• **In Lessons 12a and 12b,** students identify capitalization errors. They review the test-taking skills introduced in previous lessons, recall error types, and analyze answer choices.

Instructional Objectives

Lesson 10a	**Language Skills**	Given an oral prompt and three pictures, the student identifies which of the pictures matches the oral prompt.
Lesson 10b	**Language Skills**	Given four words, the student identifies which of the words is not in the same class as the others.
Lesson 11a	**Spelling**	Given three words, the student identifies which of the three is misspelled.
Lesson 11b	**Spelling**	
Lesson 12a	**Capitalization**	Given text divided into three parts, the student identifies which part has a capitalization mistake.
Lesson 12b	**Capitalization**	

Background

• **In Lessons 13a and 13b,** students identify a punctuation error. They review the test-taking skills introduced in previous lessons.

• **In Lessons 14a and 14b,** students identify an error in usage or expression. They review the test-taking skills introduced in previous lessons.

• **In the Test Yourself lesson,** the language skills and test-taking skills introduced and used in Lessons 10a through 14b are reinforced and presented in a format that gives students the experience of taking an achievement test.

Instructional **Objectives**

Lesson 13a	**Punctuation**	Given text divided into three parts, the student identifies which part has a punctuation mistake.
Lesson 13b	**Punctuation**	
Lesson 14a	**Usage and Expression**	Given text divided into three parts, the student identifies which part has a mistake in usage or expression.
Lesson 14b	**Usage and Expression**	
	Test Yourself	Given questions similar to those in Lessons 10a through 14b, the student utilizes language skills and test-taking strategies on achievement test formats.

Lesson 10a
Language Skills

Focus

Language Skill
• understanding oral language

Test-taking Skills
• following oral directions
• listening carefully
• considering every answer choice
• taking the best guess when unsure of the answer

Sample S

Say Turn to Lesson 10a on page 40. The page number is at the bottom of the page on the left. The answers on this page are pictures.

Check to see that the students have found the right page.

Say In this lesson you will choose a picture that matches a story I read. Let's do S together. Look at the three pictures in the row at the top of the page. They show Mr. Ladd at work. Mr. Ladd used to be a truck driver, but now he is an airplane pilot. Fill in the circle under the picture that shows Mr. Ladd at work today. *(pause)* The second answer is correct. Fill in the circle under the second answer. Be sure your answer circle is completely filled in with a dark mark and that you have marked the correct answer circle.

Check to see that the students have marked the correct circle. Explain why the second answer is correct and the other answers are wrong.

 TIPS

Say Now let's look at the tip.

Read the tip aloud to the students.

Say Listen carefully to what I say while you look at the pictures. If you are not sure which answer is correct, take your best guess. It is better to guess than to leave an item blank.

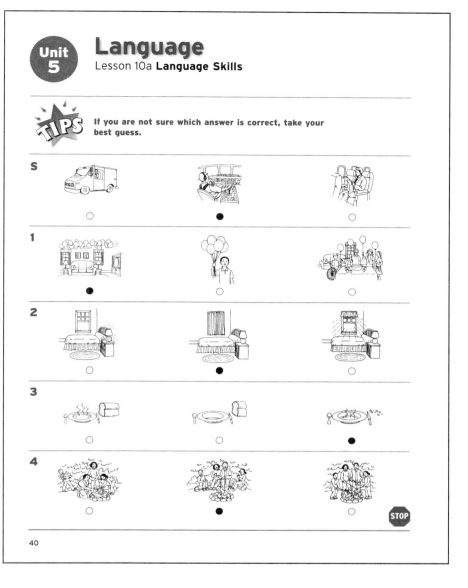

Practice

Say Now we will do the Practice items in the same way we did S. Listen to what I say and choose the answer you think is correct. Fill in the circle under the picture that goes best with what I say. Be sure your answer circle is completely filled in with a dark mark. Do you have any questions? Let's begin.

Allow time between items for students to fill in their answers.

1. Look at the pictures in row 1. The ceiling of the living room was filled with balloons for Mark's birthday party. Fill in the circle under the picture of Mark's living room.

2. Look at the pictures in row 2. Even though the morning sun was bright, the curtains in Lisa's bedroom blocked out the light. Fill in the circle under the picture of Lisa's bedroom.

3. Look at the pictures in row 3. For lunch, Mrs. Crocker made soup and homemade bread. There was plenty of soup left over, but the bread was gone in minutes. Fill in the circle under the picture that shows Mrs. Crocker's table when lunch was over.

4. Look at the pictures in row 4. The Wells family sat around a bright campfire and sang songs. Fill in the circle under the picture that shows the Wells family.

Say It's time to stop. You have finished Lesson 10a.

Review the answers with the students. Have the students indicate completion of the lesson by entering their score for this activity on the progress chart at the beginning of the book. Provide the students whatever help is necessary to record their scores.

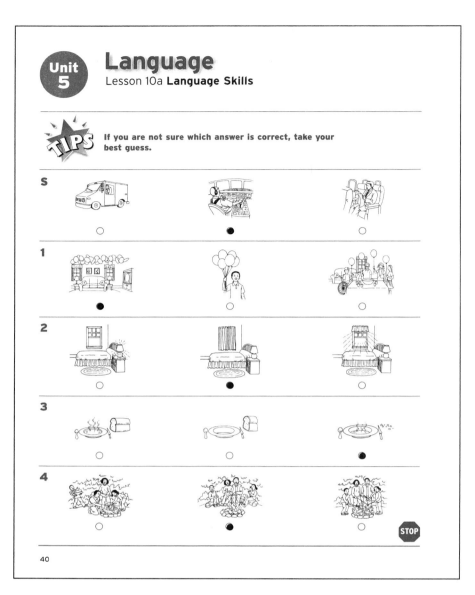

Focus

Language Skill
• identifying a word that does not fit an implied class

Test-taking Skills
• following oral directions
• listening carefully
• considering every answer choice
• using key words to find an answer

Say Look at Lesson 10b on page 41. The page number is at the bottom of the page on the right.

Check to see that the students have found the right page.

Say In this lesson you will choose a word that is different from other words. Look at S at the top of the page. Read the words to yourself while I read them out loud: *dollar, penny, dime, purse.* Which word is different from the other three? *(pause)* The last answer is correct. Three of the words are coins, but *purse* is not. Fill in the circle under the last answer. Be sure your answer circle is completely filled in with a dark mark and that you have marked the correct answer circle.

Check to see that the students have marked the correct circle.

Unit 5 **Language**
Lesson 10b **Language Skills**

S

dollar	penny	dime	purse
○	○	○	●

1

sister	friend	aunt	father
○	●	○	○

2

door	window	roof	farm
○	○	○	●

3

eyes	nose	see	mouth
○	○	●	○

4

dinner	food	lunch	breakfast
○	●	○	○

5

count	four	eight	five
●	○	○	○

STOP

41

Practice

Say Now we will do the Practice items in the same way we did S. Read the words to yourself while I read them out loud. Fill in the circle under the word that is different from the other three. Be sure your answer circle is completely filled in with a dark mark. Do you have any questions? Let's begin.

Allow time between items for students to fill in their answers.

1. The words in row 1 are *sister, friend, aunt, father*. Fill in the circle under the word that is different from the other three.

2. The words in row 2 are *door, window, roof, farm.* Fill in the circle under the word that is different from the other three.

3. The words in row 3 are *eyes, nose, see, mouth*. Fill in the circle under the word that is different from the other three.

4. The words in row 4 are *dinner, food, lunch, breakfast*. Fill in the circle under the word that is different from the other three.

5. The words in row 5 are *count, four, eight, five*. Fill in the circle under the word that is different from the other three.

Say It's time to stop. You have finished Lesson 10b.

Review the answers with the students. Have the students indicate completion of the lesson by entering their score for this activity on the progress chart at the beginning of the book. Provide the students whatever help is necessary to record their scores.

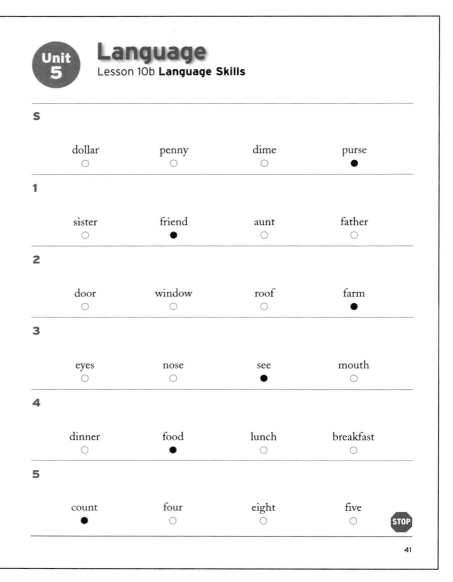

Unit 5 Lesson 11a Spelling

Focus

Language Skill
• identifying spelling errors

Test-taking Skills
• working methodically
• analyzing answer choices
• subvocalizing answer choices

Sample S

Say Turn to Lesson 11a on page 42. This page has two columns of words. In this lesson you will find misspelled words, that is, words that have a spelling mistake.

Check to see that the students have found the right page.

Say Look at the words in row S at the top of the first column. They are *car, flat, tire*. Jeff's *car* had a *flat tire*. Which answer is spelled wrong? *(the second answer)* Fill in the circle under the second answer. This is a misspelling of *f-l-a-t*. Make sure the circle is completely filled in. Press your pencil firmly so that your mark comes out dark.

Check to see that the students have filled in the correct answer circle.

★TIPS

Say Now let's look at the tips.

Read the tips aloud to the students.

Say Listen carefully to the sentence while you look at the words. The sentence will help you understand the meaning of the words so you can decide which one has a spelling mistake. You might also want to say each answer to yourself. Sometimes this will help you decide whether the word has a spelling mistake. Look at each letter while you say the word.

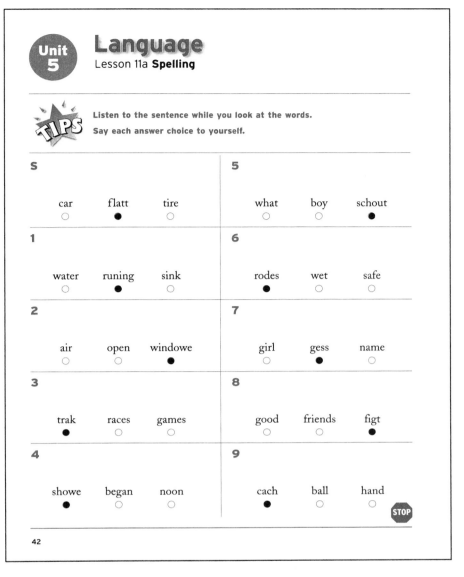

Practice

Say Now we will do the Practice items in the same way we did S. Listen to what I say while you look at the words. Fill in the circle under the word that is misspelled. Be sure your answer circle is completely filled in with a dark mark. Do you have any questions? Let's begin.

Allow time between items for students to fill in their answers.

1. Number 1: *water, running, sink*. The *water* was *running* in the *sink*.

2. Number 2: *air, open, window*. *Air* came through the *open window*.

3. Number 3: *track, races, games*. The *track* was used for *races* and *games*.

4. Number 4: *show, began, noon*. The *show began* at *noon*.

   Go to the top of the second column.

5. Number 5: *what, boy, shout*. *What* did the *boy shout*?

6. Number 6: *roads, wet, safe*. The *roads* were *wet* but *safe*.

7. Number 7: *girl, guess, name*. The *girl* tried to *guess* my *name*.

8. Number 8: *good, friends, fight*. *Good friends* do not *fight*.

9. Number 9: *catch, ball, hand*. Try to *catch* the *ball* with your *hand*.

Say It's time to stop. You have finished Lesson 11a.

Review the answers with the students. Have the students indicate completion of the lesson by entering their score for this activity on the progress chart at the beginning of the book. Provide the students whatever help is necessary to record their scores.

Unit 5

Language
Lesson 11a **Spelling**

TIPS

Listen to the sentence while you look at the words.

Say each answer choice to yourself.

S

| car | flatt | tire |
| ○ | ● | ○ |

5

| what | boy | schout |
| ○ | ○ | ● |

1

| water | runing | sink |
| ○ | ● | ○ |

6

| rodes | wet | safe |
| ● | ○ | ○ |

2

| air | open | windowe |
| ○ | ○ | ● |

7

| girl | gess | name |
| ○ | ● | ○ |

3

| trak | races | games |
| ● | ○ | ○ |

8

| good | friends | figt |
| ○ | ○ | ● |

4

| showe | began | noon |
| ● | ○ | ○ |

9

| cach | ball | hand |
| ● | ○ | ○ |

STOP

42

Unit 5 · Lesson 11b · Spelling

Focus

Language Skill
• identifying spelling errors

Test-taking Skills
• working methodically
• analyzing answer choices
• subvocalizing answer choices

Say Look at Lesson 11b on page 43. In this lesson you will find more misspelled words.

Check to see that the students have found the right page.

Practice

Say The Practice items in this lesson are the same as those we did in Lesson 11a. Listen to what I say while you look at the words. Fill in the circle under the word that is misspelled. Be sure your answer circle is completely filled in with a dark mark. Do you have any questions? Let's begin.

Allow time between items for students to fill in their answers.

1. Number 1: *toes, cold, boots*. My *toes* were *cold* inside my *boots*.

2. Number 2: *stand, back, line*. Please *stand* in the *back* of the *line*.

3. Number 3: *animals, lay, grass*. The *animals lay* in the *grass*.

4. Number 4: *talks, dinner, meal*. Our family *talks* during the *dinner meal*.

5. Number 5: *lock, gold, key*. He opened the *lock* with a *gold key*.

   Go to the top of the second column.

6. Number 6: *pay, lady, candles*. Dad will *pay* the *lady* for the *candles*.

7. Number 7: *baby, rash, arm*. The *baby* had a *rash* on her *arm*.

8. Number 8: *cleans, own, brushes*. The painter *cleans* her *own brushes*.

9. Number 9: *done, feeding, pony*. Tom was *done feeding* the *pony*.

10. Number 10: *one, light, house*. There was only *one light* on in the *house*.

Say It's time to stop. You have finished Lesson 11b.

Review the answers with the students. Have the students indicate completion of the lesson by entering their score for this activity on the progress chart at the beginning of the book. Provide the students whatever help is necessary to record their scores.

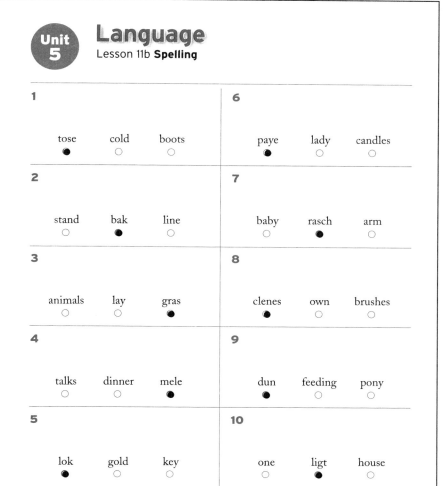

Unit 5 Lesson 12a
Capitalization

Focus

Language Skill
• identifying capitalization errors

Test-taking Skills
• following oral directions
• working methodically
• recalling error types
• analyzing answer choices

Sample S

Say Turn to Lesson 12a on page 44. The page number is at the bottom of the page on the left. In this lesson you will find capitalization errors.

Check to see that the students have found the right page.

Say Look at S at the top of the first column. It is a sentence divided into three parts. Read each part to yourself while I read it out loud.

The Docker kids sent
a card to Grandma Betty
to celebrate Mother's Day.

Which line has a word that needs another capital letter? *(the first line)* Mark the circle beside the first answer. The family name *Docker* should begin with a capital letter. Make sure the circle is completely filled in. Press your pencil firmly so that your mark comes out dark.

Check to see that the students have filled in the correct answer circle.

 TIPS

Say Now let's look at the tips.

Read the tips aloud to the students.

Unit 5 Language
Lesson 12a **Capitalization**

TIPS The first word in a sentence should be capitalized.
Important words in a sentence should be capitalized.

S
● The docker kids sent
○ a card to Grandma Betty
○ to celebrate Mother's Day.

3
○ Bring your umbrella
● to school today. it looks like
○ it is going to start raining.

1
○ Have you gone skiing
● before? Sasha and i go almost
○ every weekend in winter.

4
○ I asked my mom
○ if I could start taking music
● lessons from mrs. Greer.

2
● Jan and nick led a
○ group on a hike in the
○ mountains last summer.

5
○ The cat Garfield has a
○ comic strip named for him, but
● the dog snoopy does not.

STOP

44

Say When you do the items in this lesson, you should begin by making sure that the first word in a sentence is capitalized. Then you should look for important words in the sentence that should be capitalized.

Discuss with the students the proper nouns that should be capitalized. They include names, the pronoun I, and abbreviations like Dr., Mrs., and Mr.

Practice

Say Now we will do the Practice items in the same way we did the sample S. Listen to what I say while you look at the answers. Fill in the circle beside the line that has a word that should begin with a capital letter. Be sure your answer circle is completely filled in with a dark mark. Do you have any questions? Let's begin.

Allow time between items for the students to fill in their answers. Begin each item by reading the number using the format Number 1, Number 2, and so on.

1. Have you gone skiing before? Sasha and I go almost every weekend in winter.

2. Jan and Nick led a group on a hike in the mountains last summer.

3. Bring your umbrella to school today. It looks like it is going to start raining.

4. I asked my mom if I could start taking music lessons from Mrs. Greer.

5. The cat Garfield has a comic strip named for him, but the dog Snoopy does not.

Say It's time to stop. You have finished Lesson 12a.

Review the answers with the students. Have the students indicate completion of the lesson by entering their score for this activity on the progress chart at the beginning of the book. Provide the students whatever help is necessary to record their scores.

Unit 5 Language
Lesson 12a **Capitalization**

TIPS The first word in a sentence should be capitalized.
Important words in a sentence should be capitalized.

S
- ● The docker kids sent
- ○ a card to Grandma Betty
- ○ to celebrate Mother's Day.

1
- ○ Have you gone skiing
- ● before? Sasha and i go almost
- ○ every weekend in winter.

2
- ● Jan and nick led a
- ○ group on a hike in the
- ○ mountains last summer.

3
- ○ Bring your umbrella
- ● to school today. it looks like
- ○ it is going to start raining.

4
- ○ I asked my mom
- ○ if I could start taking music
- ● lessons from mrs. Greer.

5
- ○ The cat Garfield has a
- ○ comic strip named for him, but
- ● the dog snoopy does not.

STOP

44

Lesson 12b
Capitalization

Focus

Language Skill
• identifying capitalization errors

Test-taking Skills
• following oral directions
• working methodically
• recalling error types
• analyzing answer choices

Say Look at Lesson 12b on page 45. In this lesson you will find more capitalization errors.

Check to see that the students have found the right page.

Practice

Say The Practice items in this lesson are the same as we did in Lesson 12a. Listen to what I say while you look at the answers. Fill in the circle beside the line that has a word that should begin with a capital letter. Be sure your answer circle is completely filled in with a dark mark. Do you have any questions? Let's begin.

Allow time between items for the students to fill in their answers.

1. On Arbor Day, the
   Johnson family helped
   Uncle Leroy plant a tree.

2. Joan and I are friends.
   Both of us have relatives
   who live in other countries.

3. There is a new pool
   in town, so Fred and Mike
   are eager to go swimming.

4. It's a busy street.
   Look both ways before
   you start to cross it.

Language
Lesson 12b Capitalization

1
- ○ On Arbor Day, the
- ● johnson family helped
- ○ Uncle Leroy plant a tree.

2
- ● Joan and i are friends.
- ○ Both of us have relatives
- ○ who live in other countries.

3
- ○ There is a new pool
- ● in town, so Fred and mike
- ○ are eager to go swimming.

4
- ○ It's a busy street.
- ● look both ways before
- ○ you start to cross it.

5
- ○ I bought the book
- ○ at a garage sale and gave
- ● it to mrs. Cook as a gift.

6
- ○ My pet fish Gus swims in
- ○ a straight line. My hermit
- ● crab clyde crawls sideways.

STOP

45

5. I bought the book
   at a garage sale and gave
   it to Mrs. Cook as a gift.

6. My pet fish Gus swims in a
   straight line. My hermit crab
   clyde crawls sideways.

Say It's time to stop. You have finished Lesson 12b.

Review the answers with the students. Have the students indicate completion of the lesson by entering their score for this activity on the progress chart at the beginning of the book. Provide the students whatever help is necessary to record their scores.

Lesson 13a
Punctuation

Unit 5

Focus

Language Skill
- identifying punctuation errors

Test-taking Skills
- following oral directions
- working methodically
- recalling error types

Sample S

Say Turn to Lesson 13a on page 46. The page number is at the bottom of the page on the left. In this lesson you will find punctuation errors, for example, a missing period.

Check to see that the students have found the right page.

Say Look at S at the top of the first column. It is a little story divided into three parts. Read the story to yourself while I read it out loud.

> The girls won their
> first basketball game. Then
> they went to a pizza parlor.

> Which line needs punctuation? *(the second line)* Mark the space beside the second answer. A period should go after the word *game*. Make sure the circle is completely filled in. Press your pencil firmly so that your mark comes out dark.

Check to see that the students have filled in the correct answer circle.

TIPS

Say Now let's look at the tips.

Read the tips aloud to the students.

Language
Lesson 13a Punctuation

Unit 5

Every sentence should end with punctuation.
Someone's initials should have a period.

S
- ○ The girls won their
- ● first basketball game Then
- ○ they went to a pizza parlor.

3
- ○ Have you ever seen a lizard
- ● with a bright blue belly My
- ○ friends and I have seen a few.

1
- ○ Aunt Barb has a cozy
- ● basement We love to play and
- ○ watch movies down there.

4
- ● Bang The wind blew
- ○ the screen door against the
- ○ back of Grandma's house.

2
- ○ James Taylor got the
- ● nickname J T from his friends.
- ○ Now everyone calls him that.

5
- ○ Most of the students had
- ● finished their paintings Bryce
- ○ was taking time with his.

STOP

46

Say When you do punctuation items, always begin by looking at the end of a sentence. Be sure the sentence ends with the right kind of punctuation. You should also look for missing punctuation inside a sentence. One kind of missing punctuation is the periods after someone's initials.

Review the use of end punctuation with the students.

Practice

Say Now we will do the Practice items in the same way we did the sample. Listen to what I say while you look at the answers. Fill in the circle beside the line that needs a punctuation mark. Be sure your answer circle is completely filled in with a dark mark. Do you have any questions? Let's begin.

Allow time between items for the students to fill in their answers. Begin each item by reading the number using the format Number 1, Number 2, and so on.

1. Aunt Barb has a cozy basement. We love to play and watch movies down there.

2. James Taylor got the nickname J. T. from his friends. Now everyone calls him that.

3. Have you ever seen a lizard with a bright blue belly? My friends and I have seen a few.

4. Bang! The wind blew the screen door against the back of Grandma's house.

5. Most of the students had finished their paintings. Bryce was taking time with his.

Say It's time to stop. You have finished Lesson 13a.

Review the answers with the students. Have the students indicate completion of the lesson by entering their score for this activity on the progress chart at the beginning of the book. Provide the students whatever help is necessary to record their scores.

Every sentence should end with punctuation.
Someone's initials should have a period.

S
- ○ The girls won their
- ● first basketball game Then
- ○ they went to a pizza parlor.

1
- ○ Aunt Barb has a cozy
- ● basement We love to play and
- ○ watch movies down there.

2
- ○ James Taylor got the
- ● nickname J T from his friends.
- ○ Now everyone calls him that.

3
- ○ Have you ever seen a lizard
- ● with a bright blue belly My
- ○ friends and I have seen a few.

4
- ● Bang The wind blew
- ○ the screen door against the
- ○ back of Grandma's house.

5
- ○ Most of the students had
- ● finished their paintings Bryce
- ○ was taking time with his.

STOP

46

Lesson 13b
Punctuation

Focus

Language Skill
• identifying punctuation errors

Test-taking Skills
• following oral directions
• working methodically
• recalling error types

Say Look at Lesson 13b on page 47. In this lesson you will find more punctuation errors.

Check to see that the students have found the right page.

Practice

Say Now we will do some Practice items in the same way we did the items in Lesson 13a. Listen to what I say while you look at the answers. Fill in the circle beside the line that needs a punctuation mark. Be sure your answer circle is completely filled in with a dark mark. Do you have any questions? Let's begin.

Allow time between items for the students to fill in their answers.

1. The worker dug a small hole in the ground. Then he planted three tiny seeds.

2. We helped Aunt Meg clean her boat. Tomorrow she is taking us for a ride in it.

3. She had to find the nearest U.S. Post Office before five in the evening.

4. Will you go camping this summer? My friends and I would like to invite you.

5. Plop! Karl dropped a spoonful of yogurt on the front of his best shirt.

Language
Lesson 13b Punctuation

1
○ The worker dug a small
● hole in the ground Then he
○ planted three tiny seeds.

4
○ Will you go camping
● this summer My friends
○ and I would like to invite you.

2
○ We helped Aunt Meg
● clean her boat Tomorrow she
○ is taking us for a ride in it.

5
● Plop Karl dropped a
○ spoonful of yogurt on the
○ front of his best shirt.

3
○ She had to find the
● nearest U S Post Office
○ before five in the evening.

6
○ Many people have
● one hobby Brianna has
○ five different ones.

STOP

47

6. Many people have one hobby. Brianna has five different ones.

Say It's time to stop. You have finished Lesson 13b.

Review the answers with the students. Have the students indicate completion of the lesson by entering their score for this activity on the progress chart at the beginning of the book. Provide the students whatever help is necessary to record their scores.

Lesson 14a
Usage and Expression

Focus

Language Skill
• identifying errors in usage and expression

Test-taking Skills
• following oral directions
• working methodically
• listening carefully

Sample S

Say Turn to Lesson 14a on page 48. The page number is at the bottom of the page on the left. In this lesson you will find mistakes in the way words are used.

Check to see that the students have found the right page.

Say Look at S at the top of the first column. It is a story divided into three parts. Read each part to yourself while I read it out loud. Look for a word that is used in the wrong way and should be changed.

> Toby and Lila goes shopping on Saturdays. Their grandma goes with them.

Which line has a word that is wrong? *(the first line)* Mark the space beside the first answer. It should read *Toby and Lila go.* Make sure the circle is completely filled in. Press your pencil firmly so that your mark comes out dark.

Check to see that the students have filled in the correct answer circle. Explain why the first answer has a mistake and read the corrected story to the students.

Language
Lesson 14a Usage and Expression

TIPS Listen to the answers as you read along. Listen for a part of the answer that sounds like it is wrong.

S
● Toby and Lila goes
○ shopping on Saturdays. Their
○ grandma goes with them.

3
○ Yuri's cousins wanted to ride
○ the bus home. Yuri asked them
● if they had ever rided a bus.

1
● I borrowed yours ruler.
○ You always let me use it
○ when I can't find my own.

4
○ Laird doesn't eat a lot
○ of candy. His parents
● doesn't think it is a good habit.

2
○ Lisa told her dad she
○ needed new shoes. She needed
● them ones for playing tennis.

5
○ After Clay found his batteries
● were dead, he gone back to the
○ store to buy some new ones.

STOP

48

TIPS

Say Now let's look at the tip.

Read the tip aloud to the students.

Say Listen carefully to what I say as you read the answers to yourself. One of the words will sound like it is wrong. This is the answer that you should mark.

Practice

Say Now we will do the Practice items in the same way we did the sample. Listen to what I say while you look at the answers. Fill in the circle beside the line that has a word that is wrong and should be changed. Be sure your answer circle is completely filled in with a dark mark. Do you have any questions? Let's begin.

Allow time between items for the students to fill in their answers. Begin each item by reading the number using the format Number 1, Number 2, and so on.

1. I borrowed yours ruler. You always let me use it when I can't find my own.

2. Lisa told her dad she needed new shoes. She needed them ones for playing tennis.

3. Yuri's cousins wanted to ride the bus home. Yuri asked them if they had ever rided a bus.

4. Laird doesn't eat a lot of candy. His parents doesn't think it is a good habit.

5. After Clay found his batteries were dead, he gone back to the store to buy some new ones.

Say It's time to stop. You have finished Lesson 14a.

Review the answers with the students. Have the students indicate completion of the lesson by entering their score for this activity on the progress chart at the beginning of the book. Provide the students whatever help is necessary to record their scores.

Unit 5 **Language**
Lesson 14a **Usage and Expression**

TIPS Listen to the answers as you read along. Listen for a part of the answer that sounds like it is wrong.

S
- ● Toby and Lila goes
- ○ shopping on Saturdays. Their
- ○ grandma goes with them.

3
- ○ Yuri's cousins wanted to ride
- ○ the bus home. Yuri asked them
- ● if they had ever rided a bus.

1
- ● I borrowed yours ruler.
- ○ You always let me use it
- ○ when I can't find my own.

4
- ○ Laird doesn't eat a lot
- ○ of candy. His parents
- ● doesn't think it is a good habit.

2
- ○ Lisa told her dad she
- ○ needed new shoes. She needed
- ● them ones for playing tennis.

5
- ○ After Clay found his batteries
- ● were dead, he gone back to the
- ○ store to buy some new ones.

STOP

48

Lesson 14b
Usage and Expression

Focus

Language Skill
• identifying errors in usage and expression

Test-taking Skills
• following oral directions
• working methodically
• listening carefully

Say Look at Lesson 14b on page 49. In this lesson you will find more mistakes in the way words are used.

Check to see that the students have found the right page.

Practice

Say We will do the Practice items in this lesson in the same way we did the items in Lesson 14a. Listen to what I say while you look at the answers. Fill in the circle beside the line that has a word that is wrong and should be changed. Be sure your answer circle is completely filled in with a dark mark. Do you have any questions? Let's begin.

Allow time between items for the students to fill in their answers.

1. I haven't got no way to get to school quickly. Both tires on my bicycle need to be fixed.

2. Gil peeked inside the garage and let out a happy cry. The kittens they were so cute!

3. Jumping and spinning, the team of dancers putting on a great show for the crowd of people.

4. Rita and Heidi have been bestest of friends ever since they met in Mrs. Hashimoto's class.

Language
Lesson 14b Usage and Expression

1
- ● I haven't got no way to
- ○ get to school quickly. Both tires
- ○ on my bicycle need to be fixed.

2
- ○ Gil peeked inside the
- ○ garage and let out a happy cry.
- ● The kittens they were so cute!

3
- ○ Jumping and spinning, the
- ● team of dancers putting on a
- ○ great show for the crowd of people.

4
- ○ Rita and Heidi have been
- ● bestest of friends ever since they
- ○ met in Mrs. Hashimoto's class.

5
- ○ We save our leftover
- ○ bread. On Saturdays, we take it
- ● to the pond to feed the gooses.

6
- ● After school, I and Tony
- ○ went to the park. We sat on a
- ○ bench and did our homework.

---

5. We save our leftover bread. On Saturdays, we take it to the pond to feed the gooses.

6. After school, I and Tony went to the park. We sat on a bench and did our homework.

Say It's time to stop. You have finished Lesson 14b.

Review the answers with the students. Have the students indicate completion of the lesson by entering their score for this activity on the progress chart at the beginning of the book. Provide the students whatever help is necessary to record their scores.

Focus

Language Skills
- understanding oral language
- identifying spelling errors
- identifying capitalization errors
- identifying punctuation errors
- identifying errors in usage and expression

Test-taking Skills
- following oral directions
- listening carefully
- considering every answer choice
- taking the best guess when unsure of the answer
- working methodically
- analyzing answer choices
- subvocalizing answer choices
- recalling error types
- using key words to find an answer

This lesson simulates an actual test-taking experience. Therefore, it is recommended that the directions be read verbatim and the suggested procedures be followed.

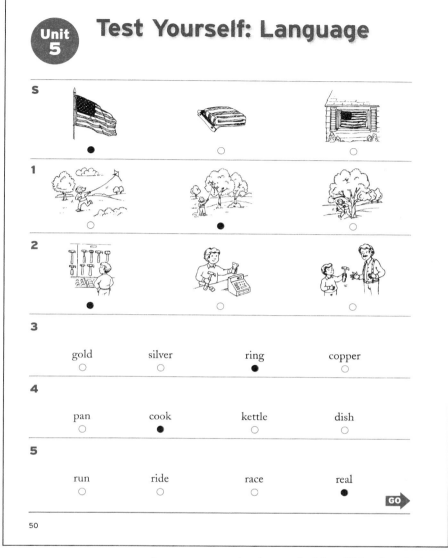

Directions

Administration Time: approximately 40 minutes

Say Turn to the Test Yourself lesson on page 50. The page number is at the bottom of the page on the left.

Check to be sure the students have found the right page. Point out to the students that this is not a real test and that they will score it themselves to see how well they are doing.

Say This lesson will check how well you understand the language skills you practiced before. Be sure that the circles for your answer choices are completely filled in. Press your pencil firmly so that your marks come out dark. Completely erase any marks for answers that you change. Do not write anything except your answer choices in your books.

Listen carefully and look at the pictures at the top of the page. This is S. The flag was old,

but someone had mended it. Fill in the circle under the picture that shows the flag. *(pause)* You should have filled in the circle under the first answer. If you did not, erase your answer and fill in the circle under the first answer now. Be sure your answer circle is completely filled in with a dark mark.

Check to see that the students have marked the correct circle.

Say Now we will do more items like S. Look at the pictures and listen to what I say. Fill in the circle under the picture that goes best with what I say. If you are not sure which answer is correct, take your best guess. Do you have any questions? Let's begin.

Allow time between items for the students to fill in their answers.

1. Look at the pictures in row 1. Susan's kite has gotten caught in the branches of a tree. Fill in the circle under the picture of Susan and her kite.

2. Look at the pictures in row 2. Ken went to buy his dad a hammer, but when he got to the store, there were too many to choose from. Fill in the circle under the picture of Ken at the store.

   Now we will do a different kind of item. Read the words to yourself while I read them out loud. Fill in the circle under the word that is different from the other three. Be sure your answer circle is completely filled in with a dark mark. Do you have any questions? Let's begin.

3. The words in row 3 are *gold, silver, ring, copper*. Fill in the circle under the word that is different from the other three.

4. The words in row 4 are *pan, cook, kettle, dish*. Fill in the circle under the word that is different from the other three.

5. The words in row 5 are *run, ride, race, real*. Fill in the circle under the word that is different from the other three.

Say Look at the next page, page 51.

Check to be sure the students have found the right page. Allow the students a moment to rest.

Say Now we will do some spelling items. Listen to what I say while you look at the words. Fill in the circle under the word that has a spelling mistake. Be sure your answer circle is completely filled in with a dark mark. Do you have any questions? Let's begin.

Allow time between items for students to fill in their answers.

6. *drank, berry, punch*. We *drank* some *berry punch*.

7. *blows, trees, shake*. When the wind *blows*, the *trees shake*.

8. *played, kick, yard*. We *played kick* ball in the *yard*.

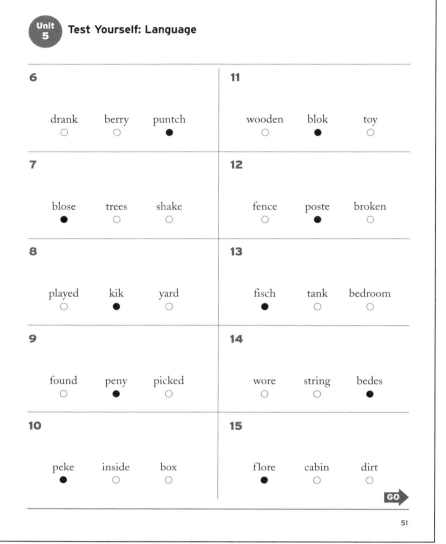

Unit 5 Test Yourself: Language

6				11		
drank	berry	puntch		wooden	blok	toy
○	○	●		○	●	○

7				12		
blose	trees	shake		fence	poste	broken
●	○	○		○	●	○

8				13		
played	kik	yard		fisch	tank	bedroom
○	●	○		●	○	○

9				14		
found	peny	picked		wore	string	bedes
○	●	○		○	○	●

10				15		
peke	inside	box		flore	cabin	dirt
●	○	○		●	○	○

GO

51

9. *found, penny, picked*. I *found* a *penny* and *picked* it up.

10. *peek, inside, box*. May I *peek inside* the *box*?

11. *wooden, block, toy*. The *wooden block* was a *toy*.

12. *fence, post, broken*. The *fence post* was *broken*.

13. *fish, tank, bedroom*. I have a *fish tank* in my *bedroom*.

14. *wore, string, beads*. She *wore* a *string* of *beads*.

15. *floor, cabin, dirt*. The *floor* of the *cabin* was made of *dirt*.

Say Turn to the next page, page 52.

Check to be sure the students have found the right page. Allow the students a moment to rest.

Say Now we will do some items that have capitalization mistakes. I will read a little story divided into three parts. Listen to what I say while you look at the answers. Fill in the circle beside the line that has a word that should begin with a capital letter. Be sure your answer circle is completely filled in with a dark mark. Do you have any questions? Let's begin.

Allow time between items for the students to fill in their answers.

16. Before the fireworks were lit, the Ryan family invited Aunt Selma to come watch.

17. There were a lot of leaves. Albert and I worked all afternoon raking them.

18. Dara and Katie make decorations to sell at the holiday gift fair at school.

19. Put our coats in the dryer. They are soaked with water after our long walk in the rain.

20. I went to the marketplace and bought some flowers for Mr. Samson's birthday party.

21. My sister Wilma can drive a car, but my brother Wayne is still too young.

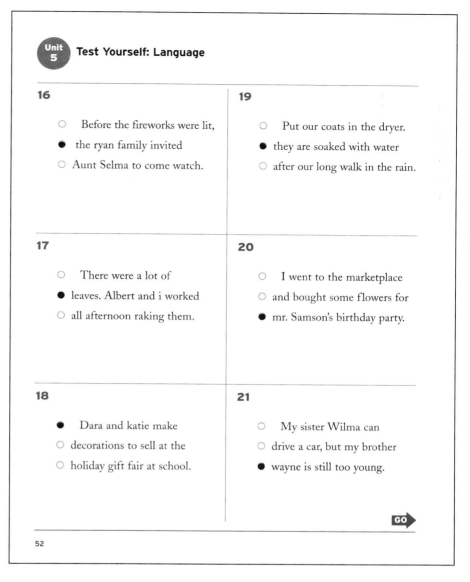

Unit 5 Test Yourself: Language

16
- ○ Before the fireworks were lit,
- ● the ryan family invited
- ○ Aunt Selma to come watch.

17
- ○ There were a lot of
- ● leaves. Albert and i worked
- ○ all afternoon raking them.

18
- ● Dara and katie make
- ○ decorations to sell at the
- ○ holiday gift fair at school.

19
- ○ Put our coats in the dryer.
- ● they are soaked with water
- ○ after our long walk in the rain.

20
- ○ I went to the marketplace
- ○ and bought some flowers for
- ● mr. Samson's birthday party.

21
- ○ My sister Wilma can
- ○ drive a car, but my brother
- ● wayne is still too young.

GO

52

Say Look at the next page, page 53.

Check to be sure the students have found the right page. Allow the students a moment to rest.

Say Now we will do some items that have punctuation mistakes. I will read a little story divided into three parts. Listen to what I say while you look at the answers. Fill in the circle beside the line that has a mistake in punctuation. Be sure your answer circle is completely filled in with a dark mark. Do you have any questions? Let's begin.

Allow time between items for the students to fill in their answers.

22. The bird collected bits of grass and twigs. Then it began to build a nest.

23. Aunt Chrissie showed us how to make bread. Next she will teach us to make noodles.

24. It was well past eleven in the evening, but D.D. and I were staying awake all night.

25. How many people can sing and dance at the same time? My mom and I can.

26. Whoosh! The kite that was in Victor's hand caught the wind like a paper rocket.

27. The bookshelf was filled with all kinds of books. Olivia picked out three to borrow.

 Unit 5 **Test Yourself: Language**

22
- ○ The bird collected bits
- ● of grass and twigs Then it
- ○ began to build a nest.

23
- ○ Aunt Chrissie showed us
- ● how to make bread Next she
- ○ will teach us to make noodles.

24
- ○ It was well past eleven in
- ● the evening, but D D and I
- ○ were staying awake all night.

25
- ○ How many people can
- ○ sing and dance at the same
- ● time My mom and I can.

26
- ● Whoosh The kite that
- ○ was in Victor's hand caught
- ○ the wind like a paper rocket.

27
- ○ The bookshelf was filled
- ● with all kinds of books Olivia
- ○ picked out three to borrow.

GO ➤

53

Say Turn to the next page, page 54.

Check to be sure the students have found the right page. Allow the students a moment to rest.

Say Now we will do some items that have mistakes in the way words are used. I will read a little story divided into three parts. Listen to what I say while you look at the answers. Fill in the circle beside the line that has a word that is used in the wrong way and should be changed. Be sure your answer circle is completely filled in with a dark mark. Do you have any questions? Let's begin.

Allow time between items for the students to fill in their answers.

28. Eddie and Orson is joining the school band. Their teacher is teaching them about music.

29. Mom asked me to help wash hers car. The inside was clean, but the outside was dirty.

30. Mr. Taylor says this here house is a hundred years old. I would like to live in it.

31. Dad went to buy more milk, but luckily mom stopped him. She had just buyed some.

32. Bart bought glasses for his grandparents. Their eyes isn't as strong as they used to be.

33. When Randy was in the second grade, he grown about three inches taller.

Say It's time to stop. You have completed the Test Yourself lesson. Check to see that you have completely filled in your answer circles with dark marks. Make sure that any marks for answers that you changed have been completely erased. Now you may close your books.

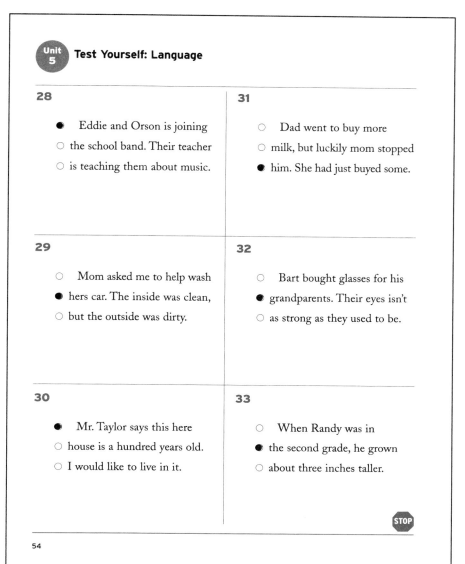

Review the answers with the students. Have the students indicate completion of the lesson by entering their score for this activity on the progress chart at the beginning of the book. Provide the students whatever help is necessary to record their scores.

Background

This unit contains three lessons that deal with mathematics skills. Students answer oral questions about mathematics concepts.

• **In Lessons 15a and 15b,** students answer oral questions about mathematics concepts. Students are encouraged to follow oral directions and listen carefully. They consider every answer choice, work methodically, and use key words to find an answer.

• **In the Test Yourself lesson,** the mathematics skills and test-taking skills introduced and used in Lessons 15a and 15b are reinforced and presented in a format that gives students the experience of taking an achievement test.

Instructional Objectives

Lesson 15a	**Mathematics Concepts**	Given an oral problem involving mathematics concepts and three or four printed answers, the student identifies which of the answers is correct.
Lesson 15b	**Mathematics Concepts**	
	Test Yourself	Given questions similar to those in Lessons 15a and 15b, the student utilizes mathematics concepts and test-taking strategies on achievement test formats.

Unit 6 Lesson 15a
Mathematics Concepts

Focus

Mathematics Skills
- using mathematical language
- counting
- naming numerals
- understanding number sentences
- recognizing plane figures
- identifying measurement tools
- recognizing value of coins and bills
- comparing and ordering whole numbers

Test-taking Skills
- following oral directions
- listening carefully
- considering every answer choice
- working methodically
- identifying and using key words, numbers, and pictures

Sample S

Say Look at Lesson 15a on page 55. The page number is at the bottom of the page on the right. There are some trees at the top of the first column.

Check to see that the students have found the right page.

Say In this lesson you will solve mathematics problems. Let's do S together. Listen carefully and look at the pictures of the trees at the top of the page. Which tree is tallest? *(pause)* The second tree is tallest. Fill in the circle under the second tree. Be sure your answer circle is completely filled in with a dark mark and that you have marked the correct answer circle.

Check to see that the students have marked the correct circle.

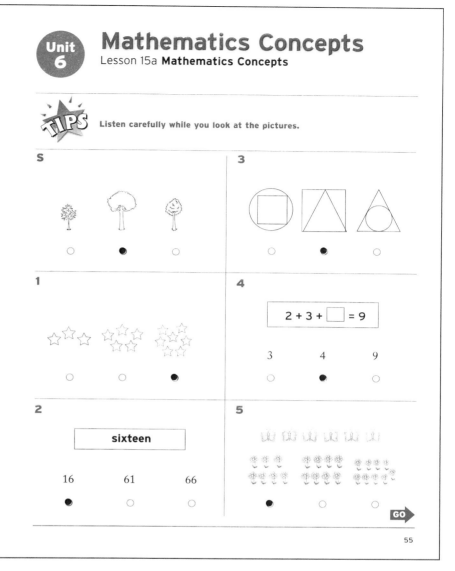

★TIPS

Say Now let's look at the tip.

Read the tip aloud to the students.

Say Listen carefully to what I say while you look at the pictures. Think about what I am saying. Listen for important words and numbers that will help you find the answer.

Practice

Say Now we will do the Practice items in the same way we did the sample. Listen to what I say and choose the answer you think is correct. Fill in the circle under the best answer. Be sure your answer circle is completely filled in with a dark mark. Do you have any questions? Let's begin.

Allow time between items for students to fill in their answers. Do not read the item numbers.

1. Look at the stars in row 1. Which group has seven stars? Fill in the circle under the group that has exactly seven stars.

2. Look at the word in the box for row 2. Which numeral means the same as the number word in the box? Fill in the circle under the numeral that means the same as the number word in the box.

3. Look at the shapes in row 3 at the top of the second column. Which answer shows a triangle inside a square? Fill in the circle under the answer that shows a triangle inside a square.

4. Look at the number sentence in row 4. Which numeral should go in the box to make the number sentence true? Fill in the circle under the numeral that should go in the box to make the number sentence true.

5. Look at the butterflies for row 5. Which answer has one more flower than there are butterflies? Fill in the circle under the answer that has one more flower than there are butterflies.

    Turn to the next page, page 56.

Check to be sure the students have found the right page. Allow the students a moment to rest.

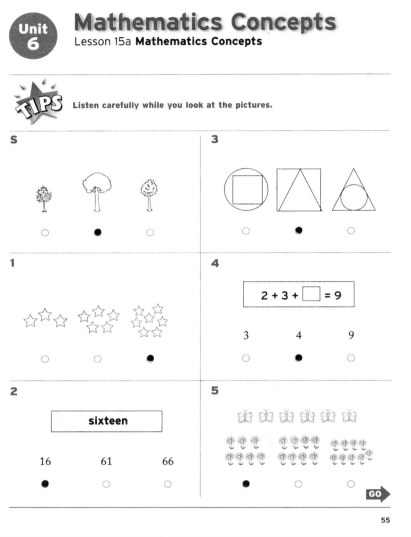

6. Look at the numerals in row 6. This row is at the top of the first column, the one with the book. Which numeral is 35? Fill in the circle under the numeral 35.

7. Look at the pictures for row 7. In which answer is there a frog on every lily pad? Fill in the circle under the answer that shows a frog on every lily pad.

8. Look at the number sentence for row 8. Which symbol will make the number sentence true? Fill in the circle under the symbol that will make the number sentence true.

9. Look at the pictures in row 9 at the top of the second column. What should you use to weigh a small package? Fill in the circle under the answer that shows what you should use to weigh a small package.

10. Look at the coins in row 10. How much money is there in all? Fill in the circle under the number that shows how much money there is in all.

11. Look at the numbers for row 11, the row with the telephone. Which answer is a number between 25 and 40? Fill in the circle under the answer that shows a number between 25 and 40.

Look at the next page, page 57.

Check to be sure the students have found the right page. Allow the students a moment to rest.

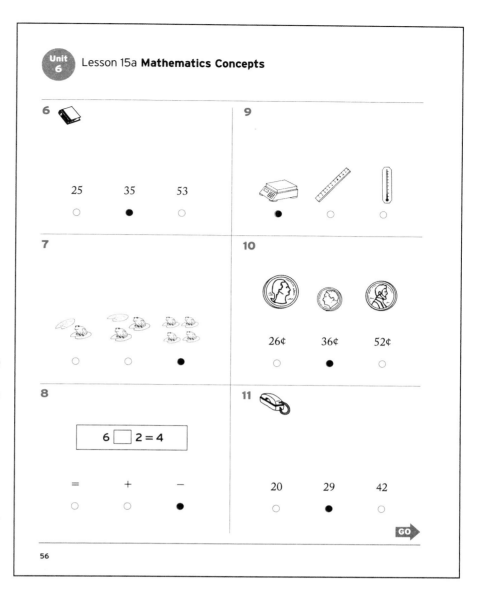

12. Look at the flowers in row 12. This row is at the top of the first column. Each vase has 10 flowers. How many flowers are there in all? Fill in the circle under the answer that shows how many flowers there are in all.

13. Look at the pictures for row 13. Which of these is closest in height to a medium-sized dog in real life? Fill in the circle under the picture that shows something that is closest in height to a medium-sized dog in real life.

14. Look at the shapes in row 14. Which answer shows the pieces that make the shape? Fill in the circle under the answer that shows the pieces that make the shape.

15. Look at the dogs in row 15. This row is at the top of the second column. Which dog is the second smallest? Fill in the circle under the dog that is the second smallest.

16. Look at the clock for row 16. What time does the clock show? Fill in the circle under the time that the clock shows.

17. Look at the numerals in row 17, the one with the leaf. Which numeral means the same as 3 tens and 5 ones? Fill in the circle under the numeral that means the same as 3 tens and 5 ones.

Say It's time to stop. You have finished Lesson 15a.

Review the answers with the students. Have the students indicate completion of the lesson by entering their score for this activity on the progress chart at the beginning of the book. Provide the students whatever help is necessary to record their scores.

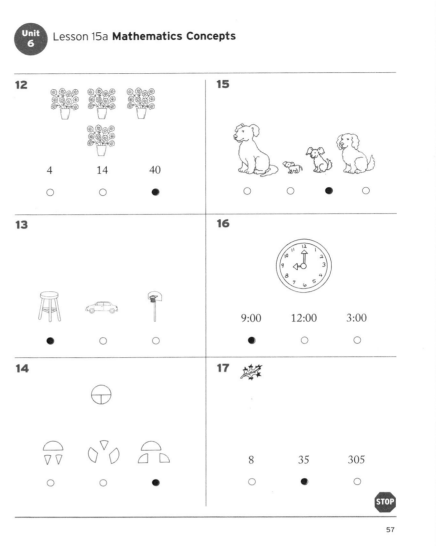

Unit 6 Lesson 15b Mathematics Concepts

Focus

Mathematics Skills
- representing problems with number sentences
- recognizing plane figures
- estimating measurement
- sequencing numbers or shapes
- recognizing fractional parts
- understanding number sentences
- recognizing value of coins and bills
- telling time
- using mathematical language
- counting
- naming numerals
- comparing and ordering whole numbers

Test-taking Skills
- following oral directions
- listening carefully
- considering every answer choice
- working methodically
- identifying and using key words, numbers, and pictures

Say Turn to Lesson 15b on page 58. In this lesson you will do more mathematics problems.

Check to see that the students have found the right page.

Practice

Say Now we will do the Practice items in the same way we did the items in Lesson 15a. Listen to what I say and choose the answer you think is correct. Fill in the circle under the best answer. Be sure your answer circle is completely filled in with a dark mark. Do you have any questions? Let's begin.

Allow time between items for students to fill in their answers. Do not read the item numbers.

1. Look at the birds in row 1. What does the picture show? Fill in the circle under the answer that best tells about the picture.

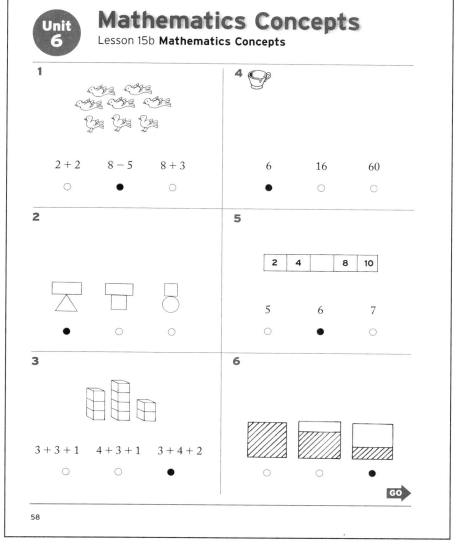

2. Look at the shapes in row 2. Which shows a rectangle on top of a triangle? Fill in the circle under the answer that shows a rectangle on top of a triangle.

3. Look at the picture and the answers in row 3. Which number expression best matches the picture? Fill in the circle under the the expression that best matches the picture.

4. Look at the numerals in row 4. It is at the top of the next column, the row with the cup. Which numeral tells about how many inches long a dollar bill is? Fill in the circle under the numeral that tells about how many inches long a dollar bill is.

5. Look at the numerals in row 5. Which numeral is missing from the pattern? Fill in the circle under the numeral that is missing from the pattern.

6. Look at the shapes in row 6. Which square is about one-third shaded? Fill in the circle under the square that is about one-third shaded.

Look at the next page, page 59.

Check to be sure the students have found the right page. Allow the students a moment to rest.

7. Look at the pizzas in row 7. Which pizza is cut into thirds? Fill in the circle under the pizza that is cut into thirds.

8. Look at the pattern in row 8. Which part of the pattern is missing? Fill in the circle under the part of the pattern that is missing.

9. Look at the number sentences in row 9. Only one number sentence is true. Which one is it? Fill in the circle under the number sentence that is true.

10. Look at the coins in row 10. This is the row at the top of the next column. Which answer shows 15¢? Fill in the circle under the answer that shows 15¢.

11. Look at the numerals in row 11, the one with the duck. Which numeral is closest in value to 32? Fill in the circle under the numeral that is closest in value to 32.

12. Look at the clock in row 12. Which numeral is missing from this clock? Fill in the circle under the numeral that is missing from the clock.

Turn to the next page, page 60.

Check to be sure the students have found the right page. Allow the students a moment to rest.

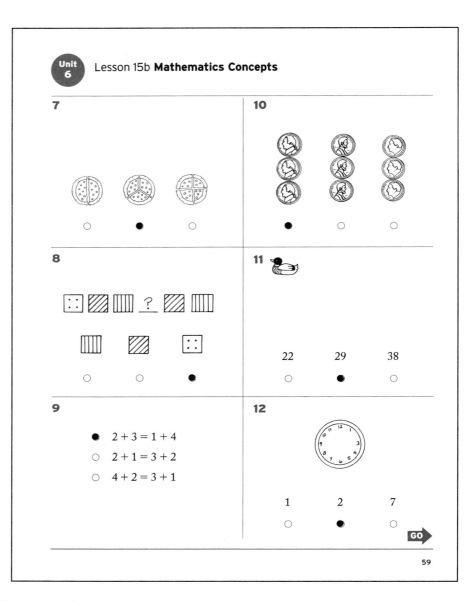

13. Look at the buildings for row 13. Which building is smallest? Fill in the circle under the building that is smallest.

14. Look at the peanuts in row 14. Which group has 9 peanuts? Fill in the circle under the group that has 9 peanuts.

15. Look at the number word in row 15. Which numeral means the same as the number word in the box? Fill in the circle under the numeral that means the same as the number word.

16. Look at the shapes in row 16, the row at the top of the next column. Which answer shows a square inside a triangle? Fill in the circle under the answer that shows a square inside a triangle.

17. Look at the number sentence in row 17. Which numeral should go in the box to make the number sentence true? Fill in the circle under the numeral that should go in the box to make the number sentence true.

18. Look at the bees and flowers for row 18. Which answer has two more flowers than there are bees? Fill in the circle under the answer that has two more flowers than there are bees.

Say It's time to stop. You have finished Lesson 15b.

Review the answers with the students. Have the students indicate completion of the lesson by entering their score for this activity on the progress chart at the beginning of the book. Provide the students whatever help is necessary to record their scores.

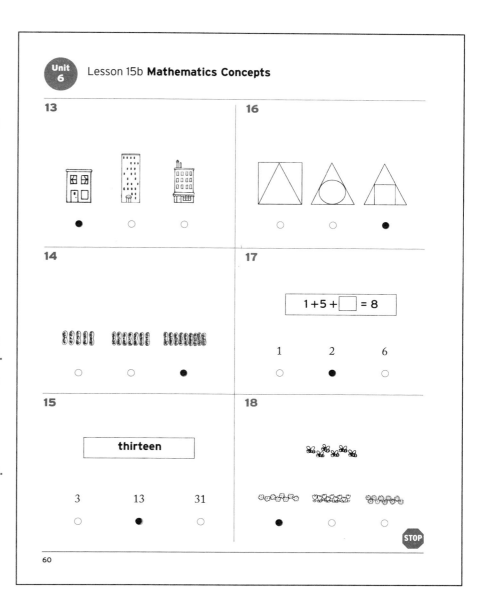

Focus

Mathematics Skills
- naming numerals
- using mathematical language
- understanding number sentences
- identifying measurement tools
- recognizing value of coins and bills
- comparing and ordering whole numbers
- counting by tens
- estimating measurement
- identifying parts of a figure
- telling time
- understanding place value
- representing problems with number sentences
- recognizing plane figures
- sequencing numbers or shapes
- recognizing fractional parts

Test-taking Skills
- following oral directions
- listening carefully
- considering every answer choice
- working methodically
- identifying and using key words, numbers, and pictures

Unit 6 Test Yourself: Mathematics Concepts

S

2	17	27
○	○	●

3

○	○	●

1

●	○	○

4

25¢	30¢	55¢
●	○	○

2

6 ☐ 2 = 8

=	+	−
○	●	○

5

17	25	31
○	●	○

GO →

61

This lesson simulates an actual test-taking experience. Therefore, it is recommended that the directions be read verbatim and the suggested procedures be followed.

Directions

Administration Time: approximately 35 minutes

Say Look at the Test Yourself lesson on page 61. The page number is at the bottom of the page on the right.

Check to be sure the students have found the right page. Point out to the students that this is not a real test and that they will score it themselves to see how well they are doing.

Say This lesson will check how well you understand the mathematics skills you practiced before. Remember to make sure that the circles for your answer choices are completely filled in. Press your pencil firmly so that your marks come out dark. Completely erase any marks for answers that you change. Do not write anything except your answer choices in your books.

Listen carefully and look at the numbers for S. This row has a picture of a pot. Which numeral is 27? Fill in the circle under the answer that is 27. *(pause)* You should have filled in the last answer. If you chose another answer, erase yours and fill in the last answer circle now. Be sure your answer circle is completely filled in with a dark mark and that you have marked the correct answer circle.

Check to see that the students have marked the correct circle.

Say Now we will do more items like the sample. Listen to what I say and choose the answer you think is correct. Fill in the circle under the best answer. Be sure your answer circle is completely filled in with a dark mark. Do you have any questions? Let's begin.

Allow time between items for students to fill in their answers. Do not read the item numbers.

1. Look at the pictures for row 1. In which answer is there a bird on every nest? Fill in the circle under the answer that shows a bird on every nest.

2. Look at the number sentence for row 2. Which symbol will make the number sentence true? Fill in the circle under the symbol that will make the number sentence true.

3. Look at the measurement tools in row 3. What should you use to find out how warm it is outside? Fill in the circle under the answer that shows what you should use to find out how warm it is outside.

4. Look at the coins in row 4. How much money is there in all? Fill in the circle under the answer that shows how much money there is in all.

5. Look at the numbers in row 5, the one with the bell. Which answer is a number between 19 and 27? Fill in the circle under the answer that shows a number between 19 and 27.

    Turn to the next page, page 62.

Check to be sure the students have found the right page. Allow the students a moment to rest.

6. Look at the flowers in row 6. Each vase has 10 flowers. How many flowers are there in all? Fill in the circle under the answer that shows how many flowers there are in all.

7. Look at the pictures in row 7. Which of these is closest in height to a child in real life? Fill in the circle under the answer that is closest in height to a child in real life.

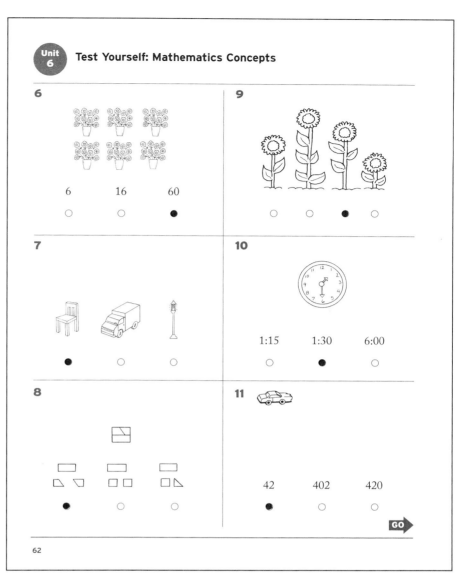

8. Look at the answers in row 8. Which answer shows the pieces that make the shape? Fill in the circle under the answer that shows the pieces that make the shape.

9. Look at the flowers in row 9. Which sunflower is the second tallest? Fill in the circle under the sunflower that is second tallest.

10. Look at the clock in row 10. What time does the clock show? Fill in the circle under the time that is shown on the clock.

11. Look at the numerals in row 11, the one with the car. Which numeral means the same as 4 tens and 2 ones? Fill in the circle under the numeral that means the same as 4 tens and 2 ones.

    Look at the next page, page 63.

Check to be sure the students have found the right page. Allow the students a moment to rest.

12. Look at the bowling pins in row 12. What does the picture show? Fill in the circle under the answer that best shows what is happening in the picture.

13. Look at the shapes in row 13. Which shows a circle on top of a square? Fill in the circle under the answer that shows a circle on top of a square.

14. Look at the dishes in row 14. Which number expression best matches the picture? Fill in the circle under the number expression that best matches the picture.

15. Look at the numerals in row 15, the one with the book. Which numeral tells about how many feet high a doorway is? Fill in the circle under the picture that shows how high a doorway is.

16. Look at the numerals in row 16. Which numeral is missing from the pattern? Fill in the circle under the numeral that is missing from the pattern.

17. Look at the circles in row 17. Which circle is about one-quarter shaded? Fill in the circle under the answer that shows a circle that is about one-quarter shaded.

Turn to the next page, page 64.

Check to be sure the students have found the right page. Allow the students a moment to rest.

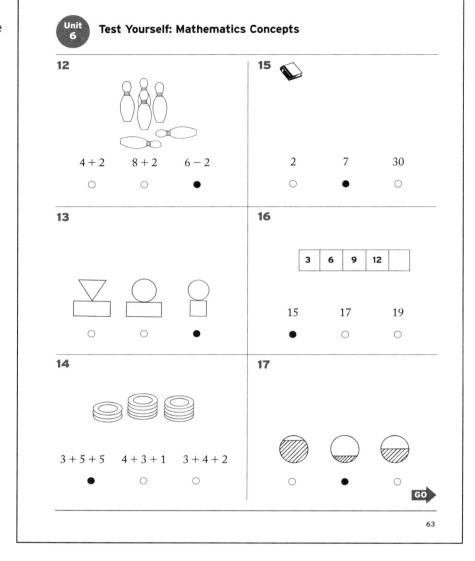

Unit 6 Test Yourself **Mathematics Concepts**

18. Look at the pizzas in row 18. Which pizza is cut into eighths? Fill in the circle under the answer that shows a pizza cut into eighths.

19. Look at the pattern in row 19. Which part of the pattern is missing? Fill in the circle under the part of the pattern that is missing.

20. Look at the number sentences in row 20. Only one number sentence is true. Which one is it? Fill in the circle beside the number sentence that is true.

21. Look at the coins in row 21. Which answer shows 30¢? Fill in the circle under the answer that shows 30¢.

22. Look at the numerals in row 22, the one with the telephone. Which numeral is closest in value to 19? Fill in the circle under the answer that is closest in value to 19.

23. Look at the clock in row 23. Which numeral is missing from this clock? Fill in the circle under the numeral that is missing from the clock.

Say It's time to stop. You have completed the Test Yourself lesson. Check to see that you have completely filled in your answer circles with dark marks. Make sure that any marks for answers that you changed have been completely erased. Now you may close your books.

Review the answers with the students. Have the students indicate completion of the lesson by entering their score for this activity on the progress chart at the beginning of the book. Provide the students whatever help is necessary to record their scores.

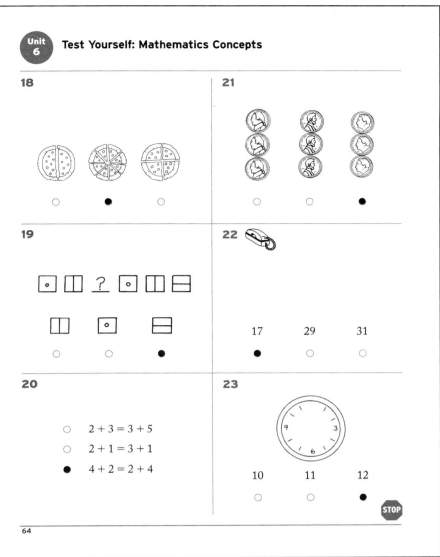

Background

This unit contains three lessons that deal with mathematics problem-solving skills. Students solve problems, identify problem solving strategies, and use graphs.

• **In Lesson 16a,** students solve oral word problems. Students are encouraged to follow oral directions and listen carefully. They practice considering every answer choice, working methodically, and indicating that the correct answer is not given.

• **In Lesson 16b,** students identify problem-solving strategies and answer questions about a graph. Students review the test-taking skills introduced in the previous lesson, analyze problems, and use graphs.

• **In the Test Yourself lesson,** the mathematics skills and test-taking skills introduced and used in Lessons 16a and 16b are reinforced and presented in a format that gives students the experience of taking an achievement test.

Instructional Objectives

Lesson 16a	**Mathematics Problems**	Given an oral word problem and four answers, the student identifies which of the answers is correct or indicates that the correct answer is not given.
Lesson 16b	**Mathematics Problems**	Given an oral word problem and three solution strategies, the student identifies which of the strategies is the correct way to solve the problem. Given a problem about a graph and three answers, the student identifies which of the answers is correct.
	Test Yourself	Given questions similar to those in Lessons 16a and 16b, the student utilizes mathematics problem-solving skills and test-taking strategies on achievement test formats.

Focus

Mathematics Skill
• solving oral word problems

Test-taking Skills
• following oral directions
• listening carefully
• considering every answer choice
• working methodically
• indicating that the correct answer is not given

Samples S1 and S2

Distribute scratch paper to the students.

Say Look at Lesson 16a on page 65. The page number is at the bottom of the page on the right. A picture of a telephone is at the top of the first column.

Check to see that the students have found the right page.

Say In this lesson you will solve word problems. I will read the problem and you will solve it. You may solve the problem in your head or use scratch paper. If the right answer to the problem is not one of the choices, fill in the circle under the N, which stands for *not given*. Are you ready? Let's do S1 together. Listen carefully and look at the numbers at the top of the page near the telephone. Amy had 1 pencil. Her mother gave her 1 more pencil. How many pencils did Amy have in all? Again, Amy had 1 pencil. Her mother gave her 1 more pencil. How many pencils did Amy have in all? *(pause)* Amy had 2 pencils in all because 1 plus 1 is 2. Fill in the circle under the number 2. Be sure your answer circle is completely filled in with a dark mark and that you have marked the correct answer circle.

Check to see that the students have marked the correct circle.

Say Now let's do the other sample, the one with the leaf. There are 3 bottles of juice in the refrigerator. Donna drank 1. How many bottles

---

Unit 7 Mathematics Problems
Lesson 16a Mathematics Problems

TIPS Listen to the problem. Decide how you should solve it.

S1				S2			
1	2	3	N	3	4	5	N
○	●	○	○	○	○	○	●

1				**4**			
2	3	5	N	7	10	11	N
○	○	●	○	●	○	○	○

2				**5**			
2	5	7	N	3	7	12	N
○	●	○	○	○	○	●	○

3				**6**			
3	7	11	N	$3	$5	$13	N
○	○	○	●	●	○	○	○

GO

65

---

of juice were left? Again, there are 3 bottles of juice in the refrigerator. Donna drank 1. How many bottles of juice were left? *(pause)* The correct answer is 2, but this is not one of the choices. Fill in the circle under N for *not given*. Be sure your answer circle is completely filled in with a dark mark and that you have marked the correct answer circle.

Check to see that the students have marked the correct circle.

★**TIPS**

Say Now let's look at the tip.

Read the tip aloud to the students.

Say Listen carefully to what I say while you look at the numbers. Think about how you should solve the problem. Then solve the problem in your head or on the scratch paper I gave you.

Practice

Say Now we will do more items like S1 and S2. Listen to what I say and choose the answer you think is correct. Fill in the circle under the best answer. Be sure your answer circle is completely filled in with a dark mark. Do you have any questions? Let's begin.

Allow time between items for students to fill in their answers. Read each problem twice. Do not read the item numbers.

1. Look at the row with the cup. Three birds were in a tree. Then 2 more birds landed in the tree. How many birds were in the tree? Again . . .

2. Look at the row with the duck. Eric has 7 tennis balls. Two of the tennis balls are in the closet. The rest are under his bed. How many tennis balls are under the bed? Again . . .

3. Look at the row with the pot. Mr. Allen used 3 eggs for breakfast. There were 7 eggs left. How many eggs did he have to begin with? Again . . .

4. Look at the row with the bell. Shelly has 2 pens, 3 pencils, and 2 crayons in her backpack. How many writing tools does she have in all? Again . . .

5. Look at the row with the car. There are 3 shelves in a bookcase. Each shelf has 4 books. How many books are there all together? Again . . .

6. Look at the row with the book. Mrs. Lyle has $5. She wants to buy groceries that cost $8. How much more money does she need? Again . . .

   Turn to the next page, page 66.

Check to be sure the students have found the right page. Allow the students a moment to relax.

Unit 7

Mathematics Problems
Lesson 16a **Mathematics Problems**

TIPS Listen to the problem. Decide how you should solve it.

S1	1	2	3	N	S2	3	4	5	N
	○	●	○	○		○	○	○	●

1	2	3	5	N	4	7	10	11	N
	○	○	●	○		●	○	○	○

2	2	5	7	N	5	3	7	12	N
	○	●	○	○		○	○	●	○

3	3	7	11	N	6	$3	$5	$13	N
	○	○	○	●		●	○	○	○

GO →

65

---

7. Look at the row with the book. Gary has 3 fish tanks. There are 4 fish in one tank and 3 in another tank. There are no fish in the third tank. How many fish does Gary have in all? Again . . .

8. Look at the row with the telephone. Ida had 7 sheets of paper. She gave 2 to her friend. The teacher then gave Ida 1 more sheet of paper. How many sheets of paper did Ida have then? Again . . .

9. Look at the row with the leaf. The science club has 5 girls, 2 boys, and 1 teacher. How many more girls than boys are in the science club? Again . . .

10. Look at the row with the cup. Millie has 3 hamsters. She has 6 carrots and wants to divide them equally among the hamsters. How many carrots will each hamster get? Again . . .

11. Look at the row with the duck. There are 5 lights in Sam's living room. One is on a table, one is on a desk, and the others are on the floor. How many lights are on the floor? Again . . .

12. Look at the row with the pot. Martina bought a bag of 8 rolls. Her family used half of them for dinner. How many rolls did they use for dinner? Again . . .

Say It's time to stop. You have finished Lesson 16a.

Review the answers with the students. Have the students indicate completion of the lesson by entering their score for this activity on the progress chart at the beginning of the book. Provide the students whatever help is necessary to record their scores.

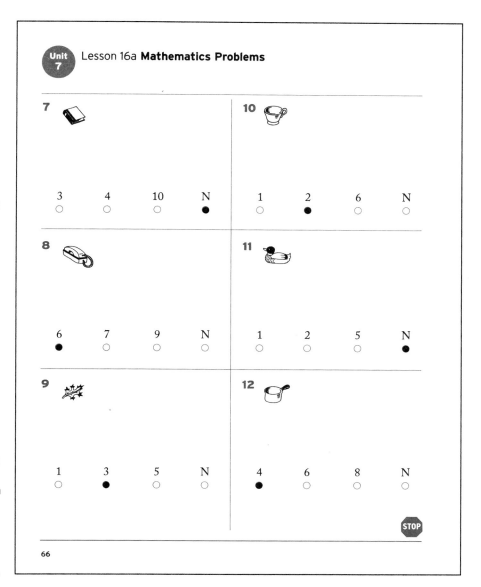

Unit 7 Lesson 16b Mathematics Problems

Focus

Mathematics Skills
- identifying problem-solving strategies
- interpreting graphs

Test-taking Skills
- following oral directions
- listening carefully
- considering every answer choice
- analyzing problems
- using graphs

Sample S1

Say Look at Lesson 16b on page 67. The page number is at the bottom of the page on the right.

Check to see that the students have found the right page.

Say In this lesson you will choose a number sentence that goes with a problem. Look at S1 at the top of the page, the row with the bell. Listen carefully. Mandy has 2 apple trees and 1 peach tree in her yard. Which number sentence tells how many trees there are in all? Again, Mandy has 2 apple trees and 1 peach tree in her yard. Which number sentence tells how many trees there are in all? *(pause)* The second answer is correct because you would add 2 plus 1 to solve the problem. Fill in the circle under the second answer. Be sure your answer circle is completely filled in with a dark mark and that you have marked the correct answer circle.

Check to see that the students have marked the correct circle.

S1

$2 - 1 =$	$2 + 1 =$	$3 + 2 =$
○	●	○

1

$5 - 4 =$	$3 + 2 =$	$5 + 4 =$
○	○	●

2

$10 - 2 =$	$10 + 2 =$	$8 + 2 =$
●	○	○

3

$4 + 5 =$	$5 - 4 =$	$5 \times 4 =$
○	○	●

4

$\$5 - \$5 =$	$\$5 - \$2 =$	$\$5 + \$2 =$
○	●	○

Practice

Say Now we will do the Practice items in the same way we did the sample. I will read a problem while you look at the answers. Fill in the circle under the answer that goes with the problem. Be sure your answer circle is completely filled in with a dark mark. Do you have any questions? Let's begin.

Allow time between items for students to fill in their answers. Read each problem twice. Do not read the item numbers.

1. Look at the row with the car. Mr. Lincoln has 5 boards in his truck. There are 4 more boards in the garage. Which number sentence tells how many boards Mr. Lincoln has all together? Again . . .

2. Look at the row with the book. A candle is 10 inches long. Two inches of the candle burned away. Which number sentence can you use to find out how much of the candle is left? Again . . .

3. Look at the row with the telephone. Mr. Jones bought 4 boxes of tile. Each box holds 5 tiles. Which number sentence can Mr. Jones use to find out how many tiles he has in all? Again . . .

4. Look at the row with the leaf. Lily had $5. She spent $2 for a movie ticket. Which number sentence can Lily use to find out how much money she has left? Again . . .

    Turn to the next page, page 68.

Check to be sure the students have found the right page. Allow the students a moment to relax.

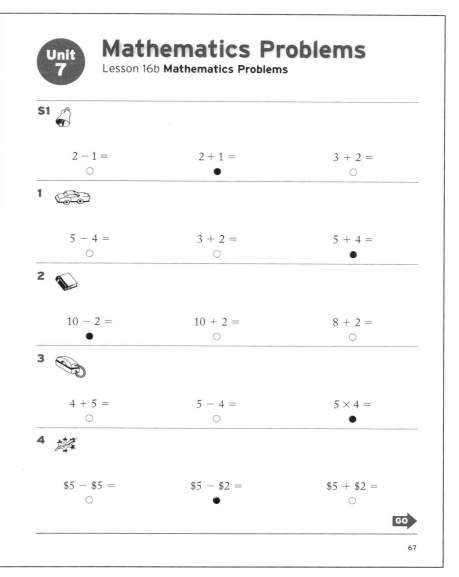

Unit 7 **Mathematics Problems**
Lesson 16b **Mathematics Problems**

S1
2 − 1 = ○   2 + 1 = ●   3 + 2 = ○

1
5 − 4 = ○   3 + 2 = ○   5 + 4 = ●

2
10 − 2 = ●   10 + 2 = ○   8 + 2 = ○

3
4 + 5 = ○   5 − 4 = ○   5 × 4 = ●

4
$5 − $5 = ○ $5 − $2 = ● $5 + $2 = ○

GO

67

Sample S2

Say Now we will do a different kind of item. Look at the circle graph at the top of the page. It shows the different kinds of fruit in a kitchen. You will use the graph to answer some questions. Look at question S2. Read the question to yourself while I read it out loud. It says, "How many bananas are in the chart?" Which answer is correct? Look at the graph to find the answer. *(pause)* There are *5* bananas in the chart. Fill in the circle beside the number *5*. Be sure your answer circle is completely filled in with a dark mark and that you have marked the correct answer circle.

Check to see that the students have marked the correct circle.

Practice

Say Let's do the rest of the problems on this page in the same way. Read each question to yourself while I read it out loud. Decide which answer is correct and fill in the circle for your answer. Let's begin.

Allow time between items for students to fill in their answers. Read each problem once.

5. Number 5: If there were another orange, how many would there be in all?

6. Number 6: How many more bananas than apples are there?

7. Number 7: How many pears and apples are there all together?

Say It's time to stop. You have finished Lesson 16b.

Review the answers with the students. Have the students indicate completion of the lesson by entering their score for this activity on the progress chart at the beginning of the book. Provide the students whatever help is necessary to record their scores.

 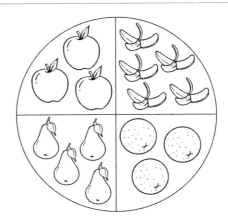

Unit 7 Lesson 16b **Mathematics Problems**

S2 How many bananas are in the chart?
- ○ 3
- ○ 4
- ● 5

5 If there were another orange, how many would there be in all?
- ● 4
- ○ 5
- ○ 6

6 How many more bananas than apples are there?
- ○ 1
- ● 2
- ○ 3

7 How many pears and apples are there all together?
- ○ 5
- ○ 6
- ● 7

68

Unit 7 Test Yourself: Mathematics Problems

Focus

Mathematics Skills
- solving oral word problems
- identifying problem-solving strategies
- interpreting graphs

Test-taking Skills
- following oral directions
- listening carefully
- considering every answer choice
- working methodically
- analyzing problems
- using graphs

This lesson simulates an actual test-taking experience. Therefore, it is recommended that the directions be read verbatim and the suggested procedures be followed.

Directions

Administration Time: approximately 25 minutes

Distribute scratch paper to the students.

Say Look at the Test Yourself lesson on page 69. The page number is at the bottom of the page on the right.

Check to be sure the students have found the right page. Point out to the students that this is not a real test and that they will score it themselves to see how well they are doing.

Say This lesson will check how well you understand the mathematics skills you practiced before. Remember to make sure that the circles for your answer choices are completely filled in. Press your pencil firmly so that your marks come out dark. Completely erase any marks for answers that you change. Do not write anything except your answer choices in your books.

In this part of the lesson you will solve word problems. I will read the problem and you will solve it. You may solve the problem in your head or use scratch paper. If the right answer

to the problem is not one of the choices, fill in the circle under the N, which stands for *not given*. Are you ready? Let's do S1 together. Listen carefully and look at the numbers at the top of the page near the cup. It takes 2 hours to get to the beach. The Hills have been driving for 1 hour. How many more hours do they have to drive? Again, it takes 2 hours to get to the beach. The Hills have been driving for 1 hour. How many more hours do they have to drive? *(pause)* The answer is *1* hour because 1 from 2 is *1*. Fill in the circle under the number 1. Be sure your answer circle is completely filled in with a dark mark and that you have marked the correct answer circle.

Check to see that the students have marked the correct circle.

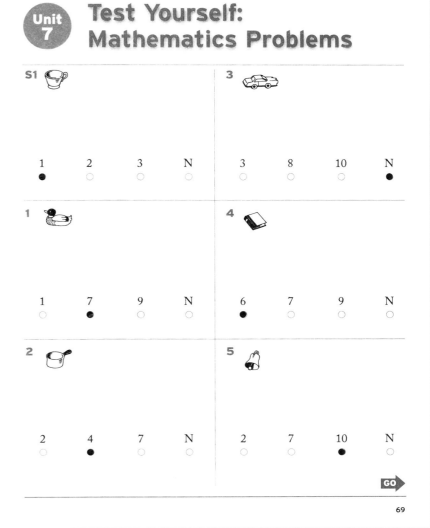

Say Now we will do more items like S1. Listen to what I say and choose the answer you think is correct. Fill in the circle under the best answer. Be sure your answer circle is completely filled in with a dark mark. Do you have any questions? Let's begin.

Allow time between items for students to fill in their answers. Read each problem twice. Do not read the item numbers.

1. Look at the row with the duck. Ms. Little had 3 cans of red paint and 4 cans of blue paint. How many cans of paint did she have in all? Again . . .

2. Look at the row with the pot. Allen collected 7 logs. He put 3 in the fire. The rest are beside the fireplace. How many logs are beside the fireplace? Again . . .

3. Look at the row with the car. Chris fed 3 cows. She had 8 more cows to feed. How many cows are there in all? Again . . .

4. Look at the row with the book. Sue bought 2 cards, 3 stamps, and 1 envelope. How many things did she buy in all? Again . . .

5. Look at the row with the bell. Don has 2 bags of carrots. Each bag has 5 carrots. How many carrots does he have in all? Again . . .

   Turn to the next page, page 70.

Check to be sure the students have found the right page. Allow the students a moment to rest.

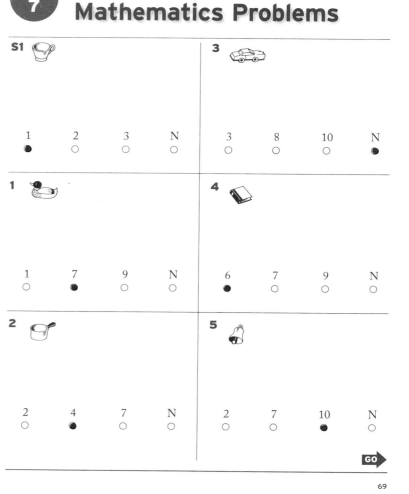

Sample S2

Say Now we will answer a different kind of question. In this part of the lesson you will choose a number sentence that goes with a problem. Look at S2 at the top of the page, the row with the cup. Listen carefully. Jennie recycled 1 box of cans and 2 boxes of glass. Which number sentence shows how many boxes she recycled in all? Again, Jennie recycled 1 box of cans and 2 boxes of glass. Which number sentence shows how many boxes she recycled in all? *(pause)* The second answer is correct because you would add 1 plus 2 to solve the problem. Fill in the circle under the second answer. Be sure your answer circle is completely filled in with a dark mark and that you have marked the correct answer circle.

Check to see that the students have marked the correct circle.

Say Now we will do more items like S2. Listen to what I say and choose the answer you think is correct. Fill in the circle under the best answer. Be sure your answer circle is completely filled in with a dark mark. Do you have any questions? Let's begin.

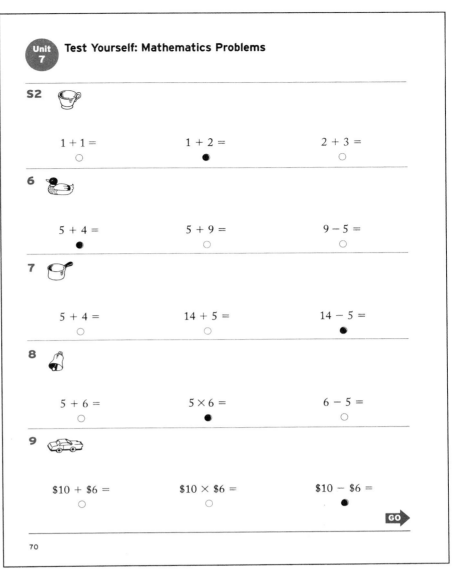

Test Yourself: Mathematics Problems (Unit 7)

S2

$1 + 1 =$ ○ $1 + 2 =$ ● $2 + 3 =$ ○

6

$5 + 4 =$ ● $5 + 9 =$ ○ $9 - 5 =$ ○

7

$5 + 4 =$ ○ $14 + 5 =$ ○ $14 - 5 =$ ●

8

$5 + 6 =$ ○ $5 \times 6 =$ ● $6 - 5 =$ ○

9

$\$10 + \$6 =$ ○ $\$10 \times \$6 =$ ○ $\$10 - \$6 =$ ●

GO

70

Allow time between items for students to fill in their answers. Read each problem twice. Do not read the item numbers.

6. Look at the row with the duck. Cora picked 5 ears of corn one day and 4 ears of corn the next day. Which number sentence shows how many ears of corn she picked in all? Again . . .

7. Look at the row with the pot. There were 14 students on the bus. Five of the students got off at the first stop. Which number sentence shows how many students were left on the bus? Again . . .

8. Look at the row with the bell. A teacher has 5 boxes of pencils. Each box has 6 pencils in it. Which number sentence can the teacher use to find out how many pencils there are in all? Again . . .

9. Look at the row with the car. A hat costs $6. Reggie paid for it with a $10 bill. Which number sentence shows how much change he received? Again . . .

Look at the next page, page 71.

Check to be sure the students have found the right page. Allow the students a moment to rest.

Say Now we will do a different kind of item. Look at the picture graph at the top of the page. It shows the different kinds of pets some students have. You will use the graph to answer some questions. Read each question to yourself while I read it out loud. Decide which answer is correct and fill in the circle for your answer. Let's begin.

Allow time between items for students to fill in their answers. Read each problem once.

10. Number 10: Which pet was chosen by 3 students?

11. Number 11: Which pet was chosen by twice as many students as fish?

12. Number 12: Which pet was chosen by the most students?

13. Number 13: How many pets were chosen by more than three students?

Say It's time to stop. You have completed the Test Yourself lesson. Check to see that you have completely filled in your answer circles with dark marks. Make sure that any marks for answers that you changed have been completely erased. Now you may close your books.

Review the answers with the students. Have the students indicate completion of the lesson by entering their score for this activity on the progress chart at the beginning of the book. Provide the students whatever help is necessary to record their scores.

 Unit 7   **Test Yourself: Mathematics Problems**

10   **Which pet was chosen by 3 students?**
- ● Dog
- ○ Cat
- ○ Fish

12   **Which pet was chosen by the most students?**
- ○ Dog
- ○ Bird
- ● Cat

11   **Which pet was chosen by twice as many students as fish?**
- ○ Horse
- ● Bird
- ○ Dog

13   **How many pets were chosen by more than three students?**
- ● 1
- ○ 2
- ○ 3

 STOP

71

Unit 8

This unit contains three lessons that deal with mathematics computation skills. Students solve addition and subtraction problems.

• **In Lesson 17a,** students solve oral addition and subtraction problems. Students are encouraged to follow oral directions and listen carefully. They practice considering every answer choice, computing carefully, and indicating that the correct answer is not given.

• **In Lesson 17b,** students solve addition and subtraction problems. Students review the test-taking skills introduced in the previous lesson and perform the correct operation. They transfer numbers accurately and convert items to a workable format.

• **In the Test Yourself lesson,** the computation skills and test-taking skills introduced and used in Lessons 17a and 17b are reinforced and presented in a format that gives students the experience of taking an achievement test.

Instructional **Objectives**

Lesson 17a	**Mathematics Computation**	Given an oral addition or subtraction problem and four answers, the student identifies which of the answers is correct or indicates that the correct answer is not given.
Lesson 17b	**Mathematics Computation**	Given an addition or subtraction problem and four answers, the student identifies which of the answers is correct or indicates that the correct answer is not given.
	Test Yourself	Given questions similar to those in Lessons 17a and 17b, the student utilizes mathematics computation skills and test-taking strategies on achievement test formats.

Lesson 17a
Mathematics Computation

Focus

Mathematics Skill
- solving oral addition and subtraction problems

Test-taking Skills
- following oral directions
- listening carefully
- considering every answer choice
- computing carefully
- indicating that the correct answer is not given

Sample S1

Distribute scratch paper to the students.

Say Turn to Lesson 17a on page 72. The page number is at the bottom of the page on the left. There is a picture of a book at the top of the first column.

Check to see that the students have found the right page.

Say In this lesson you will solve addition and subtraction problems. I will read the problem and you will solve it. You may solve the problem in your head or use scratch paper. If the right answer to the problem is not one of the choices, fill in the circle under the N, which stands for *not given*. Are you ready? Let's do S1 together. Listen carefully and look at the numbers at the top of the page near the book. What is 1 add 3? 1 plus 3 equals what number? *(pause)* 1 plus 3 is 4. Fill in the circle under the number 4. Be sure your answer circle is completely filled in with a dark mark and that you have marked the correct answer circle.

Check to see that the students have marked the correct circle.

Mathematics Computation
Lesson 17a **Mathematics Computation**

TIPS Add and subtract carefully.

S1

1	4	5	N
○	●	○	○

1

4	6	10	N
○	○	●	○

2

6	9	19	N
○	●	○	○

3

13	14	19	N
●	○	○	○

4

0	17	18	N
○	○	○	●

5

10	25	35	N
○	●	○	○

GO

72

★TIPS

Say Now let's look at the tip.

Read the tip aloud to the students.

Say Listen carefully to what I say while you look at the numbers. Add and subtract carefully in your head or on scratch paper. If you work on scratch paper, be sure to write the numbers carefully.

Practice

Say Now we will do more items like S1. Listen to what I say and choose the answer you think is correct. Fill in the circle under the best answer. Be sure your answer circle is completely filled in with a dark mark. Do you have any questions? Let's begin.

Allow time between items for students to fill in their answers. Do not read the item numbers.

1. What is 2 add 8? 2 plus 8 equals what number? Fill in the circle under your answer in the row with the telephone.

2. What is 6 add 3? 6 plus 3 equals what number? Fill in the circle under your answer in the row with the leaf.

3. What is 4 add 9? 4 plus 9 equals what number? Fill in the circle under your answer in the row with the cup.

4. What is 8 add 8? 8 plus 8 equals what number? Fill in the circle under your answer in the row with the duck.

5. What is 20 add 5? 20 plus 5 equals what number? Fill in the circle under your answer in the row with the pot.

   Look at the next page, page 73.

Check to be sure the students have found the right page. Allow the students a moment to rest.

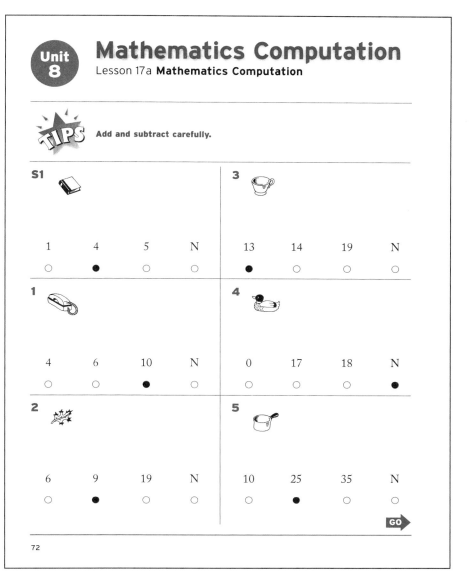

Sample S2

Say Now we will solve subtraction problems. Look at S2 at the top of the page, the row with the bell. Listen carefully. What is 3 subtract 2? 3 minus 2 equals what number? *(pause)* The second answer is correct because 3 minus 2 equals 1. Fill in the circle under the second answer. Be sure your answer circle is completely filled in with a dark mark and that you have marked the correct answer circle.

Check to see that the students have marked the correct circle.

Say Now we will do more items like S2. Listen to what I say and choose the answer you think is correct. Fill in the circle under the best answer. Be sure your answer circle is completely filled in with a dark mark. Do you have any questions? Let's begin.

Allow time between items for students to fill in their answers. Do not read the item numbers.

6. What is 6 subtract 4? 6 minus 4 equals what number? Fill in the circle under your answer in the row with the car.

7. What is 9 subtract 5? 9 minus 5 equals what number? Fill in the circle under your answer in the row with the book.

8. What is 7 subtract 6? 7 minus 6 equals what number? Fill in the circle under your answer in the row with the telephone.

9. What is 5 subtract 5? 5 minus 5 equals what number? Fill in the circle under your answer in the row with the leaf.

10. What is 10 subtract 3? 10 minus 3 equals what number? Fill in the circle under your answer in the row with the cup.

Say It's time to stop. You have finished Lesson 17a.

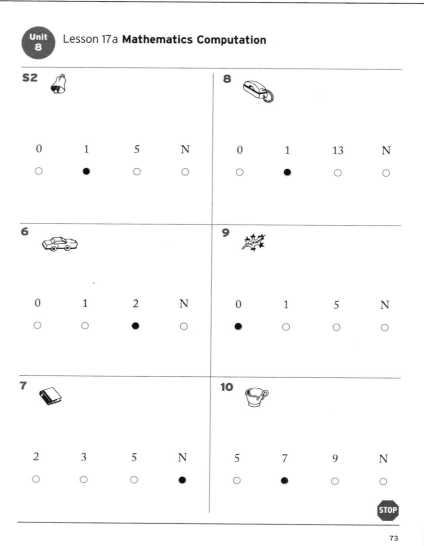

Review the answers with the students. Have the students indicate completion of the lesson by entering their score for this activity on the progress chart at the beginning of the book. Provide the students whatever help is necessary to record their scores.

Lesson 17b
Mathematics Computation

Focus

Mathematics Skill
- adding and subtracting whole numbers

Test-taking Skills
- performing the correct operation
- computing carefully
- transferring numbers accurately
- indicating that the correct answer is not given
- converting items to a workable format

Sample S

Distribute scratch paper to the students.

Say Turn to Lesson 17b on page 74. There are addition and subtraction problems on this page.

Check to see that the students have found the right page.

Say In this lesson you will solve addition and subtraction problems yourself. You may solve the problem in your head or use scratch paper. If the right answer to the problem is not one of the choices, fill in the circle under the N, which stands for *not given*. Look at the addition problem for S. It says 4 plus 1. Which answer is correct? *(pause)* 4 plus 1 is 5. Fill in the circle under the number 5. Be sure your answer circle is completely filled in with a dark mark and that you have marked the correct answer circle.

Check to see that the students have marked the correct circle.

Mathematics Computation
Lesson 17b **Mathematics Computation**

S	$\begin{array}{r} 4 \\ +\,1 \end{array}$				4	$0 + 4 =$			
	2	3	5	N		0	1	5	N
	○	○	●	○		○	○	○	●
1	$5 - 4 =$				5	$14 - 6 =$			
	0	1	9	N		2	8	10	N
	○	●	○	○		○	●	○	○
2	$\begin{array}{r} 6 \\ +\,3 \end{array}$				6	$\begin{array}{r} 16 \\ -\,4 \end{array}$			
	9	10	13	N		2	6	8	N
	●	○	○	○		○	○	○	●
3	$\begin{array}{r} 12 \\ -\,4 \end{array}$				7	$7 + 6 =$			
	6	8	12	N		13	14	16	N
	○	●	○	○		●	○	○	○

GO

74

Practice

Say We are ready for Practice. You are going to do more problems in the same way that we did the sample. Be sure to pay attention to the add or subtract symbol so you will know how to solve the problem. Do not write anything in your book except your answer choices. If you need to, use scratch paper to work the problems. When you come to the GO sign at the bottom of the page, continue working. Work until you come to the STOP sign at the bottom of the next page. Make sure that the circles for your answer choices are completely filled in with dark marks. Erase any marks for answers that you change. You may begin.

Allow time for the students to fill in their answers.

Say It's time to stop. You have finished Lesson 17b.

Review the answers with the students. Have the students indicate completion of the lesson by entering their score for this activity on the progress chart at the beginning of the book.

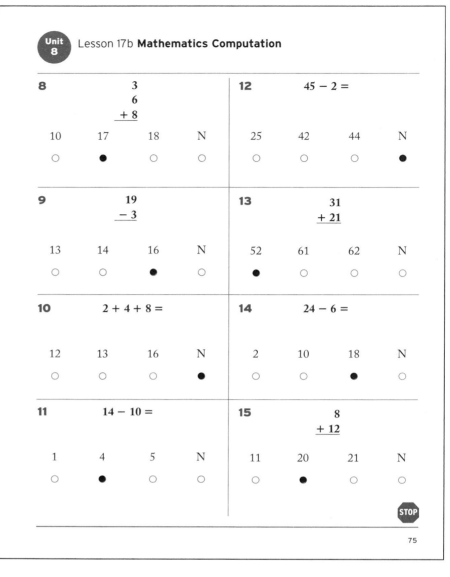

Test Yourself: Mathematics Computation

Focus

Mathematics Skills
- solving oral addition and subtraction problems
- adding and subtracting whole numbers

Test-taking Skills
- following oral directions
- listening carefully
- considering every answer choice
- computing carefully
- indicating that the correct answer is not given
- performing the correct operation
- transferring numbers accurately
- converting items to a workable format

This lesson simulates an actual test-taking experience. Therefore, it is recommended that the directions be read verbatim and the suggested procedures be followed.

Directions

Administration Time: approximately 25 minutes

Distribute scratch paper to the students.

Say Turn to the Test Yourself lesson on page 76. The page number is at the bottom of the page on the left.

Check to be sure the students have found the right page. Point out to the students that this is not a real test and that they will score it themselves to see how well they are doing.

Say This lesson will check how well you understand the addition and subtraction skills you practiced before. Remember to make sure that the circles for your answer choices are completely filled in. Press your pencil firmly so that your marks come out dark. Completely erase any marks for answers that you change. Do not write anything except your answer choices in your books.

Unit 8 Test Yourself: Mathematics Computation

S					4			
2	10	14	N		18	19	29	N
○	●	○	○		●	○	○	○

1					5			
2	7	9	N		5	16	17	N
○	○	○	●		○	●	○	○

2					6			
5	8	9	N		20	23	30	N
○	○	●	○		○	○	○	●

3					7			
2	11	12	N		0	1	10	N
○	○	●	○		○	○	●	○

GO

76

Listen as I read this problem. You may solve the problem in your head or use scratch paper. If the right answer to the problem is not one of the choices, fill in the circle under the N, which stands for *not given*. Are you ready? Let's do S together. Listen carefully and look at the numbers at the top of the page near the duck. What is 4 add 6? 4 plus 6 equals what number? *(pause)* 4 plus 6 is 10. Fill in the circle under the number 10. Be sure your answer circle is completely filled in with a dark mark and that you have marked the correct answer circle.

Check to see that the students have marked the correct circle.

Say Now we will do more items like S. Listen to what I say and choose the answer you think is correct. Fill in the circle under the best answer. Be sure your answer circle is completely filled in with a dark mark. Do you have any questions? Let's begin.

Allow time between items for students to fill in their answers. Do not read the item numbers.

1. What is 5 add 3? 5 plus 3 equals what number? Fill in the circle under your answer in the row with the pot.

2. What is 2 add 7? 2 plus 7 equals what number? Fill in the circle under your answer in the row with the bell.

3. What is 5 add 7? 5 plus 7 equals what number? Fill in the circle under your answer in the row with the car.

4. What is 9 add 9? 9 plus 9 equals what number? Fill in the circle under your answer in the row with the book.

5. What is 5 add 11? 5 plus 11 equals what number? Fill in the circle under your answer in the row with the telephone.

6. What is 30 add 2? 30 plus 2 equals what number? Fill in the circle under your answer in the row with the leaf.

7. What is 10 add 0? 10 plus 0 equals what number? Fill in the circle under your answer in the row with the cup.

   Look at the next page, page 77.

Check to be sure the students have found the right page. Allow the students a moment to rest.

Unit 8

Test Yourself: Mathematics Computation

S
2	10	14	N
○	●	○	○

4
18	19	29	N
●	○	○	○

1
2	7	9	N
○	○	○	●

5
5	16	17	N
○	●	○	○

2
5	8	9	N
○	○	●	○

6
20	23	30	N
○	○	○	●

3
2	11	12	N
○	○	●	○

7
0	1	10	N
○	○	●	○

GO

76

Say Pay attention to what I say. These problems are a little different. They are subtraction problems.

8. What is 4 subtract 1? 4 minus 1 equals what number? Fill in the circle under your answer in the row with the duck.

9. What is 6 subtract 2? 6 minus 2 equals what number? Fill in the circle under your answer in the row with the pot.

10. What is 9 subtract 8? 9 minus 8 equals what number? Fill in the circle under your answer in the row with the bell.

11. What is 10 subtract 1? 10 minus 1 equals what number? Fill in the circle under your answer in the row with the car.

12. What is 7 subtract 4? 7 minus 4 equals what number? Fill in the circle under your answer in the row with the book.

13. What is 5 subtract 5? 5 minus 5 equals what number? Fill in the circle under your answer in the row with the telephone.

14. What is 9 subtract 4? 9 minus 4 equals what number? Fill in the circle under your answer in the row with the leaf.

15. What is 8 subtract 1? 8 minus 1 equals what number? Fill in the circle under your answer in the row with the cup.

Turn to the next page, page 78.

Check to be sure the students have found the right page. Allow the students a moment to rest.

Unit 8 Test Yourself: Mathematics Computation

8 (duck)

1	2	3	N
○	○	●	○

12 (book)

3	4	11	N
●	○	○	○

9 (pot)

4	5	8	N
●	○	○	○

13 (telephone)

1	2	10	N
○	○	○	●

10 (bell)

0	1	10	N
○	●	○	○

14 (leaf)

1	5	13	N
○	●	○	○

11 (car)

0	9	11	N
○	●	○	○

15 (cup)

5	6	7	N
○	○	●	○

GO →

77

Say Now you will solve some addition and subtraction problems yourselves. We did other problems like these in Lesson 17b. Do not write anything in your book except your answer choices. If you need to, use scratch paper to work the problems. Work until you come to the STOP sign at the bottom of the page. Make sure that the circles for your answer choices are completely filled in with dark marks. Erase any marks for answers that you change. You may begin.

Allow time for the students to fill in their answers. Do not rush the students, but allow a reasonable time for all of them to finish.

Say It's time to stop. You have finished Test Yourself lesson.

Review the answers with the students. Have the students indicate completion of the lesson by entering their score for this activity on the progress chart at the beginning of the book. Provide the students whatever help is necessary to record their scores.

Unit 8 **Test Yourself: Mathematics Computation**

16
$$\begin{array}{r} 3 \\ + 4 \end{array}$$

1	6	9	N
○	○	○	●

20 6 + 13 =

7	19	20	N
○	●	○	○

17
$$\begin{array}{r} 11 \\ - 2 \end{array}$$

9	13	21	N
●	○	○	○

21
$$\begin{array}{r} 11 \\ - 5 \end{array}$$

6	7	16	N
●	○	○	○

18 0 + 2 =

0	1	2	N
○	○	●	○

22
$$\begin{array}{r} 15 \\ - 7 \end{array}$$

2	6	8	N
○	○	●	○

19 16 − 7 =

6	7	8	N
○	○	○	●

23 6 + 4 =

2	10	14	N
○	●	○	○

STOP

78

Unit 9

Background

This unit contains three lessons that deal with study skills. Students answer a variety of questions about reference sources.

• **In Lesson 18a,** students alphabetize words and answer questions about a map and a picture dictionary. Students are encouraged to follow oral directions and listen carefully. They work methodically and refer to a reference source.

• **In Lesson 18b,** students answer questions about a map and a table of contents. They review the test-taking skills introduced in Lesson 1a and evaluate answer choices.

• **In the Test Yourself lesson,** the study skills and test-taking skills introduced and used in Lessons 18a and 18b are reinforced and presented in a format that gives students the experience of taking an achievement test.

Instructional Objectives

Lesson 18a	**Sources of Information**	Given a question about a map, dictionary, table of contents, or alphabetical order, the student identifies which of three answer choices is correct.
Lesson 18b	**Sources of Information**	
	Test Yourself	Given questions similar to those in Lessons 18a and 18b, the student utilizes study skills and test-taking strategies on achievement test formats.

Lesson 18a
Sources of Information

Focus

Study Skills
- alphabetizing words
- understanding a map
- using a dictionary

Test-taking Skills
- following oral directions
- listening carefully
- working methodically
- referring to a reference source

Sample S1

Say Look at Lesson 18a on page 79. This page has pictures at the top.

Check to see that the students have found the right page.

Say In this lesson you will answer questions about different kinds of reference sources. The first thing we will do is practice putting things in alphabetical order. Look at the pictures at the top of the page. Imagine you are making a picture dictionary with the things on this page. You will want to put the pictures in alphabetical order. Let's do S1 together. Read the question to yourself while I read it out loud. Which picture should be at the very top of the page? *(pause)* The first answer, *apple,* is correct because apple comes first in alphabetical order. Fill in the circle beside the word *apple,* the first answer. Be sure your answer circle is completely filled in with a dark mark and that you have marked the correct answer circle.

Check to see that the students have marked the correct circle.

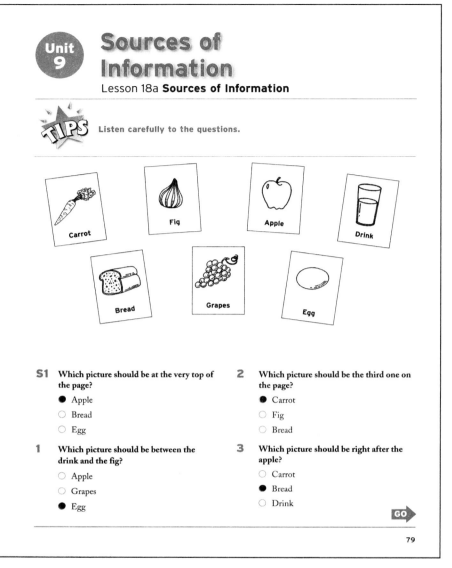

✦**TIPS**

Say Now let's look at the tip.

Read the tip aloud to the students.

Say Listen carefully to the question while I read it out loud. Listening carefully will help you understand the question if you have any trouble reading it yourself.

Practice

Say Now we will do the Practice items in the same way we did the sample. I will read the question out loud while you read it to yourself. Fill in the circle beside the best answer. Be sure your answer circle is completely filled in with a dark mark. Do you have any questions? Let's begin.

Allow time between items for students to fill in their answers.

1. Number 1: Which picture should be between the drink and the fig?

2. Number 2: Which picture should be the third one on the page?

3. Number 3: Which picture should be right after the apple?

   Turn to the next page, page 80.

Check to be sure the students have found the right page. Allow the students a moment to rest.

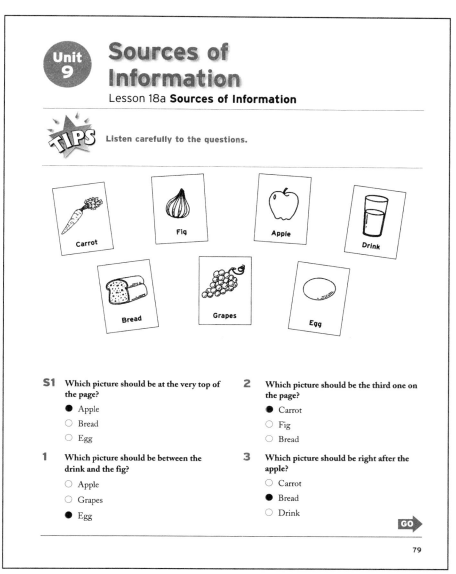

Unit 9 **Sources of Information**

Lesson 18a **Sources of Information**

TIPS Listen carefully to the questions.

Carrot   Fig   Apple   Drink

Bread   Grapes   Egg

S1 Which picture should be at the very top of the page?
- ● Apple
- ○ Bread
- ○ Egg

1 Which picture should be between the drink and the fig?
- ○ Apple
- ○ Grapes
- ● Egg

2 Which picture should be the third one on the page?
- ● Carrot
- ○ Fig
- ○ Bread

3 Which picture should be right after the apple?
- ○ Carrot
- ● Bread
- ○ Drink

GO

79

Sample S2

Say The items are a little different on this page. You will answer questions about a map. Read S2 by yourself while I read it out loud. Look at the map to find the answer. Which animal has the biggest pen? Look at the map to find the answer. *(pause)* The second answer is correct because *the llamas* have the biggest pen. Fill in the circle beside the second answer. Be sure your answer circle is completely filled in with a dark mark and that you have marked the correct answer circle.

Check to see that the students have marked the correct circle.

Say Now we will do the Practice items in the same way we did the sample. I will read a question out loud while you read it to yourself. Look at the map to find the answer. Fill in the circle beside the best answer. Be sure your answer circle is completely filled in with a dark mark. Do you have any questions? Let's begin.

Allow time between items for students to fill in their answers.

4. Number 4: Which is south of the sheep pen?

5. Number 5: Which direction do visitors go when they leave the parking lot and go to the fruit and vegetable shop?

6. Number 6: What is north of the cow pen?

7. Number 7: What do visitors pass when they go from the barn to the Fruit and Vegetable Shop?

8. Number 8: Which is closest to Fleet Street?

   Look at the next page, page 81.

Check to be sure the students have found the right page. Allow the students a moment to rest.

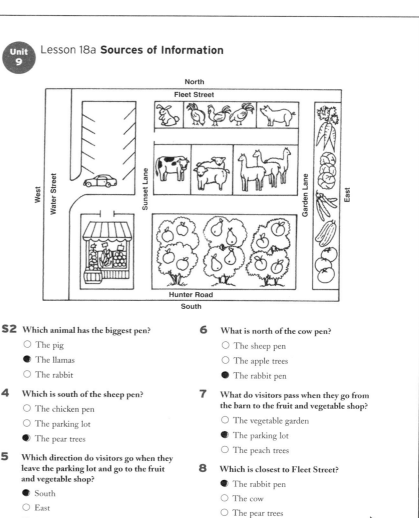

Unit 9 Lesson 18a **Sources of Information**

S2 Which animal has the biggest pen?
- ○ The pig
- ● The llamas
- ○ The rabbit

4 Which is south of the sheep pen?
- ○ The chicken pen
- ○ The parking lot
- ● The pear trees

5 Which direction do visitors go when they leave the parking lot and go to the fruit and vegetable shop?
- ● South
- ○ East
- ○ West

6 What is north of the cow pen?
- ○ The sheep pen
- ○ The apple trees
- ● The rabbit pen

7 What do visitors pass when they go from the barn to the fruit and vegetable shop?
- ○ The vegetable garden
- ● The parking lot
- ○ The peach trees

8 Which is closest to Fleet Street?
- ● The rabbit pen
- ○ The cow
- ○ The pear trees

GO

80

Say For this part of the lesson, you will answer questions about a dictionary. The words in the dictionary are *chest, funnel, jam, laundry, nails, package, sketch, soiled.* I will read a question out loud while you read it to yourself. Look at the dictionary to find the answer. Fill in the circle beside the best answer. Be sure your answer circle is completely filled in with a dark mark. Do you have any questions? Let's begin.

Allow time between items for students to fill in their answers.

9. Number 9: Which is the most like a package?

10. Number 10: How do you spell the name for a picture drawn quickly?

11. Number 11: Which of these would you be most likely to find in the refrigerator?

12. Number 12: Which is most likely to be soiled?

13. Number 13: Which word fits best in the sentence "There was treasure inside the pirate's _____"?

14. Number 14: How do you spell the name of a box you get in the mail?

Say It's time to stop. You have finished Lesson 18a.

Review the answers with the students. Have the students indicate completion of the lesson by entering their score for this activity on the progress chart at the beginning of the book. Provide the students whatever help is necessary to record their scores.

 Unit 9 Lesson 18a **Sources of Information**

Cc chest	
Ff funnel	
Jj jam	
Ll laundry	
Nn nails	
Pp package	
Ss sketch	
Ss soiled	

9 Which is the most like a package?
- ● A chest
- ○ A funnel
- ○ A sketch

10 How do you spell the name for a picture drawn quickly?
- ○ skech
- ● sketch
- ○ scetch

11 Which of these would you be most likely to find in the refrigerator?
- ○ laundry
- ○ nails
- ● jam

12 Which is most likely to be soiled?
- ○ funnels
- ● laundry
- ○ packages

13 Which word fits best in the sentence "There was treasure inside the pirate's _____"?
- ● chest
- ○ funnel
- ○ sketch

14 How do you spell the name of a box you get in the mail?
- ○ packege
- ● package
- ○ packidge

 STOP

81

Unit 9 Lesson 18b
Sources of Information

Focus

Study Skills
- understanding a map
- using a table of contents

Test-taking Skills
- following oral directions
- listening carefully
- working methodically
- referring to a reference source
- evaluating answer choices

Say Turn to Lesson 18b on page 82. There is a map of a school on this page.

Check to see that the students have found the right page.

Say Let's look at the tip at the top of the page.

Read the tip aloud to the students.

Say You should always compare your answer to the map, table of contents, or other reference source. This is the best way to find the right answer.

Practice

Say In this part of the lesson you will answer questions about a map. I will read a question out loud while you read it to yourself. Look at the map to find the answer. Fill in the circle beside the best answer. Be sure your answer circle is completely filled in with a dark mark. Do you have any questions? Let's begin.

Allow time between items for students to fill in their answers.

1. **Number 1: Where is Mr. Gibbs's room located?**

2. **Number 2: When the students walk from the main desk to the music room, what do they pass first?**

Lesson 18b **Sources of Information**

Compare your answer with the map or table of contents.

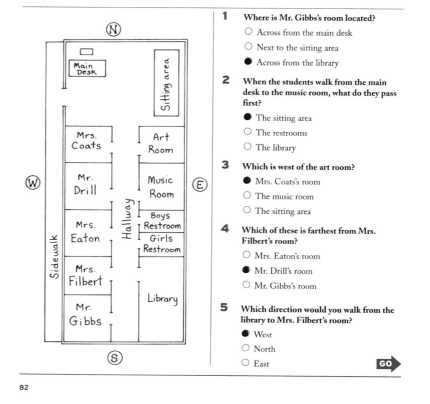

3. **Number 3: Which is west of the art room?**

4. **Number 4: Which of these is farthest from Mrs. Filbert's room?**

5. **Number 5: Which direction would you walk from the library to Mrs. Filbert's room?**

    Look at the next page, page 83.

Check to be sure the students have found the right page. Allow the students a moment to rest.

Say Now we will do some questions about a table of contents from a book about the sea. Read the title of each chapter to yourself while I read it out loud.

Sea Life
Not All Sea Plants Are Green
Exploring the Sea's Mysteries
Different Jobs at Sea
Rain or Shine at Sea
How the Sea Was Formed:
A Folktale

I will read the questions out loud while you read them to yourself. Look at the table of contents to find the answer. Fill in the circle under the best answer. Be sure your answer circle is completely filled in with a dark mark. Do you have any questions? Let's begin.

Allow time between items for students to fill in their answers.

6. Number 6: Which pages would tell you the most about the animals that live in the sea?

7. Number 7: Where should you begin reading to find out about people who work at sea?

8. Number 8: Which pages would tell you most about the weather at sea?

9. Number 9: Where should you begin reading to find a story about why there is a sea?

10. Number 10: Which pages would tell you most about colorful sea plants?

11. Number 11: Where should you begin reading to find out what a sailor does?

Say It's time to stop. You have finished Lesson 18b.

Review the answers with the students. Have the students indicate completion of the lesson by entering their score for this activity on the progress chart at the beginning of the book. Provide the students whatever help is necessary to record their scores.

 Unit 9 Lesson 18b **Sources of Information**

The Sea

CONTENTS

6 Which pages would tell you the most about the animals that live in the sea?
- ● 3–6
- ○ 7–9
- ○ 13–15

7 Where should you begin reading to find out about people who work at sea?
- ○ 10
- ● 13
- ○ 16

8 Which pages would tell you most about the weather at sea?
- ○ 10–12
- ○ 13–15
- ● 16–18

9 Where should you begin reading to find a story about why there is a sea?
- ○ 3
- ○ 13
- ● 19

10 Which pages would tell you most about colorful sea plants?
- ● 7–9
- ○ 10–12
- ○ 13–15

11 Where should you begin reading to find out what a sailor does?
- ○ 10
- ● 13
- ○ 16

83

Test Yourself:
Sources of Information
Unit 9

Focus

Study Skills
• alphabetizing words
• understanding a map
• using a dictionary
• using a table of contents

Test-taking Skills
• following oral directions
• listening carefully
• working methodically
• referring to a reference source
• evaluating answer choices

This lesson simulates an actual test-taking experience. Therefore, it is recommended that the directions be read verbatim and the suggested procedures be followed.

Directions

Administration Time:
approximately 30 minutes

Say Turn to the Test Yourself lesson on page 84. There are some pictures at the top of the page.

Check to be sure the students have found the right page. Point out to the students that this is not a real test and that they will score it themselves to see how well they are doing.

Say This lesson will check how well you understand sources of information. Remember to make sure that the circles for your answer choices are completely filled in. Press your pencil firmly so that your marks come out dark. Completely erase any marks for answers that you change. Do not write anything except your answer choices in your books.

The first thing we will do is practice putting things in alphabetical order. Look at the pictures at the top of the page. Imagine you are making a picture dictionary with the things on this page. You will want to put the pictures in alphabetical order. Let's do S1 together. Read the question to yourself while I read it out loud. Which picture should be at

Test Yourself:
Sources of Information
Unit 9

S1 Which picture should be at the very top of the page?
● Attic
○ Chair
○ Envelope

1 Which picture should be between the chair and the envelope?
○ Bed
● Door
○ Fireplace

2 Which picture should be the second one on the page?
○ Chair
○ Door
● Bed

3 Which picture should be right after the envelope?
● Fireplace
○ Door
○ Grass

4 Which picture should be the last one on the page?
○ Attic
● Grass
○ Envelope

5 Which picture should be right before the door?
○ Envelope
○ Grass
● Chair

GO

84

the very top of the page? *(pause)* The first answer, *attic,* is correct because attic comes first in alphabetical order. Fill in the circle beside the word *attic,* the first answer. Be sure your answer circle is completely filled in with a dark mark and that you have marked the correct answer circle.

Check to see that the students have marked the correct circle.

Say Now we will do more items in the same way we did the sample. I will read a question out loud while you read it to yourself. Fill in the circle beside the best answer. Be sure your answer circle is completely filled in with a dark mark. Do you have any questions? Let's begin.

Allow time between items for students to fill in their answers.

1. **Number 1:** Which picture should be between the chair and the envelope?

2. **Number 2:** Which picture should be the second one on the page?

3. **Number 3:** Which picture should be right after the envelope?

4. **Number 4:** Which picture should be the last one on the page?

5. **Number 5:** Which picture should be right before the door?

   Look at the next page, page 85.

Check to be sure the students have found the right page. Allow the students a moment to rest.

 Unit 9

Test Yourself: Sources of Information

Chair   **Fireplace**   **Door**   **Attic**

Bed   **Grass**   **Envelope**

S1 Which picture should be at the very top of the page?
- ● Attic
- ○ Chair
- ○ Envelope

1 Which picture should be between the chair and the envelope?
- ○ Bed
- ● Door
- ○ Fireplace

2 Which picture should be the second one on the page?
- ○ Chair
- ○ Door
- ● Bed

3 Which picture should be right after the envelope?
- ● Fireplace
- ○ Door
- ○ Grass

4 Which picture should be the last one on the page?
- ○ Attic
- ● Grass
- ○ Envelope

5 Which picture should be right before the door?
- ○ Envelope
- ○ Grass
- ● Chair

 GO

84

Say The items on this page are about a map of a camping area. Read S2 by yourself while I read it out loud. Look at the map to find the answer. Which is the smallest campsite? Look at the map to find the answer. *(pause)* The second answer is correct because Campsite 38 is the smallest. Fill in the circle beside the second answer. Be sure your answer circle is completely filled in with a dark mark and that you have marked the correct answer circle.

Check to see that the students have marked the correct circle.

Say Now we will do more items in the same way we did S2. I will read a question out loud while you read it to yourself. Look at the map to find the answer. Fill in the circle beside the best answer. Be sure your answer circle is completely filled in with a dark mark. Do you have any questions? Let's begin.

Allow time between items for students to fill in their answers.

6. Number 6: Which campsite is south of the gift shop?

7. Number 7: Which direction do campers walk from campsite 25 to the restrooms?

8. Number 8: What is south of campsite 32?

9. Number 9: If you walked from the gift shop to the picnic area, which campsite might you pass through?

10. Number 10: Which campsite is closest to the entrance?

Turn to the next page, page 86.

Check to be sure the students have found the right page. Allow the students a moment to rest.

Test Yourself: Sources of Information

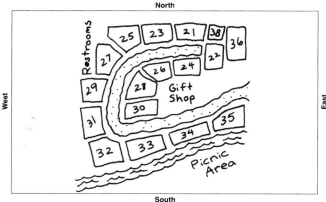

S2 Which is the smallest campsite?
- ○ Campsite 21
- ● Campsite 38
- ○ Campsite 33

6 Which campsite is south of the gift shop?
- ○ Campsite 25
- ● Campsite 34
- ○ Campsite 36

7 Which direction do campers walk from campsite 25 to the restrooms?
- ● West
- ○ South
- ○ East

8 What is south of campsite 32?
- ○ The picnic area
- ○ Campsite 31
- ● The river

9 If you walked from the gift shop to the picnic area, which campsite might you pass through?
- ● Campsite 34
- ○ Campsite 36
- ○ Campsite 24

10 Which campsite is closest to the entrance?
- ○ Campsite 24
- ○ Campsite 29
- ● Campsite 35

85

Say For this part of the lesson, you will answer questions about a dictionary. The words in the dictionary are *bucket, frame, loaf, sword, toast, vine, well, wrinkle*. I will read the question out loud while you read it to yourself. Look at the dictionary to find the answer. Fill in the circle beside the best answer. Be sure your answer circle is completely filled in with a dark mark. Do you have any questions? Let's begin.

Allow time between items for students to fill in their answers.

11. Number 11: Which is most like a bucket?

12. Number 12: How do you spell the name for a line on the skin?

13. Number 13: Which of these would you be most likely to find in a backyard?

14. Number 14: Which is most likely to be sliced?

15. Number 15: Which word fits best in the sentence "Around the picture was a carved _____"?

16. Number 16: How do you spell the name of a sharp metal weapon?

   Look at the next page, page 87.

Check to be sure the students have found the right page. Allow the students a moment to rest.

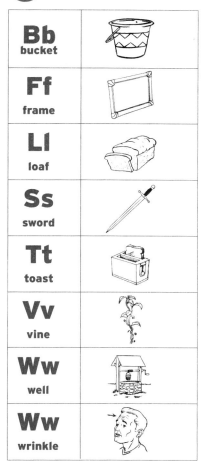

 Test Yourself: Sources of Information

Bb bucket	
Ff frame	
Ll loaf	
Ss sword	
Tt toast	
Vv vine	
Ww well	
Ww wrinkle	

11 Which is most like a bucket?
- ● A well
- ○ A frame
- ○ A loaf

12 How do you spell the name for a line on the skin?
- ○ rinkle
- ● wrinkle
- ○ wrinkel

13 Which of these would you be most likely to find in a backyard?
- ○ A sword
- ○ A frame
- ● A vine

14 Which is most likely to be sliced?
- ● A loaf
- ○ A well
- ○ A bucket

15 Which word fits best in the sentence "Around the picture was a carved _____"?
- ○ well
- ○ loaf
- ● frame

16 How do you spell the name of a sharp metal weapon?
- ○ sowrd
- ● sword
- ○ soard

GO

86

Say In this part of the lesson you will answer questions about a map. I will read the question out loud while you read it to yourself. Look at the map to find the answer. Fill in the circle beside the best answer. Be sure your answer circle is completely filled in with a dark mark. Do you have any questions? Let's begin.

Allow time between items for students to fill in their answers.

17. Number 17: Where is the park located?

18. Number 18: When the King children walk from home to school, what do they pass first?

19. Number 19: Which is west of the hospital?

20. Number 20: Who lives farthest from the school?

21. Number 21: Who lives east of the food store?

22. Number 22: Which direction would the Stone children walk to get to school?

　Turn to the next page, page 88.

Check to be sure the students have found the right page. Allow the students a moment to rest.

Test Yourself: Sources of Information

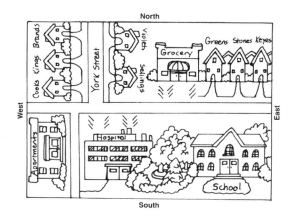

17　Where is the park located?
　○　At the north end of the hospital
　●　Next to the school
　○　On the edge of the apartments

18　When the King children walk from home to school, what do they pass first?
　●　The Cooks' house
　○　The Greens' house
　○　The Keyes' house

19　Which is west of the hospital?
　○　The food store
　●　The apartments
　○　The school

20　Who lives farthest from the school?
　●　The Brands
　○　The Violets
　○　The Stones

21　Who lives east of the food store?
　○　The Sellings
　○　The Brands
　●　The Greens

22　Which direction would the Stone children walk to get to school?
　○　East
　○　North
　●　South

87

Say Now we will do some questions about a table of contents from a book about nuts. Read the title of each chapter to yourself while I read it out loud.

Kinds of Nuts
A Healthy Life With Nuts
Cooking With Nuts
Oil From Nuts
How Nuts Are Grown
Nuts From Far-Off Lands

I will read the questions out loud while you read them to yourself. Look at the table of contents to find the answer. Fill in the circle beside the best answer. Be sure your answer circle is completely filled in with a dark mark. Do you have any questions? Let's begin.

Allow time between items for students to fill in their answers.

23. Number 23: Which pages would tell you the difference between a walnut and an almond?

24. Number 24: Where should you begin reading to find out if nuts grow on trees?

25. Number 25: Which pages would tell you most about nut farms?

26. Number 26: Where should you begin reading to find out how to include nuts in your everyday meals?

27. Number 27: Which pages would tell you why nuts are good for you?

28. Number 28: Where should you begin reading to find out about nuts grown in China?

Say It's time to stop. You have completed the Test Yourself lesson. Check to see that you have completely filled in your answer circles with dark marks. Make sure that any marks for answers that you changed have been completely erased. Now you may close your books.

Test Yourself: Sources of Information

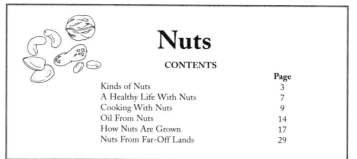

Nuts

CONTENTS

	Page
Kinds of Nuts	3
A Healthy Life With Nuts	7
Cooking With Nuts	9
Oil From Nuts	14
How Nuts Are Grown	17
Nuts From Far-Off Lands	29

23 Which pages would tell you the difference between a walnut and an almond?
● 3–6
○ 7–8
○ 14–16

24 Where should you begin reading to find out if nuts grow on trees?
○ 7
○ 14
● 17

25 Which pages would tell you most about nut farms?
○ 3–6
○ 14–16
● 17–28

26 Where should you begin reading to find out how to include nuts in your everyday meals?
○ 3
○ 7
● 9

27 Which pages would tell you why nuts are good for you?
○ 3–6
● 7–8
○ 9–13

28 Where should you begin reading to find out about nuts grown in China?
○ 14
○ 17
● 29

88

Review the answers with the students. Have the students indicate completion of the lesson by entering their score for this activity on the progress chart at the beginning of the book. Provide the students whatever help is necessary to record their scores.

Background

This unit contains three lessons that deal with science skills. Students answer a variety of questions about science.

• **In Lesson 19a,** students answer questions about science. Students are encouraged to follow oral directions and listen carefully. They work methodically and choose a picture to answer a question.

• **In Lesson 19b,** students answer questions about science. They review the test-taking skills introduced in Lesson 19a and evaluate answer choices.

• **In the Test Yourself lesson,** the science skills and test-taking skills introduced and used in Lessons 19a and 19b are reinforced and presented in a format that gives students the experience of taking an achievement test.

Instructional Objectives

Lesson 19a	**Science Skills**	Given a question about science, the student identifies which of three answer choices is correct.
Lesson 19b	**Science Skills**	
	Test Yourself	Given questions similar to those in Lessons 19a and 19b, the student utilizes science skills and test-taking strategies on achievement test formats.

Focus

Science Skills
- understanding plant and animal behaviors and characteristics
- recognizing health and safety practices
- understanding magnetism
- understanding scientific instruments, measurement, and processes
- recognizing characteristics of a habitat
- recognizing states and properties of matter
- understanding characteristics of bodies of water
- understanding diseases and their sources
- understanding weather, climate, and seasons
- differentiating real and imaginary living things
- understanding foods and food groups

Test-taking Skills
- following oral directions
- listening carefully
- working methodically
- choosing a picture to answer a question

Sample S

Say Look at Lesson 19a on page 89. This page has pictures at the top.

Check to see that the students have found the right page.

Say In this lesson you will answer questions about science. Find S at the top of the page. Look at the pictures of a robin, a pigeon, and a duck. Which bird is the best swimmer? *(pause)* The third answer, *the duck*, is correct. Fill in the circle under the duck, the third answer. Be sure your answer circle is completely filled in with a dark mark and that you have marked the correct answer circle.

Check to see that the students have marked the correct circle.

 TIPS

Say Now let's look at the tip.

Read the tip aloud to the students.

Say Listen carefully while you look at all the pictures. When you find the picture you think is correct, put your finger on it. Then mark the circle for your answer.

Practice

Say Now we will do the Practice items in the same way we did the sample. I will read the question out loud. Fill in the circle under the best answer. Be sure your answer circle is completely filled in with a dark mark. Do you have any questions? Let's begin.

Allow time between items for students to fill in their answers.

1. Look at the pictures in row 1. Which picture shows a bud that will turn into a flower? Fill in the circle under the picture that shows a bud that will turn into a flower.

2. Look at the pictures in row 2. Which picture shows a person dressed for protection against strong sun? Fill in the circle under the picture that shows a person dressed for protection against strong sun.

   Turn to the next page, page 90.

Check to be sure the students have found the right page. Allow the students a moment to rest.

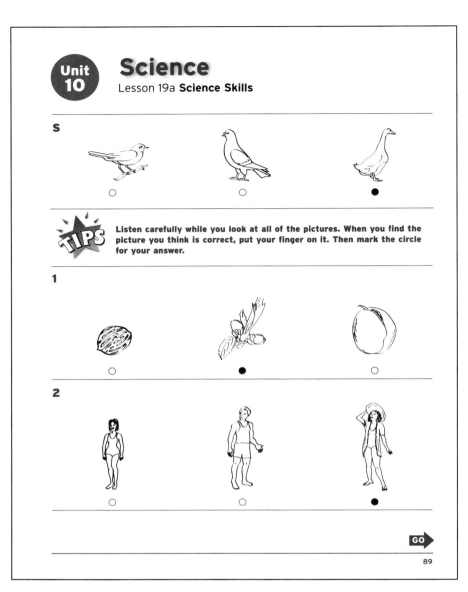

3. Look at the pictures in row 3 at the top of the page. Which picture shows something that would move toward a magnet without a person touching it? Fill in the circle under the picture that shows something that would move toward a magnet without a person touching it.

4. Look at the pictures in row 4. Which thing shows what day it is? Fill in the circle under the picture of the object that shows what day it is.

5. Look at the pictures in row 5. Which habitat would be best for a frog? Fill in the circle under the picture of the habitat that would be best for a frog.

6. Look at the pictures in row 6. Which of these things would probably float if you dropped it in water? Fill in the circle under the picture that would probably float if you dropped it in water.

   Look at the next page, page 91.

Check to be sure the students have found the right page. Allow the students a moment to rest.

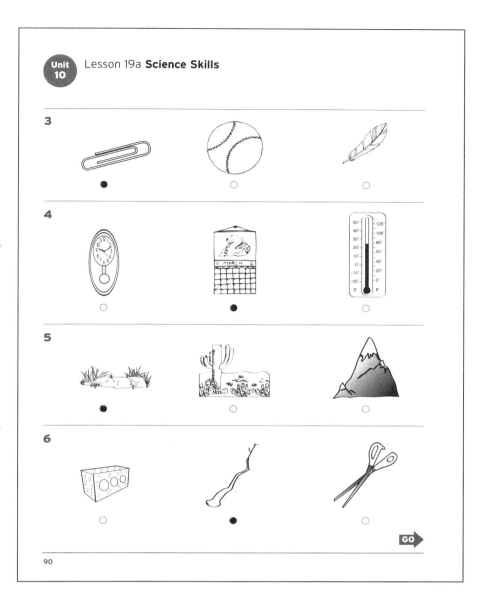

7. Look at the pictures in row 7 at the top of the page. A scientist has a jar full of water that is salty. From which place did the scientist probably get the salty water? Fill in the circle under the picture that shows where the salty water came from.

8. Look at the pictures in row 8. Which balloon probably weighs the most? Fill in the circle under the picture that shows the balloon that probably weighs the most.

9. Look at the pictures in row 9. Leo wants to add just a few drops of water to a mixture. Which tool should he use? Fill in the circle under the picture that would let Leo add just a few drops of water to a mixture.

10. Look at the pictures in row 10. Which of these objects that you could find in a kitchen will remove dirt? Fill in the circle under the picture that shows something in a kitchen that will remove dirt.

   Turn to the next page, page 92.

Check to be sure the students have found the right page. Allow the students a moment to rest.

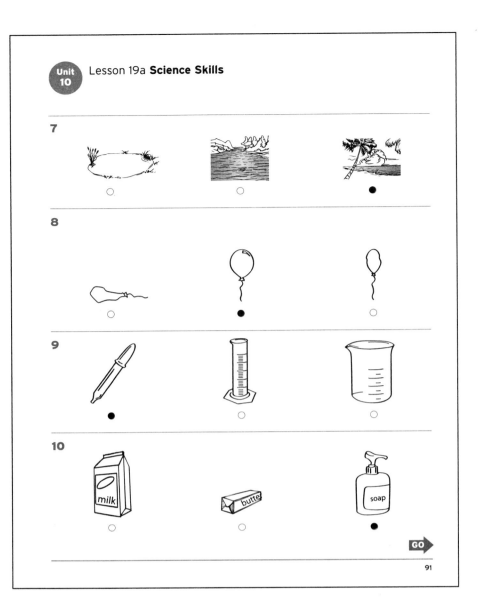

Unit 10   Lesson 19a **Science Skills**

91

11. Look at the pictures in row 11. Which of these is an insect? Fill in the circle under the picture that shows an insect.

12. Look at the pictures in row 12. Which of these would a scientist use to look at faraway stars? Fill in the circle under the picture that shows what a scientist would use to look at faraway stars.

13. Look at the pictures in row 13. Which of these living things uses energy from the sun to make food? Fill in the circle under the picture that shows living things that use energy from the sun to make food.

14. Look at the pictures in row 14. Kevin looked outside and saw that the pond in their yard was frozen. Then he looked at the thermometer. What temperature did the outside thermometer probably show? Fill in the circle under the picture that shows the temperature when the pond was frozen.

    Look at the next page, page 93.

Check to be sure the students have found the right page. Allow the students a moment to rest.

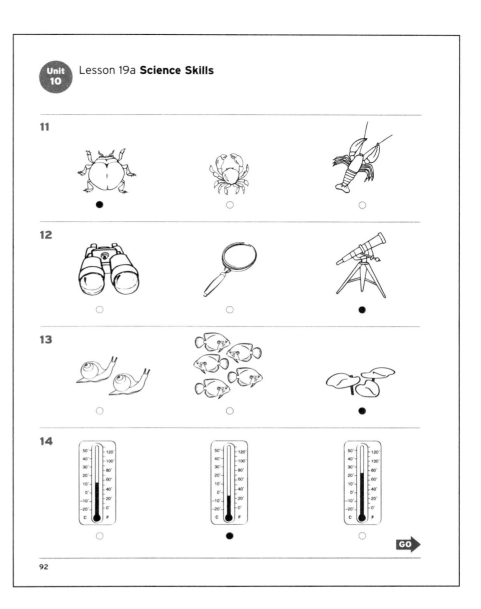

15. Look at the pictures in row 15. Lisa saw these signs on a trail through a national park. Which sign means no motorcycles on the trail? Fill in the circle under the picture that means no motorcycles on the trail.

16. Look at the pictures in row 16. Which one shows the habitat with the most water? Fill in the circle under the picture that shows the habitat with the most water.

17. Look at the pictures in row 17. Which fish tank can hold the most water? Fill in the circle under the picture of the fish tank that can hold the most water.

18. Look at the pictures in row 18. In which picture does the arrow point to the part of the mountain where the snow will probably melt most slowly? Fill in the circle under the picture that shows where the snow will probably melt most slowly.

   Turn to the next page, page 94.

Check to be sure the students have found the right page. Allow the students a moment to rest.

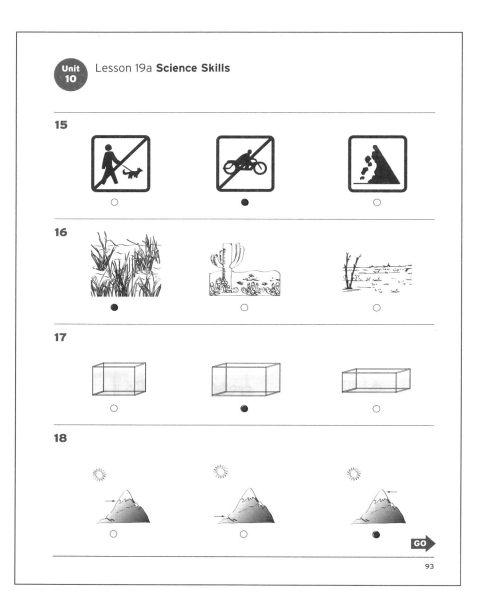

Unit 10 **Lesson 19a Science Skills**

19. Look at the pictures of animals in row 19. One is alive today, one lived long ago, and one is imaginary. Which of the animals is imaginary? Fill in the circle under the picture of the imaginary animal.

20. Look at the pictures in row 20. Eric's science teacher had two pieces of wood that were exactly the same size. She then burned one piece of wood outside and collected the ashes. The teacher put the ashes on one pan of a balance scale and the other piece of wood on the other pan. Which picture shows what the balance scale would look like? Fill in the circle for your answer.

21. Look at the pictures of hospital workers in row 21. Which person is wearing something that will protect against germs in the air? Fill in the circle under the picture that shows a person wearing something that will protect against germs in the air.

22. Look at the pictures in row 22. Which food is in the same food group as bread? Fill in the circle under the picture of the food that is in the same group as bread.

It's time to stop. You have finished Lesson 19a.

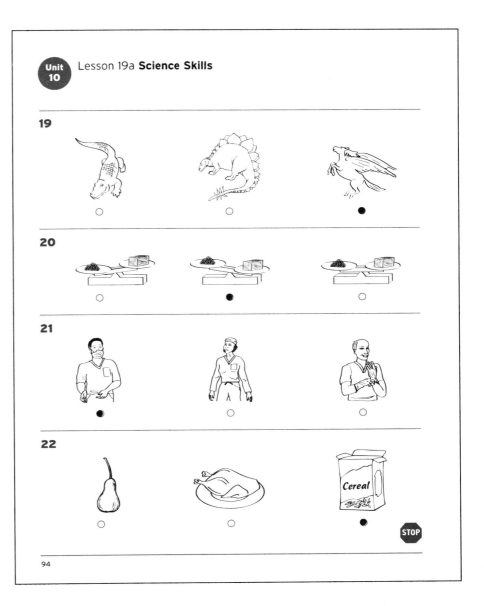

Unit 10 Lesson 19a **Science Skills**

19

20

21

22

94

Review the answers with the students. If any questions caused particular difficulty, work through each of the answer choices.

Have the students indicate completion of the lesson by entering their score for this activity on the progress chart at the beginning of the book. Provide the students whatever help is necessary to record their scores.

Focus

Science Skills
- understanding plant and animal behaviors and characteristics
- understanding the history and language of science
- understanding foods and food groups
- recalling characteristics of Earth and bodies in space
- differentiating the source of natural and manufactured products
- understanding properties of light
- understanding work and the principles of machines
- recalling characteristics and functions of the human body
- understanding weather, climate, and seasons
- understanding scientific instruments, measurement, and processes
- recognizing health and safety practices
- recognizing forms, sources, and principles of energy

Test-taking Skills
- following oral directions
- listening carefully
- working methodically
- evaluating answer choices

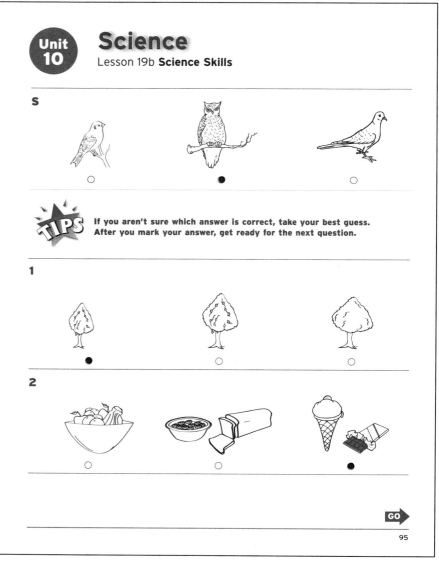

Unit 10 **Science**
Lesson 19b **Science Skills**

S

If you aren't sure which answer is correct, take your best guess. After you mark your answer, get ready for the next question.

1

2

GO

95

Sample S

Say Look at Lesson 19b on page 95. This page has pictures of birds at the top.

Check to see that the students have found the right page.

Say In this lesson you will answer questions about science. Find S at the top of the page. Look at the pictures of the birds. Which bird is a hunter, not a seed eater? *(pause)* The second answer, *the owl*, is correct. Fill in the circle under the second answer. Be sure your answer circle is completely filled in with a dark mark and that you have marked the correct answer circle.

Check to see that the students have marked the correct circle.

 TIPS

Say Now let's look at the tips.

Read the tips aloud to the students.

Say If you aren't sure which answer is correct, take your best guess. After you mark your answer, get ready for the next question.

Practice

Say Now we will do the Practice items in the same way we did the sample. I will read the question out loud. Fill in the circle under the best answer. Be sure your answer circle is completely filled in with a dark mark. Do you have any questions? Let's begin.

Allow time between items for students to fill in their answers.

1. Look at the pictures in row 1. Which is the shorter tree that has fruit? Fill in the circle under the picture that shows the shorter tree that has fruit.

2. Look at the pictures in row 2. You should eat more of some foods than others. Which of these foods should you eat just a little of? Fill in the circle under the picture that shows food you should eat just a little of.

   Turn to the next page, page 96.

Check to be sure the students have found the right page. Allow the students a moment to rest.

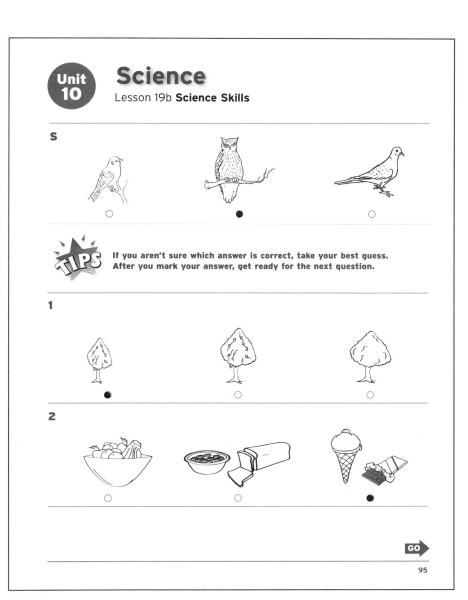

3. Look at the pictures in row 3. They are the sun, the moon, and a star. Which one goes around Earth? Fill in the circle under the picture of something that goes around Earth.

4. Look at the pictures in row 4. They are bread, chicken, and a hot dog. Which of these foods comes from a plant? Fill in the circle under the picture of a food that comes from a plant.

5. Look at the pictures in row 5. Which picture shows the person's shadow in the right place? Fill in the circle under the picture that shows the person's shadow in the right place.

6. Look at the pictures of the fish, the bird, and the tree in row 6. Which one do you think lives the longest? Fill in the circle under the picture that shows the thing that lives the longest.

Look at the next page, page 97.

Check to be sure the students have found the right page. Allow the students a moment to rest.

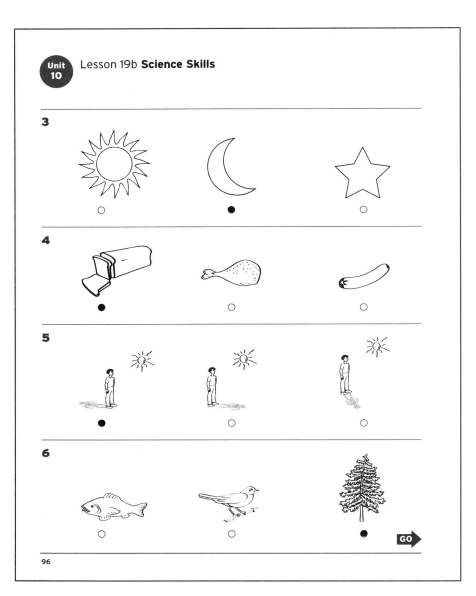

7. Look at the pictures in row 7. A person is trying to move the log. In which picture will the person have the easiest time moving it? Fill in the circle under the picture that shows when the person has the easiest time moving the log.

8. Look at the pictures in row 8. Which body organ beats about 70 times each minute? Fill in the circle under the picture of the body organ that beats about 70 times each minute.

9. Look at the pictures in row 9. If the wind blew, which pile would it move most easily? Fill in the circle under the picture that shows what the wind would move most easily.

10. Look at the pictures in row 10. They show three science tools. Which one did scientists probably use hundreds of years ago? Fill in the circle under the picture that shows a science tool that scientists probably used hundreds of years ago.

    Turn to the next page, page 98.

Check to be sure the students have found the right page. Allow the students a moment to rest.

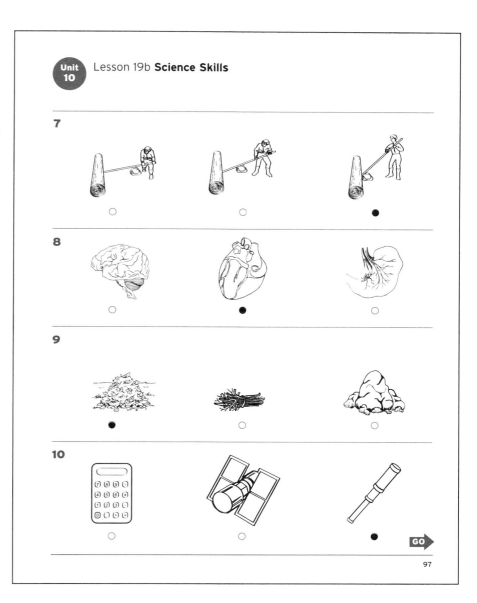

11. Look at the pictures in row 11. Which symbol probably means that there are sharp curves on the road ahead? Fill in the circle under the picture that shows a symbol that probably means that there are sharp curves on the road ahead.

12. Look at the pictures in row 12. Which part of a bike makes the wheels turn? Fill in the circle under the picture of part of a bike that makes the wheels turn.

13. Look at the pictures in row 13. A particular type of corn takes about 3 months to grow. Cassie planted a kernel of corn. About how tall would it be after two weeks of growing? Fill in the circle under the picture that shows how tall the corn would be after two weeks of growing.

14. Look at the pictures of a seesaw in row 14. Which one shows that the two children weigh about the same? Fill in the circle under the picture that shows two children who weigh about the same.

Look at the next page, page 99.

Check to be sure the students have found the right page. Allow the students a moment to rest.

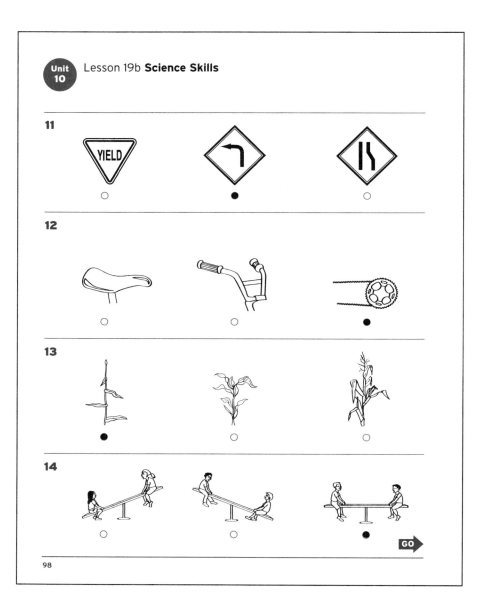

15. Look at the pictures in row 15. They show a pile of leaves, a pile of wood chips, and a pile of plastic bottles. If these things were buried, which would not be broken down for a long, long time by natural forces? Fill in the circle under the picture of something that would not be broken down for a long, long time by natural forces.

16. Look at the pictures of thermometers in row 16. Which one shows the normal temperature of a person? Fill in the circle under the picture that shows the normal temperature of a person.

17. Look at the pictures in row 17. Which telescope is probably most powerful? Fill in the circle under the picture of the most powerful telescope.

18. Look at the pictures in row 18. They are a paved driveway, a lawn, and a path made of wood chips. Suppose you walked on each of these surfaces on a sunny day. Which one would feel hottest on your feet? Fill in the circle under the picture that shows what would feel hottest on your feet.

Turn to the next page, page 100.

Check to be sure the students have found the right page. Allow the students a moment to rest.

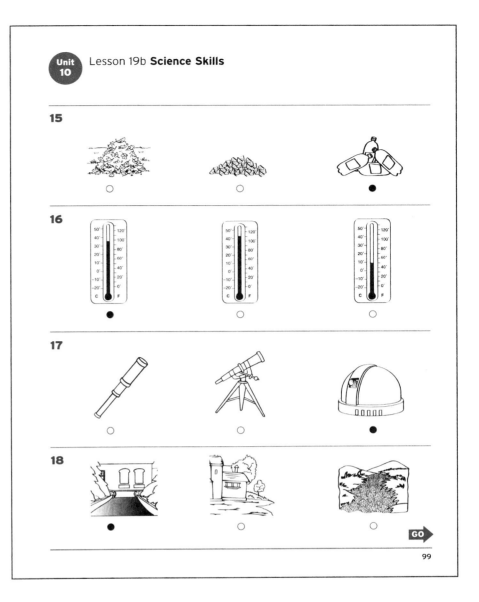

Unit 10 Lesson 19b **Science Skills**

15

16

17

18

GO

99

19. Look at the pictures in row 19. Which animal has a backbone and flies? Fill in the circle under the picture that shows an animal that has a backbone and flies.

20. Look at the pictures in row 20. Which picture shows a person doing something that will make the person's legs stronger? Fill in the circle under the picture that shows a person doing something that will make the person's legs stronger.

21. Look at the pictures in row 21. Lisa wants to test if sand gets hotter than soil when they are placed in the sun. Which picture shows how she might test for this? Fill in the circle under the picture that shows how to test if sand gets hotter than soil.

22. Look at the pictures in row 22. Which of these foods contains seeds that can grow into a new plant? Fill in the circle under the picture that shows the food containing seeds that can grow into a new plant.

Say It's time to stop. You have finished Lesson 19b.

Review the answers with the students. If any questions caused particular difficulty, work through each of the answer choices.

Have the students indicate completion of the lesson by entering their score for this activity on the progress chart at the beginning of the book. Provide the students whatever help is necessary to record their scores.

Unit 10 Test Yourself: Science

Focus

Science Skills

- understanding plant and animal behaviors and characteristics
- recalling characteristics of Earth and bodies in space
- classifying things based on characteristics
- recognizing characteristics of a habitat
- recognizing states and properties of matter
- understanding scientific instruments, measurement, and processes
- understanding foods and food groups
- understanding the history and language of science
- recognizing health and safety practices
- differentiating living and nonliving things
- understanding work and the principles of machines
- differentiating the source of natural and manufactured products
- recognizing moon phases
- recalling characteristics and functions of the human body
- understanding diseases and their sources
- understanding life cycles and reproduction

Test-taking Skills

- following oral directions
- listening carefully
- working methodically
- choosing a picture to answer a question
- evaluating answer choices

This lesson simulates an actual test-taking experience. Therefore, it is recommended that the directions be read verbatim and the suggested procedures be followed.

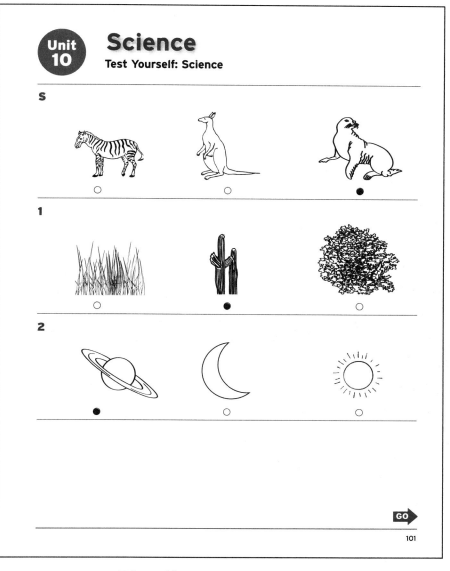

Directions

Administration Time: approximately 45 minutes

Say Look at the Test Yourself lesson on page 101. There are some pictures at the top of the page.

Check to be sure the students have found the right page. Point out to the students that this is not a real test and that they will score it themselves to see how well they are doing.

Say This lesson will check how well you understand science. Remember to make sure that the circles for your answer choices are completely filled in. Press your pencil firmly so that your marks come out dark. Completely erase any marks for answers that you change. Do not write anything except your answer choices in your books.

Say Let's do S together. Look at the pictures at the top of the page. Listen carefully. Which of these animals spends the most time in the water? *(pause)* The last answer, *the seal*, is correct. Fill in the circle under the last answer. Be sure your answer circle is completely filled in with a dark mark and that you have marked the correct answer circle.

Check to see that the students have marked the correct circle.

Say Now we will do more items in the same way we did the sample. I will read a question out loud while you read it to yourself. Fill in the circle under the best answer. Be sure your answer circle is completely filled in with a dark mark. Do you have any questions? Let's begin.

Allow time between items for students to fill in their answers.

1. Look at the pictures in row 1. Which plant is hardest for an animal to eat? Fill in the circle under the picture of the plant that is hardest for an animal to eat.

2. Look at the pictures in row 2. Connie looked through a telescope and saw a planet with rings. Which of these did she see? Fill in the circle under the picture of the planet with rings.

    Turn to the next page, page 102.

Check to be sure the students have found the right page. Allow the students a moment to rest.

Unit 10 **Science**
Test Yourself: Science

S

1

2

GO

101

3. Look at the pictures in row 3. Which of these is most like a rocket? Fill in the circle under the picture of something that is most like a rocket.

4. Look at the pictures in row 4. Which picture shows a place that is cared for by people? Fill in the circle under the picture of a place that is cared for by people.

5. Look at the pictures in row 5. Which of these burns most easily? Fill in the circle under the picture of the thing that burns most easily.

6. Look at the pictures in row 6. Helium is lighter than air. Which picture shows a person holding a balloon filled with helium? Fill in the circle under the picture of a person holding a balloon filled with helium.

   Look at the next page, page 103.

Check to be sure the students have found the right page. Allow the students a moment to rest.

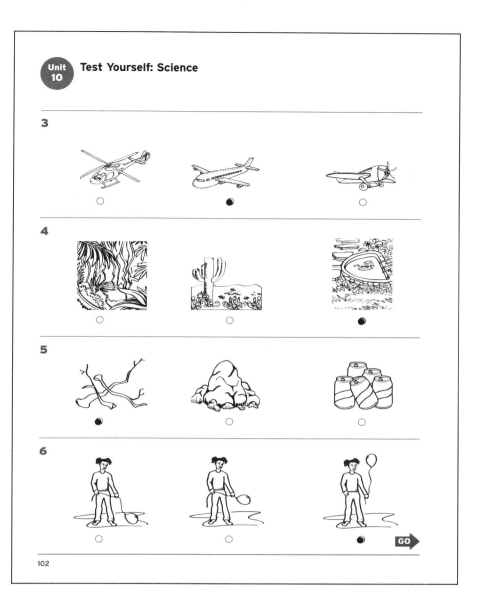

7. **Which food is in a different food group from the others?** Fill in the circle under the picture of a food that is in a different group from the others.

8. **Look at the pictures in row 8. Which of these sources of light was used first?** Fill in the circle under the picture that shows the source of light that was used first.

9. **Look at the pictures in row 9. Which part of your body should you brush after you eat?** Fill in the circle under the picture that shows the part of your body you should brush after you eat.

10. **Look at the rock, the clam, and the ice cube in row 10. Which of these has to eat to survive?** Fill in the circle under the picture that shows the thing that has to eat to survive.

    Turn to the next page, page 104.

Check to be sure the students have found the right page. Allow the students a moment to rest.

Unit 10 Test Yourself: Science

103

11. Look at the orange, the pineapple, and the pear in row 11. Which fruit has an outside skin that most people usually eat? Fill in the circle under the picture that shows the fruit that has an outside skin that most people usually eat.

12. Look at the pictures of steps in row 12. Which steps would be hardest to climb? Fill in the circle under the picture of the steps that would be hardest to climb.

13. Look at the pictures of trees in row 13. Which one is about as old as a puppy? Fill in the circle under the picture that shows a tree that is about as old as a puppy?

14. Look at the pictures in row 14. Which one will let you compare the weight of two objects? Fill in the circle under the picture of the tool that will let you compare the weight of two objects.

Look at the next page, page 105.

Check to be sure the students have found the right page. Allow the students a moment to rest.

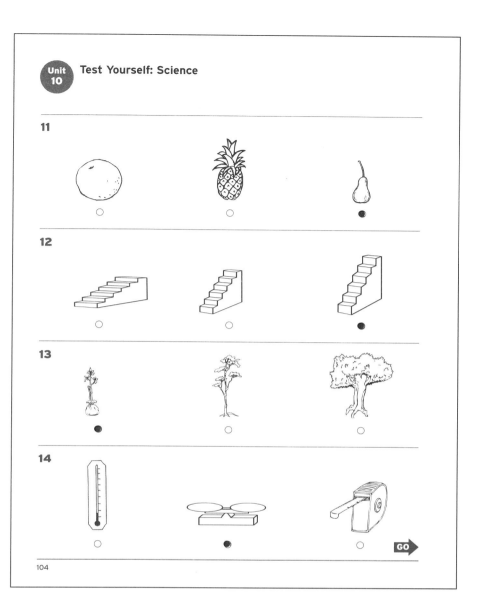

15. Look at the pictures in row 15. Which place has the best soil for plants to grow? Fill in the circle under the picture that shows the place with the best soil for plants to grow.

16. Look at the pictures in row 16. Which person probably has a fever? Fill in the circle under the picture that shows the person who probably has a fever.

17. Look at the pictures in row 17. Which scientist is probably looking into space? Fill in the circle under the picture of the scientist who is probably looking into space.

18. Look at the pictures in row 18. Which child probably feels warmest? Fill in the circle under the picture that shows the child who probably feels warmest.

Turn to the next page, page 106.

Check to be sure the students have found the right page. Allow the students a moment to rest.

19. Look at the pictures in row 19. Which animal has a shell and a backbone? Fill in the circle under the picture of the animal that has a shell and a backbone.

20. Look at the pictures in row 20. They show milk, juice, and soda. Which drink is least healthy for you? Fill in the circle under the picture that shows the drink that is the least healthy for you.

21. Look at the pictures in row 21. Carrie wants to compare the strength of a piece of string and a piece of thin wire. What is the best way to compare the strength of the wire and the string? Fill in the circle under the picture that shows the best way to compare the strength of the wire and the string.

22. Look at the potato, carrot, and corn in row 22. Which one contains the seeds of the plant on which it grew? Fill in the circle under the picture that shows a food containing seeds that can grow into a new plant.

Look at the next page, page 107.

Check to be sure the students have found the right page. Allow the students a moment to rest.

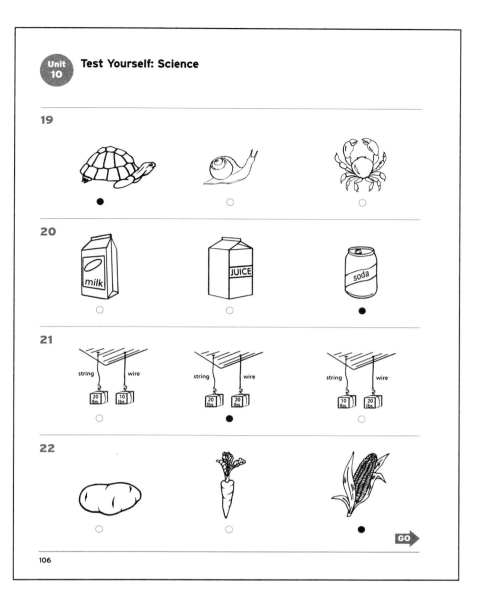

Unit 10 — Test Yourself: Science

19

20

21

22

106

23. Look at the ruler, the tape measure, and the yardstick in row 23. Which one would a scientist probably use to measure the length of a fallen tree? Fill in the circle under the picture of the tool a scientist would probably use to measure the length of a fallen tree.

24. Look at the pictures in row 24. Which machine is pushing something? Fill in the circle under the picture that shows a machine pushing something.

25. Look at the picture of the newspaper, the jug, and the glass in row 25. Which one came from a tree? Fill in the circle under the picture that shows something that came from a tree.

26. Look at the pictures in row 26. In which picture is the student doing the experiment safely? Fill in the circle under the picture that shows the student doing the experiment safely.

Turn to the next page, page 108.

Check to be sure the students have found the right page. Allow the students a moment to rest.

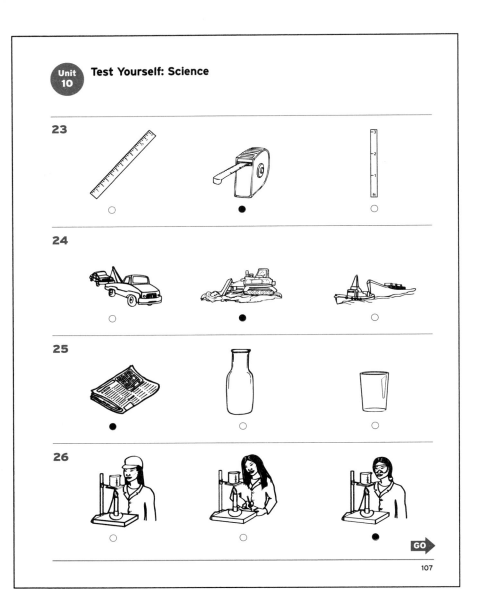

27. Look at the pictures in row 27. Which picture shows a full moon? Fill in the circle under the picture that shows a full moon.

28. Look at the pictures in row 28. Which part of the body do you use most when you think? Fill in the circle under the picture that shows the part of the body you use most when you think.

29. Look at the pictures in row 29. Which picture shows how an iceberg floats in the ocean? Fill in the circle under the picture that shows how an iceberg floats in the ocean.

30. Look at the pictures in row 30. Which part of your body senses invisible chemicals floating in the air? Fill in the circle under the picture that shows the part of your body that senses invisible chemicals floating in the air.

Look at the next page, page 109.

Check to be sure the students have found the right page. Allow the students a moment to rest.

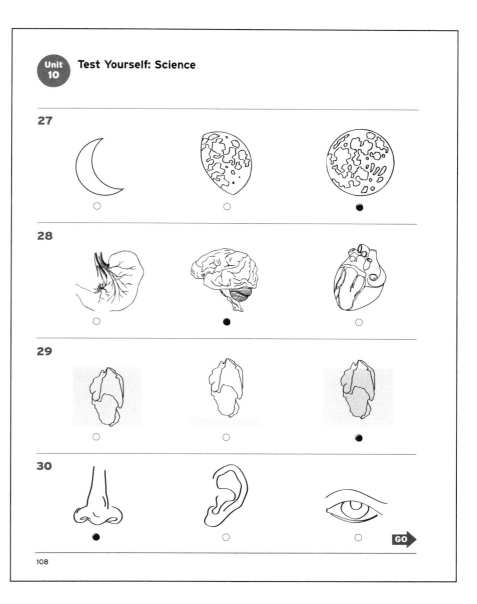

31. Look at the pictures in row 31. Which of these is least likely to lead to good health? Fill in the circle under the picture of something that is least likely to lead to good health.

32. Look at the pictures in row 32. They show a dandelion, an acorn, and a maple seed. Which one probably falls from the plant and is not moved by the wind? Fill in the circle under the picture that shows something that falls from a plant but is not moved by the wind.

33. Look at the pictures in row 33. Which thing almost always moves down, not up? Fill in the circle under the picture of something that almost always moves down, not up.

34. Look at the pictures in row 34. In which picture does the arrow point to the part of the fish that moves it through the water? Fill in the circle under the picture in which the arrow points to the part of the fish that moves it through the water.

Turn to the next page, page 110.

Check to be sure the students have found the right page. Allow the students a moment to rest.

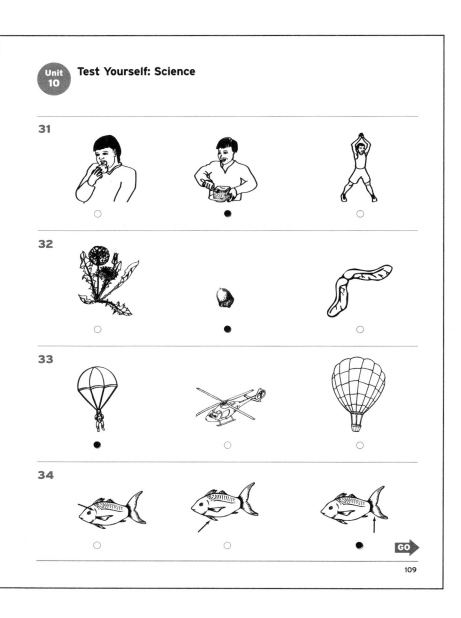

35. Look at the pictures in row 35. Which of these things will not burn? Fill in the circle under the picture of something that will not burn.

36. Look at the pictures in row 36. Which balloon contains the most air? Fill in the circle under the picture of the balloon that contains the most air.

37. Look at the candy bar, the cereal, and the orange in row 37. Which of these foods should you eat the least of? Fill in the circle under the picture that shows a food you should eat the least of.

38. Look at the pictures in row 38. Which thing you see in the sky does not make its own light? Fill in the circle under the picture that shows something in the sky that does not make its own light.

It's time to stop. You have completed the Test Yourself lesson. Check to see that you have completely filled in your answer circles with dark marks. Make sure that any marks for answers that you changed have been completely erased. Now you may close your books.

Review the answers with the students. Have the students indicate completion of the lesson by entering their score for this activity on the progress chart at the beginning of the book. Provide the students whatever help is necessary to record their scores.

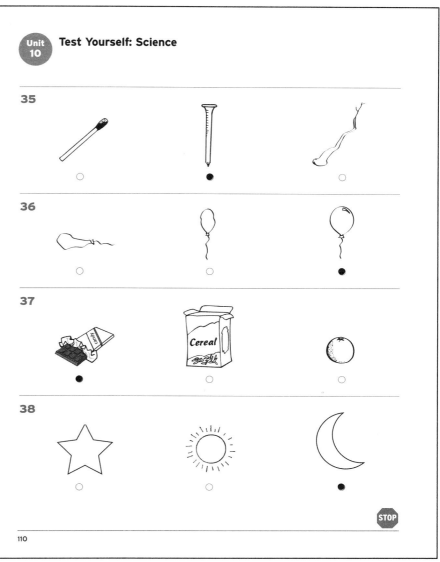

 Practice

To the Teacher:

The Test Practice unit provides the students with an opportunity to apply the reading, spelling, language arts, mathematics, study, test-taking and science skills practiced in the lessons of this book. It is also a final practice activity to be used prior to administering the *Iowa Tests of Basic Skills*®. By following the step-by-step instructions on the subsequent pages, you will be able to simulate the structured atmosphere in which achievement tests are given. Take time to become familiar with the administrative procedures before the students take the tests.

Preparing for the Tests

1. **Put a "Testing—Do Not Disturb" sign on the classroom door to eliminate unnecessary interruptions.**

2. **Make sure the students are seated at comfortable distances from each other and that their desks are clear.**

3. **Provide each student sharpened pencils with erasers. Have an extra supply of pencils available. For the mathematics items, provide each student scratch paper.**

4. **Distribute the students' books.**

5. **Encourage the students with a "pep talk."**

Scheduling the Tests

Each test should be administered in a separate session. Two sessions may be scheduled for the same day if a sufficient break in time is provided between sessions.

Test	Administration Time (minutes)
1 Vocabulary	20
2 Word Analysis	25
3 Reading	30
4 Listening	15
5 Language	25
6 Mathematics Concepts	25
7 Mathematics Problems	25
8 Mathematics Computation	20
9 Sources of Information	25
10 Science	35

Administering the Tests

1. Read the "Say" copy verbatim to the students and follow all the instructions given.

2. Make sure the students understand the directions for each test before proceeding.

3. Move about the classroom during testing to see that the directions are being followed. Make sure the students are working on the correct page and are marking their answers properly.

4. Without distracting the students, provide test-taking tips at your discretion. If you notice a student is working independently and is unable to answer a question, encourage him or her to skip the question and go on to the next one. If students finish the test before time is called, suggest they go back to any skipped questions within that part of the test. However, do not provide help with the content of any question.

Test 1
Vocabulary

Administration Time: 20 minutes

Say Turn to the Test Practice section of your book on page 111. There are pictures and words on this page.

Check to see that the students have found page 111.

Say This test will check how well you know vocabulary words. Remember to make sure that the circles for your answer choices are completely filled in. Press your pencil firmly so that your marks come out dark. Completely erase any marks for answers that you change.

Look at the picture for S. It is at the top of the first column. Now look at the words beside the picture. Which word best tells about the picture? *(pause)* The last answer, *cliff*, is correct because it best tells about the picture. Fill in the circle beside the word *cliff*, the last answer. Be sure your answer circle is completely filled in with a dark mark and that you have marked the correct answer circle.

Check to see that the students have marked the correct circle.

Say Now we will do more items in the same way we did the sample. You will work by yourself. Look at each picture. Read each answer choice. Fill in the circle beside the word that goes best with the picture. If you are not sure which answer is correct, take your best guess.

Work until you come to the STOP sign at the bottom of the page. Fill in your answer circles with dark marks and completely erase any marks for answers that you change. Do you have any questions? Start working now.

Allow time for the students to do Numbers 1 through 5.

Say Turn to the next page, page 112.

Check to see that the students have found the right page. Allow the students a moment to rest.

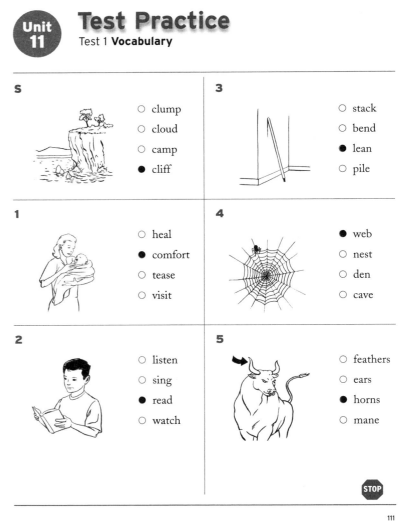

Say Now you will answer different questions. In this part of the test, you will read a sentence in which a word is missing. You will choose the word that fits best at the end of the sentence. Fill in the circle beside the answer you think is best. Work until you come to the STOP sign at the bottom of the page. When you have finished, you can check over your answers to this test. Then wait for the rest of the group to finish. Any questions?

Answer any questions that the students have.

Say Start working now.

Allow time for the students to do Numbers 6 through 11.

Say It's time to stop. You have completed Test 1. Check to see that you have completely filled in your answer circles with dark marks. Make sure that any marks for answers that you changed have been completely erased. Now you may close your books.

Review the items with the students. Have students indicate completion of the lesson by entering their score for this activity on the progress chart at the beginning of the book. Provide the students whatever help is necessary to record their scores. Then collect the students' books and answer sheets if this is the end of the testing session.

Unit 11 Test 1 **Vocabulary**

6 A quiet voice is a …

● whisper   ○ shout   ○ yell   ○ swallow

7 To be worried is to be …

○ tired   ● nervous   ○ alone   ○ comfortable

8 To look quickly is to …

○ blink   ○ grin   ○ rip   ● peek

9 Something that is not real is …

● pretend   ○ easy   ○ wonderful   ○ terrible

10 To go up a ladder is to …

○ walk   ○ dance   ○ spin   ● climb

11 To become different is to …

○ agree   ○ think   ● change   ○ promise STOP

112

Administration Time: 25 minutes

Say Look at the Test Practice section of your book on page 113. There are two columns of words on this page.

Check to see that the students have found page 113.

Say This test will check how well you know letters and sounds. Remember to make sure that the circles for your answer choices are completely filled in. Press your pencil firmly so that your marks come out dark. Completely erase any marks for answers that you change. Do not write anything except your answer choices in your books.

Find S1, the row of words below the picture of the book. Listen carefully. Which word begins with the same sound as *grade... grade*? Fill in the circle for your answer.

Allow time for the students to fill in their answers.

Say The second answer, *grow*, is correct. If you chose another answer, erase yours and fill in the circle for the word *grow* now.

Check to see that the students have correctly filled in their answer circles with a dark mark.

Say Now you will do more items like S1. Listen carefully to what I say. Fill in the circle under the answer you think is correct. If you are not sure which answer is correct, take your best guess. Are you ready? Let's begin.

Allow time between items for the students to mark their answers.

1. Look at the row with the phone. Which word in this row begins with the same sound as *sneak*? Fill in the circle under the word that begins with the same sound as *sneak... sneak*.

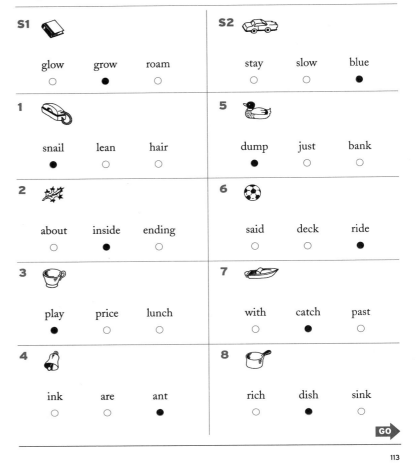

2. Look at the row with the leaf. Which word in this row begins with the same sound as *into*? Fill in the circle under the word that begins with the same sound as *into... into*.

3. Look at the row with the cup. Which word in this row begins with the same sound as *plant*? Fill in the circle under the word that begins with the same sound as *plant... plant*.

4. Look at the row with the bell. Which word in this row begins with the same sound as *ask*? Fill in the circle under the word that begins with the same sound as *ask... ask*.

Look at S2, the row of words below the picture of the car. It is at the top of the next column. Listen carefully. Which word rhymes with *shoe*? Fill in the circle under the word that rhymes with *shoe...shoe*.

Allow time for the students to fill in their answers.

Say The third answer, *blue*, is correct. If you chose another answer, erase yours and fill in the circle for the word *blue* now.

Check to see that the students have correctly filled in their answer circles with a dark mark.

Say Now you will do more items like S2. Listen carefully to what I say. Fill in the circle under the answer you think is correct.

5. Look at the row with the duck. Fill in the circle under the word that rhymes with *lump...lump*.

6. Look at the row with the ball. Fill in the circle under the word that rhymes with *hide...hide*.

7. Look at the row with the boat. Fill in the circle under the word that rhymes with *match...match*.

8. Move down to the last row, the one with the pot. Fill in the circle under the word that rhymes with *fish...fish*.

    Turn to the next page, page 114.

Check to be sure the students have found the right page. Allow the students a moment to rest.

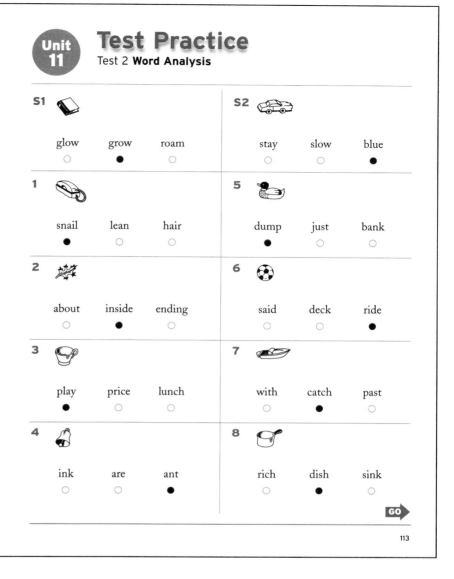

9. The items on this page are different. Listen carefully to what I say. Look at row 9. The word is *rag*. Take away the *r* and put *f-l* in its place. Fill in the circle under the picture of the new word.

10. Look at row 10. The word is *say*. Take away the *s* and put *h* in its place. Fill in the circle under the picture of the new word.

11. Look at row 11. The word is *tail*. Take away the *t* and put *s-n* in its place. Fill in the circle under the picture of the new word.

12. Look at row 12. The word is *tell*. Take away the *t* and put *s-h* in its place. Fill in the circle under the picture of the new word.

13. Look at row 13. The word is *sunk*. Take away the *s* and put *t-r* in its place. Fill in the circle under the picture of the new word.

14. Look at row 14. The word is *sick*. Take away the *s* and put *b-r* in its place. Fill in the circle under the picture of the new word.

Say Look at the next page, page 115.

Check to see that the students have found the right page. Allow the students a moment to rest.

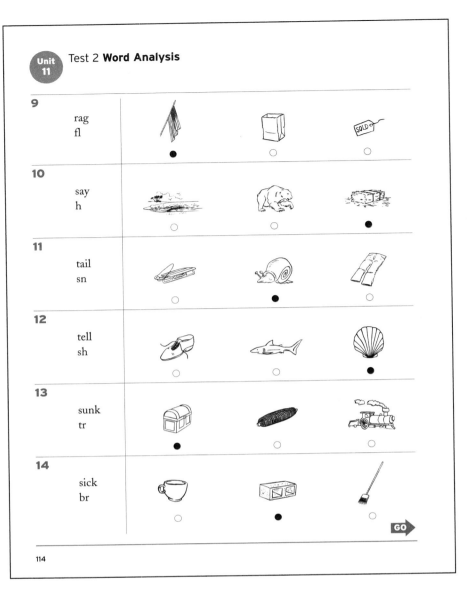

15. Look at row 15, the picture of the *basket*. Fill in the circle under the letter that goes before *a-s-k-e-t* to make the word *basket*.

16. Look at row 16, the picture of a *coat*. Fill in the circle under the letter that goes before *o-a-t* to make the word *coat*.

17. Look at row 17, the picture of the *jar*. Fill in the circle under the letter that goes before *a-r* to make the word *jar*.

18. Look at row 18, the picture of the *pony*. Fill in the circle under the letter that goes before *o-n-y* to make the word *pony*.

19. Look at row 19, the picture of the *pocket*. Fill in the circle under the letter that goes in the middle to make the word *pocket*.

20. Look at row 20, the picture of the baby learning to *crawl*. Fill in the circle under the letters that go in the middle to make the word *crawl*.

Turn to the next page, page 116.

Check to be sure the students have found the right page. Allow the students a moment to rest.

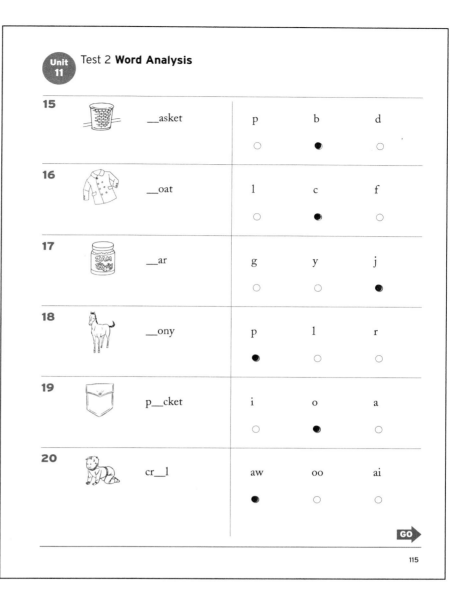

21. Look at row 21. Fill in the circle under the picture whose name has the same vowel sound as *tape... tape*.

22. Look at row 22. Fill in the circle under the picture whose name has the same vowel sound as *hear... hear*.

23. Look at row 23. Fill in the circle under the picture whose name has the same vowel sound as *took... took*.

24. Look at the row with the ball. Fill in the circle under the word that has the same vowel sound as *lace... lace*.

25. Look at the row with the boat. Fill in the circle under the word that has the same vowel sound as *ride... ride*.

26. Look at the row with the pot. Fill in the circle under the word that has the same vowel sound as *must... must*.

Say It's time to stop. You have completed Test 2. Check to see that you have completely filled in your answer circles with dark marks. Make sure that any marks for answers that you changed have been completely erased. Now you may close your books.

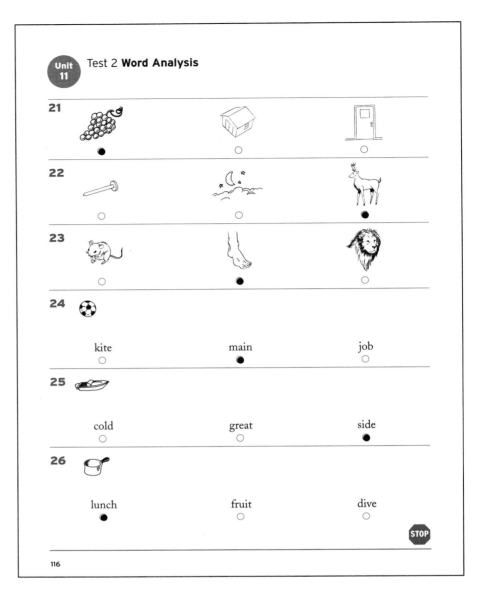

Review the items with the students.
Have them indicate completion of the lesson by entering their score for this activity on the progress chart at the beginning of the book. Provide the students whatever help is necessary to record their scores. Then collect the students' books and answer sheets if this is the end of the testing session.

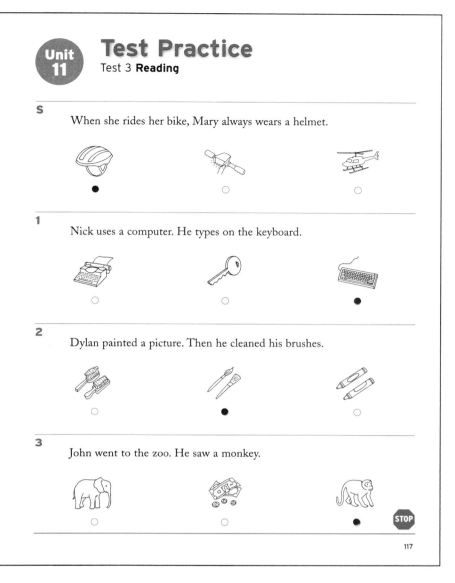

Unit 11 Test 3 Reading

Administration Time: 30 minutes

Say Look at the Test Practice section of your book on page 117. This is Test 3, Reading.

Check to see that the students have found page 117.

Say In this part of the test you will choose a picture that matches the last word in a sentence. Read the story for S1. It is at the top of the page. Now look at the pictures under the story. Which picture best matches the last word of the story? *(pause)* The first answer, *the helmet*, is correct. Fill in the circle under the first answer. Be sure your answer circle is completely filled in with a dark mark and that you have marked the correct answer circle.

Check to see that the students have marked the correct circle.

Say Now we will do more items in the same way we did the sample. You will work by yourself. Read each story and look at the pictures. Fill in the circle under the picture that goes best with the last word in the story. If you don't know what the last word is, use letter clues to help you find the right answer. Work until you come to the STOP sign at the bottom of the page. Do you have any questions? Start working now.

Allow time for the students to do Numbers 1 through 3.

Say Turn to the next page, page 118.

Check to be sure the students have found the right page. Allow the students a moment to rest.

Test Practice
Test 3 Reading

S When she rides her bike, Mary always wears a helmet.

1 Nick uses a computer. He types on the keyboard.

2 Dylan painted a picture. Then he cleaned his brushes.

3 John went to the zoo. He saw a monkey.

117

Say In this part of the lesson you will read sentences about a picture. The sentences have a missing word. You will fill in the circle under the word that fits best in each sentence. Work until you come to the STOP sign at the bottom of the page. Do you have any questions? Start working now.

Allow time for the students to do Numbers 4 through 6.

Say Look at the next page, page 119.

Check to be sure the students have found the right page. Allow the students a moment to rest.

Test 3 **Reading**

4   Max and Annie are playing in the ———.

    ○ bathtub   ● pool   ○ park   ○ driveway

5   Max is holding a ———.

    ● hose   ○ bucket   ○ towel   ○ sprinkler

6   Annie is ——— Max with water.

    ○ scaring   ○ shouting   ○ shaking   ● splashing

STOP

118

Say Now you will answer questions about stories you read. Read each story and the questions that follow it. Fill in the circle beside the answer you think is correct for each question. If you are not sure which answer is correct, take your best guess. When you come to the GO sign at the bottom of a page, turn the page and continue working. Work until you come to the STOP sign at the bottom of page 121. Fill in your answer circles with dark marks and completely erase any marks for answers that you change. Do you have any questions? Start working now.

Allow time for students to fill in their answers.

Jody's mother loves to spin her own yarn. First, she buys fluffy wool from a farm. Then she cleans it and combs it into long pieces. She puts the pieces through a spinning wheel. The wheel twists the wool tight and makes yarn.

After Jody's mother is finished spinning, she knits with the yarn. She makes mittens, scarves, and socks. Her wool socks keep Jody's feet warm in winter. Jody loves the socks her mom makes.

7 **Where does Jody's mom get her wool?**
- ○ From a store
- ○ From her friend
- ● From a farm

8 **What does the spinning wheel do?**
- ○ Rolls on the ground
- ● Twists the wool into yarn
- ○ Makes mittens

9 **Which of these did mother make for Jody?**
- ○ Scarves
- ○ Mittens
- ● Socks

It was the last day of school. Sarah, Josh, and the other students couldn't wait for school to be out for the summer. Their class was noisy and restless. Suddenly the door opened. The principal walked in.

"Sarah and Josh, come with me," she said. They followed the principal down the hall.

"Are we in trouble?" whispered Josh. Sarah didn't know. She was scared.

They went to the library. There were many other children inside. There was a cake and punch.

"This is a special party," the principal said. "I want to thank you all for having perfect attendance all year!" Everyone clapped and cheered. Sarah and Josh clapped too.

10 Who came for Sara and Josh?
○ The teacher
● The principal
○ Their friends

11 What was the surprise?
○ A game
○ A day off
● A party

12 Why were the children noisy and restless?
○ They didn't have any homework.
○ The teacher was sick.
● They wanted to start their vacation.

13 What was true about all the children in the library?
● They all had perfect attendance.
○ They were library helpers.
○ They were friends.

GO

120

Say It's time to stop. You have completed Test 3. Check to see that you have completely filled in your answer circles with dark marks. Make sure that any marks for answers that you changed have been completely erased. Now you may close your books.

Review the items with the students. Have them indicate completion of the lesson by entering their score for this activity on the progress chart at the beginning of the book. Provide the students whatever help is necessary to record their scores. Then collect the students' books and answer sheets if this is the end of the testing session.

 Test 3 **Reading**

> I went to Aunt Lily's house last week to cheer her up. I knew she was sad because her son had moved away. He had gotten married and had a new job.
> I found a big, old book at Aunt Lily's house. It was tied with string. Inside I found a red rose pressed in the pages.
> "Your cousin Joe gave me that rose a long time ago," Aunt Lily told me. "Every time I see red roses I think of him."
> The next time I went to Aunt Lily's house I took her some roses.
> "The red roses are so you will remember Joe," I said.
> "What is the yellow rose for?" Aunt Lily asked.
> "That one is so that you will think of me," I said.

14 What is this story mostly about?
- ● Remembering people you love
- ○ Buying flowers for the kitchen
- ○ Visiting family

15 Why did Aunt Lily press the rose in the book?
- ○ To keep the flower fresh
- ● To remind her of Joe
- ○ To mark a page

16 Why did the child think Aunt Lily would forget Joe?
- ○ He was away at school.
- ● He had moved.
- ○ He was coming home soon.

17 How do red roses remind her of Joe?
- ○ They grew in his yard.
- ○ They are pretty.
- ● He gave her one long ago.

121

Test 4
Listening

Administration Time: 15 minutes

Say Turn to Test 4 on page 122. There are rows of pictures on the top part of the page.

Check to see that the students have found page 122.

Say In this part of the test you will choose a picture that matches what you hear. Let's do S together. Listen carefully and look at the pictures at the top of the page. In the morning a tree was covered with bright golden leaves. A strong afternoon wind blew all the leaves down, leaving the tree bare. Fill in the circle under the picture of the tree in the evening. *(pause)* The second answer is correct. Fill in the circle under the second answer. Be sure your answer circle is completely filled in with a dark mark and that you have marked the correct answer circle.

Check to see that the students have filled in the correct answer circle.

Say Now we will do more items in the same way we did the sample. Listen to what I say and choose the answer you think is correct. Fill in the circle under the picture that goes best with what I say. Be sure your answer circle is completely filled in with a dark mark. Do you have any questions? Let's begin.

Allow time between items for students to fill in their answers.

1. Look at the pictures in row 1. Clara will push her younger brother in the swing at the park. Fill in the circle under the picture that shows that Clara will push her younger brother in the swing.

2. Look at the pictures in row 2. Ellen loved sleeping with the teddy bear because it belonged to her great-grandmother when she was a little girl. Fill in the circle under the picture that shows where Ellen put the teddy bear.

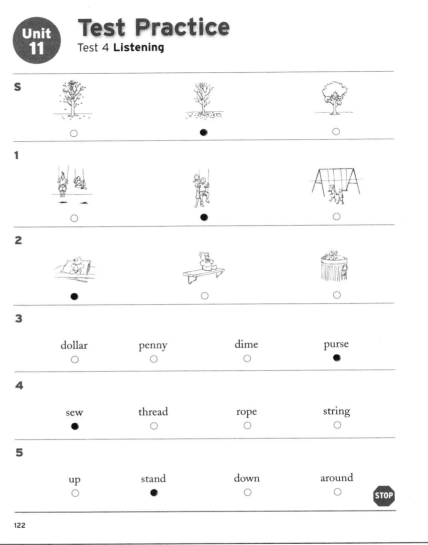

Test Practice
Test 4 **Listening**

S			
1			
2			
3	dollar ○	penny ○	dime ○ / purse ●
4	sew ●	thread ○	rope ○ / string ○
5	up ○	stand ●	down ○ / around ○

122

Say Now we will do a different kind of item. For Numbers 3 through 5, you will read the words to yourself while I read them out loud. Fill in the circle under the word that is different from the other three. Be sure your answer circle is completely filled in with a dark mark. Do you have any questions? Let's begin.

Allow time between items for students to fill in their answers.

3. The words in row 3 are *dollar, penny, dime, purse.* Fill in the circle under the word that is different from the other three.

4. The words in row 4 are *sew, thread, rope, string.* Fill in the circle under the word that is different from the other three.

5. The words in row 5 are *up, stand, down, around.* Fill in the circle under the word that is different from the other three.

Say It's time to stop. You have completed Test 4. Check to see that you have completely filled in your answer circles with dark marks. Make sure that any marks for answers that you changed have been completely erased. Now you may close your books.

Review the items with the students. Have them indicate completion of the lesson by entering their score for this activity on the progress chart at the beginning of the book. Provide the students whatever help is necessary to record their scores. Then collect the students' books and answer sheets if this is the end of the testing session.

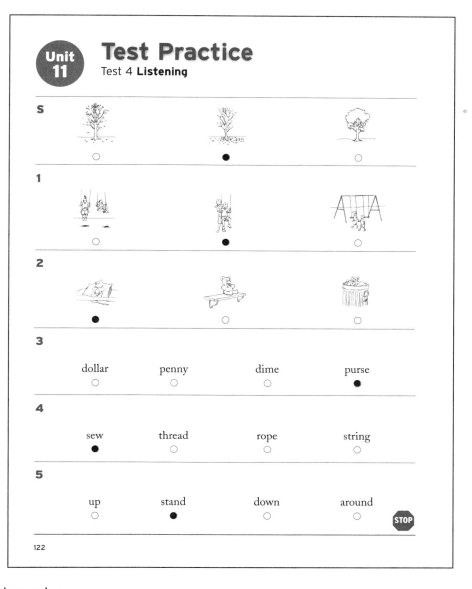

Unit 11

Test Practice

Test 4 **Listening**

3. dollar   penny   dime   purse

4. sew   thread   rope   string

5. up   stand   down   around

122

Administration Time: 25 minutes

Say Look at Test 5 on page 123. There are two columns of words on this page.

Check to see that the students have found page 123.

Say This part of the test will check how well you can find spelling mistakes. Look at the words in row S at the top of the first column. They are *found, penny, picked.* I *found* a *penny* and *picked* it up. Fill in the circle under the word that is not spelled correctly. Which answer did you choose? *(the second answer, p-e-n-y)* Mark the space under the second answer. This is a misspelling of *p-e-n-n-y*. Make sure the circle is completely filled in. Press your pencil firmly so that your mark comes out dark.

Check to see that the students have filled in the correct answer circle.

Say Now we will do more items. Listen to what I say while you look at the words. Fill in the circle under the word that is misspelled. Be sure your answer circle is completely filled in with a dark mark. Do you have any questions? Let's begin.

Allow time between items for students to fill in their answers.

1. **Number 1:** *peek, inside, box.* May I *peek inside* the *box*?

2. **Number 2:** *wooden, block, toy.* The *wooden block* was a *toy*.

3. **Number 3:** *fence, post, broken.* The *fence post* was *broken*.

4. **Number 4:** *fish, tank, bedroom.* I have a *fish tank* in my *bedroom*.

   Go to the top of the second column.

S			5		
found ○	peny ●	picked ○	wore ○	string ○	bedes ●
1			**6**		
peke ●	inside ○	box ○	flore ●	cabin ○	dirt ○
2			**7**		
wooden ○	blok ●	toy ○	lamp ○	brigt ●	read ○
3			**8**		
fence ○	poste ●	broken ○	reatch ●	top ○	shelf ○
4			**9**		
fisch ●	tank ○	bedroom ○	new ○	shoos ●	tight ○

GO

123

5. **Number 5:** *wore, string, beads.* She *wore* a *string* of *beads*.

6. **Number 6:** *floor, cabin, dirt.* The *floor* of the *cabin* was made of *dirt*.

7. **Number 7:** *lamp, bright, read.* The *lamp* was *bright* enough for me to *read*.

8. **Number 8:** *reach, top, shelf.* I could not *reach* the *top shelf*.

9. **Number 9:** *new, shoes, tight.* My *new shoes* were very *tight*.

   Turn to the next page, page 124

Check to be sure the students have found the right page. Allow the students a moment to rest.

Say Now we will do some capitalization items. Listen to what I say while you look at the answers. Fill in the circle beside the line that has a word that should begin with a capital letter. Be sure your answer circle is completely filled in with a dark mark. Do you have any questions? Let's begin.

Allow time between items for the students to fill in their answers. Begin each item by reading the number using the format Number 1, Number 2, and so on.

10. The Carver family spends every Independence Day at a campsite near the beach.

11. Where is the nearest bank? My mom and I have not been able to find it.

12. Matt and Anna are members of a postcard club that meets once a month.

Say Now we will do some punctuation items. Listen to what I say while you look at the answers. Fill in the circle beside the line that needs a punctuation mark. Be sure your answer circle is completely filled in with a dark mark. Do you have any questions? Let's begin.

Allow time between items for the students to fill in their answers. Begin each item by reading the number using the format Number 1, Number 2, and so on.

13. The street cleaner asked the people to move their cars. Then he swept and washed the street.

14. We planted a strawberry patch with Uncle Shelby. Soon we will be eating fresh strawberries.

15. The new kid on the block is O. P. Barnes, and Saturday at six he is joining us for dinner.

    Look at the next page, page 125.

Check to be sure the students have found the right page. Allow the students a moment to rest.

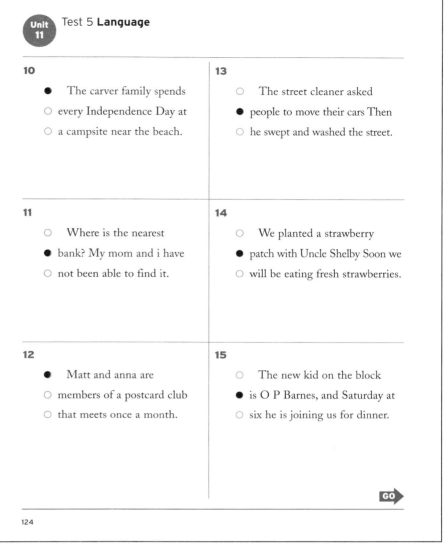

Unit 11 Test 5 **Language**

10
- ●   The carver family spends
- ○ every Independence Day at
- ○ a campsite near the beach.

11
- ○   Where is the nearest
- ● bank? My mom and i have
- ○ not been able to find it.

12
- ●   Matt and anna are
- ○ members of a postcard club
- ○ that meets once a month.

13
- ○   The street cleaner asked
- ● people to move their cars Then
- ○ he swept and washed the street.

14
- ○   We planted a strawberry
- ● patch with Uncle Shelby Soon we
- ○ will be eating fresh strawberries.

15
- ○   The new kid on the block
- ● is O P Barnes, and Saturday at
- ○ six he is joining us for dinner.

GO

124

Say On this page you will look for mistakes in the use of words. Listen to what I say while you look at the answers. Fill in the circle beside the line that has a word that is wrong and should be changed. Be sure your answer circle is completely filled in with a dark mark. Do you have any questions? Let's begin.

Allow time between items for the students to fill in their answers. Begin each item by reading the number using the format Number 1, Number 2, and so on.

16. I haven't never won a prize in a contest. I keep hoping that someday I will.

17. Mom could not believe what she saw in the car mirror. The kids they were sleeping!

18. Frank watched how his dad made his famous pancakes. Mixed and fried.

19. Ella was hungry, and the warm soup made her stomach feel much gooder.

20. A group of deers stood in the middle of the large meadow behind the barn.

21. Sundays are my favorite days. That is when I and Luis work on our backyard tree fort.

Say It's time to stop. You have completed Test 4. Check to see that you have completely filled in your answer circles with dark marks. Make sure that any marks for answers that you changed have been completely erased. Now you may close your books.

Review the items with the students. Have them indicate completion of the lesson by entering their score for this activity on the progress chart at the beginning of the book. Provide the students whatever help is necessary to record their scores. Then collect the students' books and answer sheets if this is the end of the testing session.

Unit 11 Test 5 **Language**

16
● I haven't never won a
○ prize in a contest. I keep
○ hoping that someday I will.

17
○ Mom could not believe
○ what she saw in the car mirror.
● The kids they were sleeping!

18
○ Frank watched how
○ his dad made his famous
● pancakes. Mixed and fried.

19
○ Ella was hungry, and
○ the warm soup made her
● stomach feel much gooder.

20
● A group of deers stood
○ in the middle of the large
○ meadow behind the barn.

21
○ Sundays are my favorite
● days. That is when I and Luis
○ work on our backyard tree fort.

STOP

125

Unit 11 Test 6
Mathematics Concepts

Administration Time: 25 minutes

Say Turn to Test 6 on page 126. This part of the test is about mathematics.

Check to see that the students have found page 126.

Say Let's do S together. Listen carefully and look at the shapes at the top of the first column. Which shape is widest? *(pause)* The second shape is widest. Fill in the circle under the second shape. Be sure your answer circle is completely filled in with a dark mark and that you have marked the correct answer circle.

Check to see that the students have marked the correct circle.

Say Now we will do more mathematics items in the same way we did the sample. Listen to what I say and choose the answer you think is correct. Fill in the circle under the best answer. Be sure your answer circle is completely filled in with a dark mark. Do you have any questions? Let's begin.

Allow time between items for students to fill in their answers. Do not read the item numbers.

1. Look at the stars in row 1. Which group has six stars? Fill in the circle under the answer that has exactly six stars.

2. Look at the number word in the box in row 2. Which numeral means the same as the number word in the box? Fill in the circle under the numeral that means the same as the number word in the box.

3. Look at the shapes in row 3 at the top of the next column. Which answer shows a circle inside a triangle? Fill in the circle under the answer that shows a circle inside a triangle.

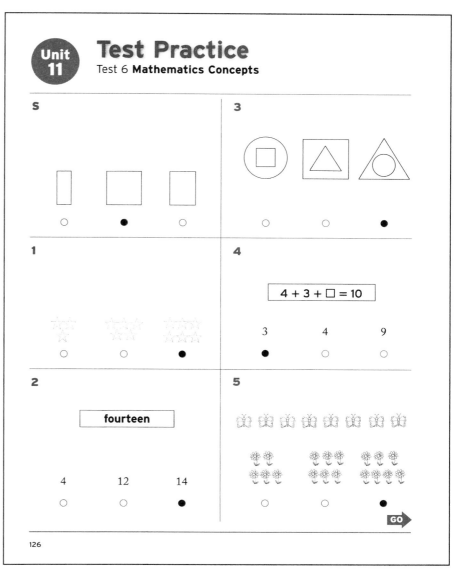

4. Look at the number sentence in row 4. Which numeral should go in the box to make the number sentence true? Fill in the circle under the numeral that should go in the box to make the number sentence true.

5. Look at the butterflies in row 5. Which answer has one less flower than there are butterflies? Fill in the circle under the answer that has one less flower than there are butterflies.

   Look at the next page, page 127.

Check to be sure the students have found the right page. Allow the students a moment to rest.

6. Look at the row with the book at the top of the page. Which numeral is 37? Fill in the circle under the numeral 37.

7. Look at the pictures in row 7. In which answer is there a bird in every cage? Fill in the circle under the answer that shows a bird in every cage.

8. Look at the number sentence in row 8. Which symbol will make the number sentence true? Fill in the circle under the symbol that will make the number sentence true.

9. Look at the pictures in row 9 at the top of the next column. What should you use to measure how long a puppy's tail is? Fill in the circle that shows what you should use to measure how long a puppy's tail is.

10. Look at the coins in row 10. How much money is there in all? Fill in the circle under the answer that shows how much money there is in all.

11. Look at the numbers in row 11, the one with the telephone. Which answer is a number between 33 and 46? Fill in the circle under the number that is between 33 and 46.

Turn to the next page, page 128.

Check to be sure the students have found the right page. Allow the students a moment to rest.

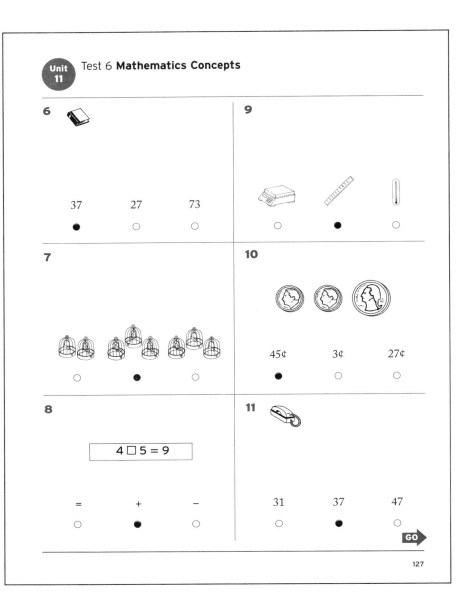

Unit 11   Test 6 **Mathematics Concepts**

6

37	27	73
●	○	○

9

○	●	○

7

○	●	○

10

45¢	3¢	27¢
●	○	○

8

$$4 \ \square \ 5 = 9$$

=	+	−
○	●	○

11

31	37	47
○	●	○

GO

127

12. Look at the flowers in row 12. Each vase has 10 flowers. How many flowers are there in all? Fill in the circle under the answer that shows how many flowers there are in all.

13. Look at the pictures in row 13. Which of these is about the same height as a first grade student in real life? Fill in the circle under the picture of something that is about the same height as a first grade student in real life.

14. Look at the pieces in row 14. Which answer shows the pieces that make the shape? Fill in the circle under the answer that shows the pieces that make the shape.

15. Look at the dogs in row 15 at the top of the next column. Which dog is smaller than the others? Fill in the circle under the dog that is smaller than the others.

16. Look at the clock in row 16. What time does the clock show? Fill in the circle under the time that the clock shows.

17. Look at the numerals in the last row, the one with the leaf. Which numeral means the same as 1 ten and 7 ones? Fill in the circle under the numeral that means the same as 1 ten and 7 ones.

   It's time to stop. You have completed Test 6. Check to see that you have completely filled in your answer circles with dark marks. Make sure that any marks for answers that you changed have been completely erased. Now you may close your books.

Review the items with the students. Have them indicate completion of the lesson by entering their score for this activity on the progress chart at the beginning of the book. Provide the students whatever help is necessary to record their scores. Then collect the students' books and answer sheets if this is the end of the testing session.

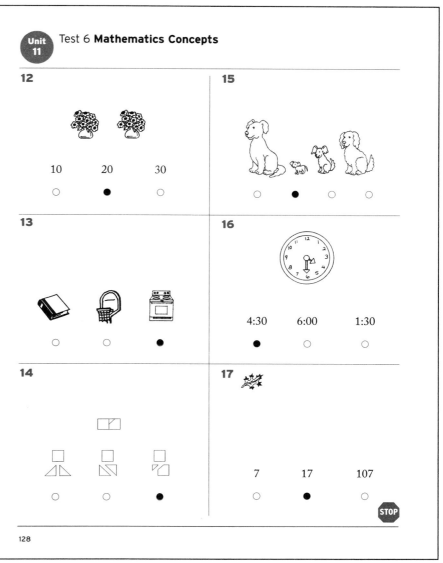

Unit 11 Test 6 **Mathematics Concepts**

12

10   20   30
○   ●   ○

13

○   ○   ●

14

○   ○   ●

15

○   ●   ○   ○

16

4:30   6:00   1:30
●   ○   ○

17

7   17   107
○   ●   ○

STOP

128

Test 7 Mathematics Problems

Administration Time: 25 minutes

Distribute scratch paper to the students.

Say Look at Test 7 on page 129.

Check to see that the students have found page 129.

Say In this lesson you will solve word problems. I will read the problem and you will solve it. You may solve the problem in your head or use scratch paper. If the right answer to the problem is not one of the choices, fill in the circle under the N, which stands for *not given*. Are you ready? Let's do S together. Listen carefully and look at the numbers at the top of the page near the cup. Lou had 3 books. He read 1 book. How many books were left for Lou to read? Again, Lou had 3 books. He read 1 book. How many books were left for Lou to read? *(pause)* Lou had *2* books left to read because 3 minus 1 is *2*. Fill in the circle under the number *2*. Be sure your answer circle is completely filled in with a dark mark and that you have marked the correct answer circle.

Check to see that the students have filled in the correct answer circle.

Say Now we will do more items like S. Listen to what I say and choose the answer you think is correct. Fill in the circle under the best answer. Be sure your answer circle is completely filled in with a dark mark. Do you have any questions? Let's begin.

Allow time between items for students to fill in their answers. Read each problem twice. Do not read the item numbers.

Test Practice
Test 7 Mathematics Problems

S

1	2	4	N
○	●	○	○

4

7	8	10	N
○	●	○	○

1

2	3	9	N
○	○	○	●

5

8	10	18	N
○	○	○	●

2

2	5	7	N
○	●	○	○

6

$3	$4	$10	N
○	●	○	○

3

4	10	12	N
○	○	●	○

7

0	1	4	N
●	○	○	○

GO

129

1. Look at the row with the duck. Five cars were in the school parking lot. Three more cars came into the lot. How many cars in all were in the parking lot? Again . . .

2. Look at the row with the pot. Mrs. Lane has 8 light bulbs in a box. Three are clear glass and the rest are colored. How many light bulbs are made of colored glass? Again . . .

3. Look at the row with the bell. Keith used 4 ice cubes. There were 8 left in the tray. How many ice cubes were in the tray to begin with? Again . . .

4. Look at the row with the car. Fran has 3 shells, 4 buttons, and 1 rock in a box. How many things are in the box all together? Again . . .

5. Look at the row with the book. Some students are standing in 2 rows. There are 8 students in each row. How many students are there in all? Again . . .

6. Look at the row with the telephone. Beth is saving to buy a pair of gloves. She has $6. The gloves cost $10. How much more money does she need? Again . . .

7. Look at the row with the leaf. Andy baked 8 rolls. He brought the 8 rolls to school and shared all of them with his friends. How many rolls were left? Again . . .

Turn to the next page, page 130.

Check to be sure the students have found the right page. Allow the students a moment to rest.

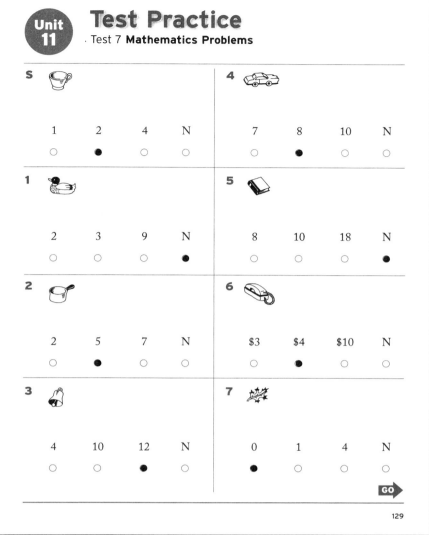

Unit 11 · Test Practice — Test 7 Mathematics Problems

S 1 2 4 N

4 7 8 10 N

1 2 3 9 N

5 8 10 18 N

2 2 5 7 N

6 $3 $4 $10 N

3 4 10 12 N

7 0 1 4 N

GO

129

Say In this part of the test you will do something different. You will choose a number sentence that goes with a problem. I will read a problem while you look at the answers. Fill in the circle under the answer that goes with the problem. Be sure your answer circle is completely filled in with a dark mark. Do you have any questions? Let's begin.

Allow time between items for students to fill in their answers. Read each problem twice. Do not read the item numbers.

8. Look at the row with the cup at the top of the page. Rick's plant was 3 inches tall. It grew 4 more inches. Which number sentence can Rick use to find out how tall the plant is? Again . . .

9. Look at the row with the duck. Gill had 9 trading cards. He gave 3 to his sister. Which number sentence can Gill use to find out how many trading cards he has left?

10. Look at the row with the pot. Monica saw 11 butterflies in her garden. Three of the butterflies went away. Which number sentence can Monica use to find out how many butterflies are left in her garden?

11. Look at the row with the bell. There are 4 rows of desks in Mr. Day's class. Each row has 3 students in it. Which number sentence tells how many students are in Mr. Day's class?

12. Look at the row with the car. Mrs. Teller bought flowers that cost $10. She paid for the flowers with a $20 bill. Which number sentence shows how much change she should receive?

Look at the next page, page 131.

Check to be sure the students have found the right page. Allow the students a moment to rest.

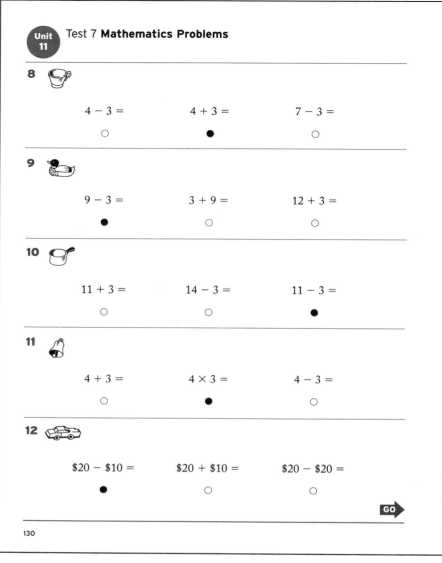

8.
$4 - 3 =$	$4 + 3 =$	$7 - 3 =$
○	●	○

9.
$9 - 3 =$	$3 + 9 =$	$12 + 3 =$
●	○	○

10.
$11 + 3 =$	$14 - 3 =$	$11 - 3 =$
○	○	●

11.
$4 + 3 =$	$4 \times 3 =$	$4 - 3 =$
○	●	○

12.
$\$20 - \$10 =$	$\$20 + \$10 =$	$\$20 - \$20 =$
●	○	○

GO

130

Say Now we will do a different kind of item. Look at the chart at the top of the page. It shows the number of birds some students counted on different days in two different places, at school and at a park. Read each question to yourself while I read it out loud. Look at the chart to find the answer to each question. Decide which answer is correct and fill in the circle for your answer. Let's begin.

Allow time between items for students to fill in their answers. Read each problem once.

13. Number 13: How many birds were counted in the park on Wednesday?

14. Number 14: The number of birds counted in the park on Tuesday was the same as the number of birds counted at school on which day?

15. Number 15: On which day were the fewest number of birds counted in the park?

16. Number 16: How many more birds were counted at school than in the park on Wednesday?

It's time to stop. You have completed Test 7. Check to see that you have completely filled in your answer circles with dark marks. Make sure that any marks for answers that you changed have been completely erased. Now you may close your books.

Review the items with the students. Have them indicate completion of the lesson by entering their score for this activity on the progress chart at the beginning of the book. Then collect the students' books and answer sheets if this is the end of the testing session.

 Unit 11 Test 7 **Mathematics Problems**

Number of Birds Counted in One Week

	School	Park
Monday	9	12
Tuesday	5	9
Wednesday	18	14
Thursday	6	4
Friday	3	9

13 How many birds were counted in the park on Wednesday?
- ○ 9
- ○ 12
- ● 14

14 The number of birds counted in the park on Tuesday was the same as the number of birds counted at school on which day?
- ● Monday
- ○ Tuesday
- ○ Thursday

15 On which day were the fewest number of birds counted in the park?
- ○ Wednesday
- ● Thursday
- ○ Friday

16 How many more birds were counted at school than in the park on Wednesday?
- ○ 3
- ● 4
- ○ 6

131

Administration Time: 20 minutes

Distribute scratch paper to the students.

Say Turn to Test 8 on page 132. There are numbers on this page.

Check to see that the students have found page 132.

Say In this part of the test you will solve addition and subtraction problems. I will read the problem and you will solve it. You may solve the problem in your head or use scratch paper. If the right answer to the problem is not one of the choices, fill in the circle under the N, which stands for *not given*. Are you ready? Let's do S1 together. Listen carefully and look at the numbers at the top of the page near the book. What is 1 add 6? 1 plus 6 equals what number? *(pause)* 1 plus 6 is 7. Fill in the circle under the number 7. Be sure your answer circle is completely filled in with a dark mark and that you have marked the correct answer circle.

Check to see that the students have filled in the correct answer circle.

Say Now we will do more items like S. Listen to what I say and choose the answer you think is correct. Fill in the circle under the best answer. Be sure your answer circle is completely filled in with a dark mark. Do you have any questions? Let's begin.

Allow time between items for students to fill in their answers. Do not read the item numbers.

Test Practice
Test 8 Mathematics Computation

S

5	7	16	N
○	●	○	○

1

9	10	14	N
●	○	○	○

2

10	12	14	N
○	○	●	○

3

10	15	25	N
○	○	●	○

4

2	3	10	N
●	○	○	○

5

5	7	11	N
○	●	○	○

6

1	5	10	N
○	○	○	●

7

4	6	14	N
○	●	○	○

GO

132

1. What is 4 add 5? 4 plus 5 equals what number? Fill in the circle under your answer in the row with the telephone.

2. What is 5 add 9? 5 plus 9 equals what number? Fill in the circle under your answer in the row with the leaf.

3. What is 20 add 5? 20 plus 5 equals what number? Fill in the circle under your answer in the row with the cup.

   The rest of the items on this page are subtraction. Listen carefully to what I say.

4. What is 6 subtract 4? 6 minus 4 equals what number? Fill in the circle under your answer in the row with the duck.

5. What is 9 subtract 2? 9 minus 2 equals what number? Fill in the circle under your answer in the row with the pot.

6. What is 5 subtract 5? 5 minus 5 equals what number? Fill in the circle under your answer in the row with the bell.

7. What is 10 subtract 4? 10 minus 4 equals what number? Fill in the circle under your answer in the row with the car.

   Look at the next page, page 133.

Check to be sure the students have found the right page. Allow the students a moment to rest.

Unit 11

Test Practice
Test 8 **Mathematics Computation**

S

5	7	16	N
○	●	○	○

1

9	10	14	N
●	○	○	○

2

10	12	14	N
○	○	●	○

3

10	15	25	N
○	○	●	○

4

2	3	10	N
●	○	○	○

5

5	7	11	N
○	●	○	○

6

1	5	10	N
○	○	○	●

7

4	6	14	N
○	●	○	○

GO

132

Say In this part of the test you will solve addition and subtraction problems yourself. You may solve the problem in your head or use scratch paper. If the right answer to the problem is not one of the choices, fill in the circle under the N, which stands for *not given*. Be sure to pay attention to the add or subtract symbol so you will know how to solve the problem. Do not write anything in your book except your answer choices. Work until you come to the STOP sign at the bottom of the page. Make sure that the circles for your answer choices are completely filled in with dark marks. Erase any marks for answers that you change. You may begin.

Allow time for the students to fill in their answers.

Say It's time to stop. You have completed Test 9. Check to see that you have completely filled in your answer circles with dark marks. Make sure that any marks for answers that you changed have been completely erased. Now you may close your books.

Review the items with the students. Have them indicate completion of the lesson by entering their score for this activity on the progress chart at the beginning of the book. Then collect the students' books and answer sheets if this is the end of the testing session.

Unit 11 Test 8 **Mathematics Computation**

8

$$\begin{array}{r} 3 \\ + 6 \\ \hline \end{array}$$

3	8	9	N
○	○	●	○

12

$$\begin{array}{r} 16 \\ - 7 \\ \hline \end{array}$$

1	11	9	N
○	○	●	○

9

$$\begin{array}{r} 12 \\ - 2 \\ \hline \end{array}$$

2	10	22	N
○	●	○	○

13

$$7 + 9 =$$

16	17	19	N
●	○	○	○

10

$$0 + 9 =$$

0	10	90	N
○	○	○	●

14

$$4 + 14 =$$

10	17	24	N
○	○	○	●

11

$$14 - 8 =$$

6	8	22	N
●	○	○	○

15

$$\begin{array}{r} 11 \\ - 9 \\ \hline \end{array}$$

1	2	20	N
○	●	○	○

STOP

133

Test 9
Sources of Information

Administration Time: 25 minutes

Say Turn to Test 9 on page 134. There are pictures at the top of the page.

Check to see that the students have found page 134.

Say In this lesson you will answer questions about different kinds of reference sources. The first thing we will do is practice putting things in alphabetical order. Look at the pictures at the top of the page. Imagine you are making a picture dictionary with the things on this page. You will want to put the things in alphabetical order. Let's do S1 together. Read the question to yourself while I read it out loud. Which picture should be at the very top of the page? *(pause)* The first answer, *apron*, is correct because apron comes first in alphabetical order. Fill in the circle beside the word *apron*, the first answer. Be sure your answer circle is completely filled in with a dark mark and that you have marked the correct answer circle.

Check to see that the students have marked the correct circle.

Say Now we will do more items in the same way we did the sample. I will read a question out loud while you read it to yourself. Fill in the circle beside the best answer. Be sure your answer circle is completely filled in with a dark mark. Do you have any questions? Let's begin.

Allow time between items for students to fill in their answers.

1. Number 1: Which picture should be between the broom and the dish?

2. Number 2: Which picture should be the second one on the page?

3. Number 3: Which picture should be right after the easel?

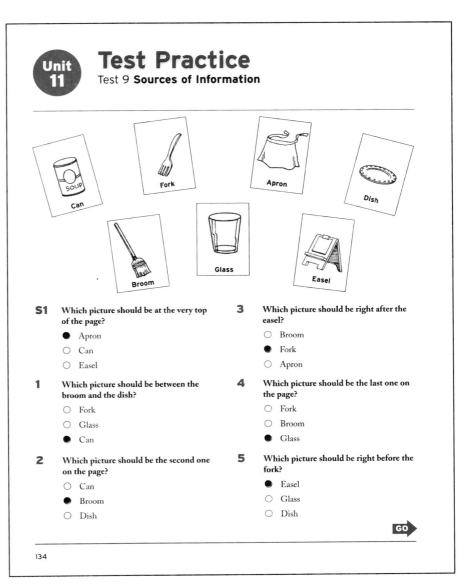

Test Practice
Test 9 **Sources of Information**

S1 Which picture should be at the very top of the page?
- ● Apron
- ○ Can
- ○ Easel

1 Which picture should be between the broom and the dish?
- ○ Fork
- ○ Glass
- ● Can

2 Which picture should be the second one on the page?
- ○ Can
- ● Broom
- ○ Dish

3 Which picture should be right after the easel?
- ○ Broom
- ● Fork
- ○ Apron

4 Which picture should be the last one on the page?
- ○ Fork
- ○ Broom
- ● Glass

5 Which picture should be right before the fork?
- ● Easel
- ○ Glass
- ○ Dish

GO

134

4. Number 4: Which picture should be the last one on the page?

5. Number 5: Which picture should be right before the fork?

   Look at the next page, page 135.

Check to be sure the students have found the right page. Allow the students a moment to rest.

Say The items are a little different on this page. You will answer questions about the map of an amusement park. Read S2 by yourself while I read it out loud. Look at the map to find the answer. Which is the smallest stand in the food court? Look at the map to find the answer. *(pause)* The first answer is correct because *the ice cream stand* is the smallest. Fill in the circle beside the first answer. Be sure your answer circle is completely filled in with a dark mark and that you have marked the correct answer circle.

Check to see that the students have marked the correct circle.

Say Now we will do more items in the same way we did the sample. I will read a question out loud while you read it to yourself. Look at the map to find the answer. Fill in the circle under the best answer. Be sure your answer circle is completely filled in with a dark mark. Do you have any questions? Let's begin.

Allow time between items for students to fill in their answers.

6. Number 6: Which of these is south of the bumper cars?

7. Number 7: Which direction do people go when they leave the food court and walk to the art show?

8. Number 8: What is south of the fun house?

9. Number 9: What does John pass when he goes from the log ride to the rest area?

10. Number 10: Which is the closest to Logan Road?

    Turn to the next page, page 136.

Check to be sure the students have found the right page. Allow the students a moment to rest.

Test 9 **Sources of Information**

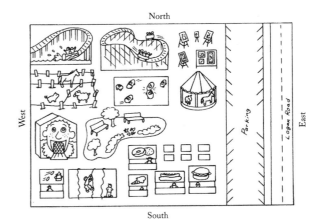

North

West

East

Parking

Logan Road

South

S2 Which is the smallest stand in the food court?
- ● The ice cream stand
- ○ The bakery stand
- ○ The hamburger stand

6 Which of these is south of the bumper cars?
- ○ The carousel
- ○ The petting zoo
- ● The climbing wall

7 Which direction do people go when they leave the food court and walk to the art show?
- ○ East
- ● North
- ○ South

8 What is south of the fun house?
- ○ The bumper cars
- ○ The rest area
- ● The ring toss

9 What does John pass when he goes from the log ride to the rest area?
- ● The roller coaster
- ○ The carousel
- ○ The food court

10 Which is closest to Logan Road?
- ○ The petting zoo
- ○ The bumper cars
- ● The hamburger stand

135

Say For this part of the lesson, you will answer questions about a dictionary. The words in the dictionary are *bundle, corner, glitter, mystery, necklace, officer, puzzle, stampede.* I will read the question out loud while you read it to yourself. Look at the dictionary to find the answer. Fill in the circle beside the best answer. Be sure your answer circle is completely filled in with a dark mark. Do you have any questions? Let's begin.

Allow time between items for students to fill in their answers.

11. Number 11: Which is most like a mystery?

12. Number 12: How do you spell the name for something that is tied up?

13. Number 13: Which of these would you be most likely to see at a ranch?

14. Number 14: Which is most likely to glitter?

15. Number 15: Which word fits best in the sentence "Jack stood on the _____ and waited for his ride"?

16. Number 16: How do you spell what the stars do at night?

Look at the next page, page 137.

Check to be sure the students have found the right page. Allow the students a moment to rest.

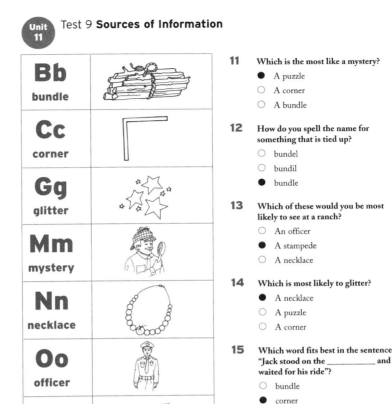

Unit 11 Test 9 **Sources of Information**

Bb bundle	
Cc corner	
Gg glitter	
Mm mystery	
Nn necklace	
Oo officer	
Pp puzzle	
Ss stampede	

136

11 Which is the most like a mystery?
- ● A puzzle
- ○ A corner
- ○ A bundle

12 How do you spell the name for something that is tied up?
- ○ bundel
- ○ bundil
- ● bundle

13 Which of these would you be most likely to see at a ranch?
- ○ An officer
- ● A stampede
- ○ A necklace

14 Which is most likely to glitter?
- ● A necklace
- ○ A puzzle
- ○ A corner

15 Which word fits best in the sentence "Jack stood on the _____ and waited for his ride"?
- ○ bundle
- ● corner
- ○ stampede

16 How do you spell what the stars do at night?
- ○ gliter
- ○ glider
- ● glitter

GO ▶

Say Now we will do some questions about a table of contents from a book about turtles. Read the title of each chapter to yourself while I read it out loud.

Turtles and Their Armor
Places Turtles Call Home
Early Turtles in History
Laying Eggs Turtle Style
Turtles Get Hungry
Help Save the Turtles

I will read the questions out loud while you read them to yourself. Look at the table of contents to find the answer. Fill in the circle under the best answer. Be sure your answer circle is completely filled in with a dark mark. Do you have any questions? Let's begin.

Allow time between items for students to fill in their answers.

17. Number 17: Which pages would tell you most about what different turtles look like?

18. Number 18: Where should you begin reading to find out about when the first turtles lived?

19. Number 19: Which pages would tell you most about how baby turtles are born?

20. Number 20: Where should you begin reading to find out about what turtles eat?

21. Number 21: Which pages would tell you most about where turtles live?

22. Number 22: Where should you begin reading to find out how to protect turtles?

It's time to stop. You have completed Test 9. Check to see that you have completely filled in your answer circles with dark marks. Make sure that any marks for answers that you changed have been completely erased. Now you may close your books.

 Test 9 **Sources of Information**

Turtles
CONTENTS

17 Which pages would tell you most about what different turtles look like?
- ● 2–4
- ○ 5–7
- ○ 8–9

18 Where should you begin reading to find out about when the first turtles lived?
- ○ 5
- ● 8
- ○ 15

19 Which pages would tell you most about how bably turtles are born?
- ○ 2–4
- ○ 5–7
- ● 10–11

20 Where should you begin reading to find out about what turtles eat?
- ○ 5
- ● 12
- ○ 15

21 Which pages would tell you most about where turtles live?
- ● 5–7
- ○ 8–9
- ○ 10–11

22 Where should you begin reading to find out how to protect turtles?
- ○ 2
- ○ 8
- ● 15

137

Review the items with the students. Have them indicate completion of the lesson by entering their score for this activity on the progress chart at the beginning of the book. Provide the students whatever help is necessary to record their scores. Then collect the students' books and answer sheets if this is the end of the testing session.

Administration Time: 25 minutes

Say Turn to Test 10 on page 138. There are pictures at the top of the page.

Check to see that the students have found page 138.

Say In this lesson you will answer questions about science. Let's do S together. Look at the pictures of a rabbit, fox, and mouse. Two of the animals eat plants and one hunts other animals. Which animal does <u>not</u> eat plants? *(pause)* **The second answer, *the fox*, is correct because a fox does not eat plants. Fill in the circle under the picture of the fox. Be sure your answer circle is completely filled in with a dark mark and that you have marked the correct answer circle.**

Check to see that the students have marked the correct circle.

Say Now we will do more items in the same way we did the sample. I will read a question out loud while you read it to yourself. Fill in the circle under the best answer. Be sure your answer circle is completely filled in with a dark mark. Do you have any questions? Let's begin.

Allow time between items for students to fill in their answers.

1. Look at the pictures in row 1. Which one shows the arrow pointing to the root of the tree? Fill in the circle under the picture that shows the arrow pointing to the root of the tree.

2. Look at the pictures in row 2. If you looked at the moon through a telescope, what would it look like? Fill in the circle under the picture of what the moon would look like if you saw it through a telescope.

    Look at the next page, page 139.

Check to be sure the students have found the right page. Allow the students a moment to rest.

S

1

2

GO

138

3. Look at the pictures in row 3. Which thing floats because it is lighter than air? Fill in the circle under the picture of something that floats because it is lighter than air.

4. Look at the pictures in row 4. Which picture shows trees that have been planted and cared for by humans? Fill in the circle under the picture that shows trees that have been planted and cared for by humans.

5. Look at the pictures in row 5. Which one shows the thing that would burn most easily if lit with a match? Fill in the circle under the picture of something that would burn most easily if lit with a match.

6. Look at the pictures in row 6. Danielle wanted to prove that air has weight. She created a simple demonstration for her science project. Which of these did she probably make? Fill in the circle under the picture that shows how Danielle proved that air has weight.

Look at the next page, page 140.

Check to be sure the students have found the right page. Allow the students a moment to rest.

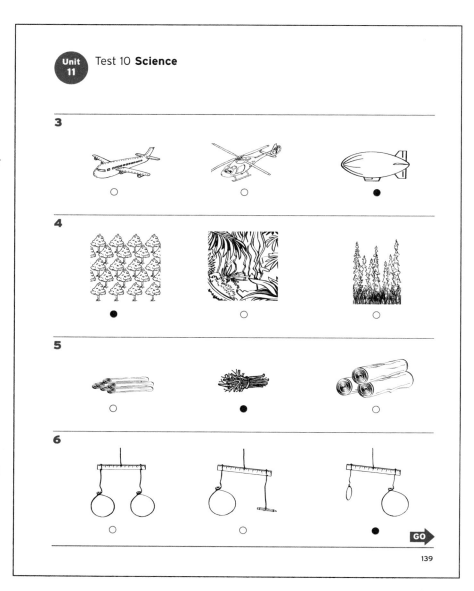

Unit 11 Test 10 **Science**

3

4

5

6

GO

139

7. Look at the pictures in row 7. Two of the foods are in the same food group. One is different. Fill in the circle under the food that is in a different group from the other two.

8. Look at the pictures in row 8. Which of these three things is largest in real life? Fill in the circle under the picture of the thing that is largest in real life.

9. Look at the pictures in row 9. When you have a cold, which part of your body is usually affected the most? Fill in the circle under the picture that shows the part of your body that is usually affected the most when you have a cold.

10. Look at the pictures in row 10. Which picture shows an animal that prefers to live near water? Fill in the circle under the picture of an animal that prefers to live near water.

   Look at the next page, page 141.

Check to be sure the students have found the right page. Allow the students a moment to rest.

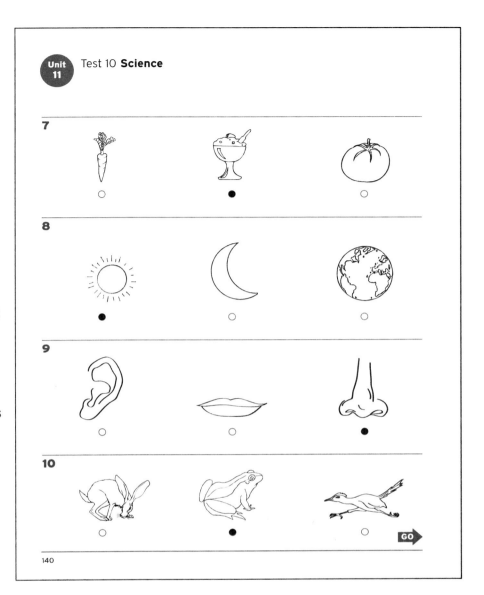

11. Look at the shapes in row 11. Which shape is a safety sign that means you should stop? Fill in the circle under the picture that shows a sign that means you should stop.

12. Look at the pictures in row 12. Which picture shows the person who will have the easiest time moving the box into the truck? Fill in the circle under the picture that shows the person who will have the easiest time moving the box into the truck.

13. Look at the pictures in row 13. Which tree is less than one year old? Fill in the circle under the picture of the tree that is less than one year old.

14. Look at the pictures in row 14. Which scale shows that the orange weighs more than the apple? Fill in the circle under the picture that shows the orange weighs more than the apple.

Turn to the next page, page 142.

Check to be sure the students have found the right page. Allow the students a moment to rest.

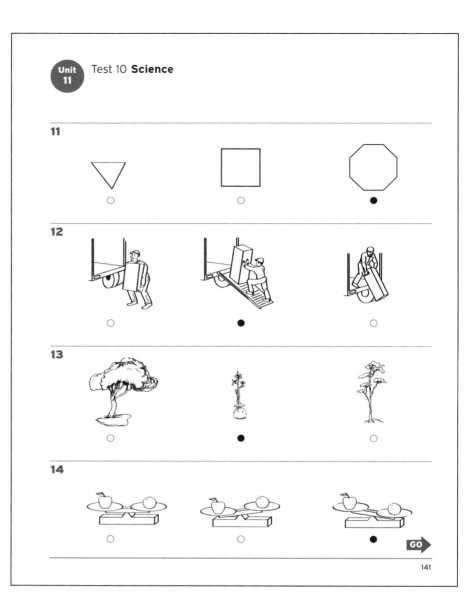

Unit 11 **Test Practice**

15. Look at the pictures in row 15. Which of these things will decay and form soil? Fill in the circle under the picture that shows things that will decay and form soil.

16. Look at the pictures in row 16. Which of these animals makes its own heat? Fill in the circle under the picture of the animal that makes its own heat.

17. Look at the pictures in row 17. Which of these would you probably use to get a better look at an ant? Fill in the circle under the picture that shows something that will give you a better look at an ant.

18. Look at the pictures in row 18. If you put each of these things in the hot sun, which would start to melt first? Fill in the circle under the picture of the thing that would melt first in the hot sun.

Look at the next page, page 143.

Check to be sure the students have found the right page. Allow the students a moment to rest.

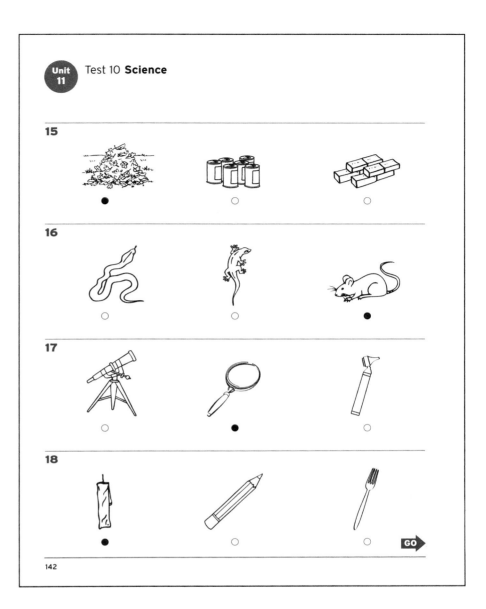

19. Look at the pictures in row 19. Which of these animals has a backbone? Fill in the circle under the picture of the animal that has a backbone.

20. Look at the pictures in row 20. Which picture shows a person doing something to stay healthy? Fill in the circle under the picture that shows a person doing something to stay healthy.

21. Look at the pictures in row 21. Edward wants to see which seed becomes a plant first, beans or corn. Which picture shows a good way to do this? Fill in the circle under the picture that shows how to find out which seed becomes a plant first.

22. Look at the pictures in row 22. Which part of a pine tree contains its seeds? Fill in the circle under the picture that shows the part of a pine tree that contains its seeds.

Turn to the next page, page 144.

Check to be sure the students have found the right page. Allow the students a moment to rest.

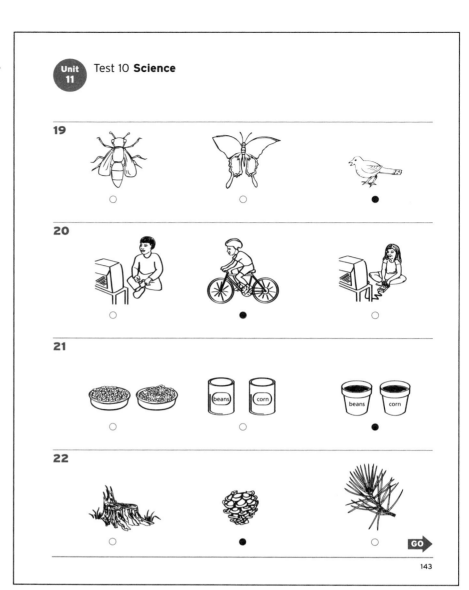

Unit 11

Test 10 **Science**

19

20

21

22

GO

143

23. Look at the pictures in row 23. Which tool would be best to measure milk for a recipe? Fill in the circle under the picture that shows the best tool to measure milk for a recipe.

24. Look at the pictures in row 24. Which picture shows someone using force to pull something? Fill in the circle under the picture that shows someone using force to pull something.

25. Look at the pictures in row 25. Which of these foods came from an animal? Fill in the circle under the picture of a food that comes from an animal.

26. Look at the pictures in row 26. Which science tool should you use only with the help of an adult? Fill in the circle under the picture that shows a science tool you should use only with the help of an adult.

Look at the next page, page 145.

Check to be sure the students have found the right page. Allow the students a moment to rest.

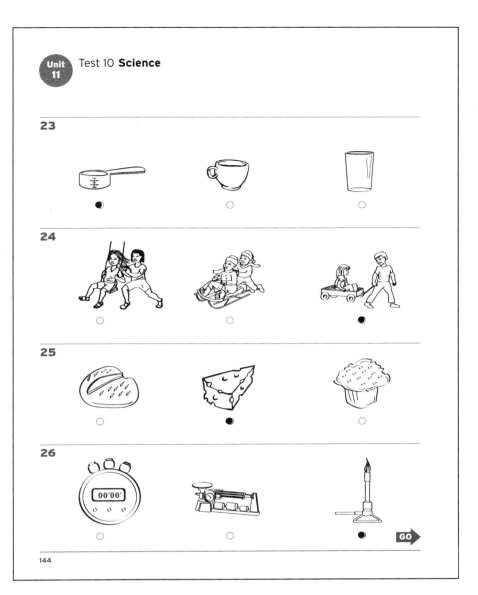

23

24

25

26

GO

144

27. Look at the pictures of the moon, the sun, and the Big Dipper in row 27. Which thing is farthest from Earth? Fill in the circle under the picture of the thing that is farthest from Earth.

28. Look at the pictures in row 28. Which picture shows the organ that helps digest food? Fill in the circle under the picture that shows the organ that helps digest food.

29. Look at the pictures in row 29. Karen filled a glass with ice cubes. She then let the ice cubes melt. Which picture shows how much water would be in the glass? Fill in the circle under the picture that shows how much water would be in the glass after the ice cubes melted.

30. Look at the pictures in row 30. Imagine that you are walking through the woods. You and your friends are pretty sure that a skunk is nearby. Which part of your body did you probably use to discover this? Fill in the circle under the picture that shows the part of your body that would help you discover that a skunk is nearby.

Look at the next page, page 146.

Check to be sure the students have found the right page. Allow the students a moment to rest.

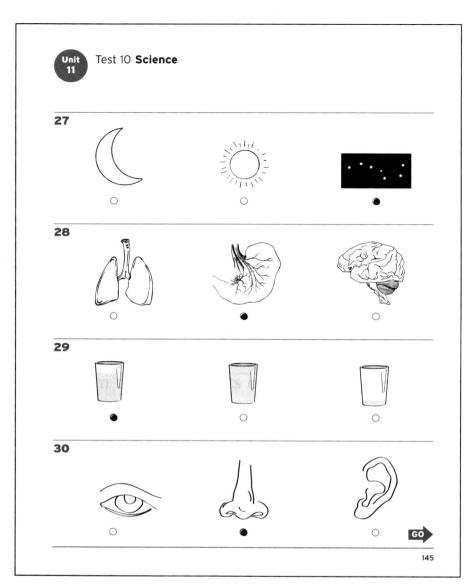

31. Look at the pictures in row 31. Which picture shows how you can help other people avoid getting sick? Fill in the circle under the picture that shows how you can help other people avoid getting sick.

32. Look at the pictures in row 32. Ben looked through three different telescopes at a lighthouse. Which picture shows what he saw through the most powerful telescope? Fill in the circle under the picture that shows the lighthouse through the most powerful telescope.

33. Look at the pictures in row 33. Which picture shows something that is moved by the power of a person? Fill in the circle under the picture that shows something moved by the power of a person.

34. Look at the pictures in row 34. Which picture shows plants that are grown by people? Fill in the circle under the picture of plants that are grown by people.

    Look at the next page, page 147.

Check to be sure the students have found the right page. Allow the students a moment to rest.

Unit 11 Test 10 **Science**

31

32

33

34

146

35. Look at the pictures in row 35. Which of these won't burn? Fill in the circle under the picture of something that won't burn.

36. Look at the pictures in row 36. Kayla has a glass of water. Kayla wants to show her class how to find out how much just the water in a glass weighs. Fill in the circle under the picture that shows how she could do this.

37. Look at the pictures in row 37. Which food is in the same food group as an apple? Fill in the circle under the picture of the food that is in the same group as an apple.

38. Look at the pictures in row 38. Which picture shows the time of day when it is probably warmest. Fill in the circle showing the time of day it is probably warmest.

It's time to stop. You have completed Test 10. Check to see that you have completely filled in your answer circles with dark marks. Make sure that any marks for answers that you changed have been completely erased. Now you may close your books.

Review the items with the students. Have them indicate completion of the lesson by entering their score for this activity on the progress chart at the beginning of the book. Provide the students whatever help is necessary to record their scores. Then collect the students' books and answer sheets if this is the end of the testing session.

Go over any questions that caused difficulty. If necessary, review the skills that will help the students score their highest.

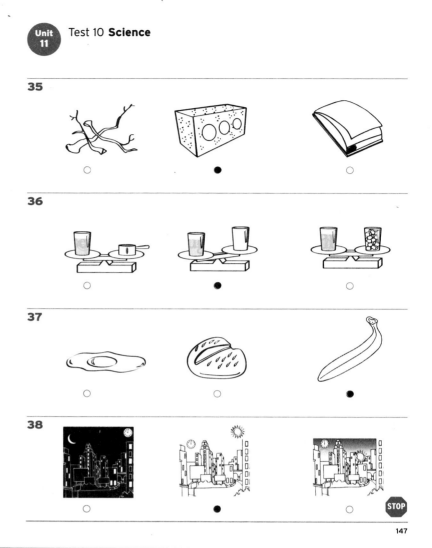

Unit 11 Test 10 **Science**

35

36

37

38

147